ACQUISITIONS
AND
MERGERS

GEORGE D. McCARTHY

Partner,
Price Waterhouse & Co.

THE RONALD PRESS COMPANY · NEW YORK

11-27-63
of2

$15.00

Library of Congress Catalog Card Number: 63-15017

PRINTED IN THE UNITED STATES OF AMERICA

PREFACE

This work is the result of a survey of some ten thousand corporate acquisitions and mergers, with particular emphasis on those occurring since World War II. It attempts to present the reader with a thorough study of the various facets of this economic phenomenon, which has been a major factor in the growth and development of our country.

The work has been arranged so that the steps and procedures involved in the planning, preparation, and completion of a corporate acquisition or merger can be followed by the reader. A large number of case studies of various phases of corporate combinations have been presented to illustrate and clarify the many aspects of these corporate transformations. The book also contains many footnote annotations for those desiring to explore further particular topics. Though legal aspects of the subject are discussed, when specific problems arise that require reference to laws, regulations, and decisions, it is suggested that legal counsel be consulted.

It also has an immediate, practical purpose—that is, to offer a comprehensive guide and useful reference work to show, in concrete form, the factors to be considered and steps undertaken in effecting the many types of corporate acquisitions and mergers. Success in the consummation of a business combination is not assured by good intentions, but by careful advance planning.

The author was fortunate in having been active in a professional capacity in many acquisitions and mergers over a period of some thirty years. In the course of studying this subject, the author comprehensively reviewed pertinent data on hundreds of business combinations by reference to Federal Trade Commission and other governmental records, Moody's Investors Service, Standard & Poor's Corp. service, published annual reports to stockholders, proxy and registration statements filed with the Securities and Exchange Commission, and reports filed with stock exchanges, as well as the voluminous files to which he had access in his own firm.

No work of this magnitude could have been completed without the generous help of the author's associates with experience and insight in this field. While the responsibility for the opinions and conclusions in the book are those of the author, he gratefully acknowledges the help furnished by such associates, particularly Joseph D. Coughlan, Clyde H. Folley, John P. Glynn, Michael F. Klein, Jr., and Edwin K. Walker.

GEORGE D. MCCARTHY

Newark, N. J.
April, 1963

CONTENTS

Finders' Fees and Brokers' Commissions, 256; Corporate Raiders, 257; Public Announcements of Business Combinations, 260

APPENDIXES

ACQUISITIONS
AND
MERGERS

Chapter 1

BUSINESS COMBINATIONS TODAY

Corporate acquisitions and mergers (the combination of two or more businesses into a single enterprise) have played a dominant role in the economic expansion of our country. The pooling of the talents and resources of enterprises whose growth, in large measure, was achieved through such combinations has accelerated technological developments and the nationwide distribution of goods and services.

THE THREE MAJOR MERGER MOVEMENTS

Since the turn of the century, three major waves of manufacturing and mining concern mergers can be identified: one running from 1895 to 1904; the movement from 1925 to 1931; and the post-World War II movement, commencing in 1945 and still at a high rate in 1962. The latter wave is not characterized by a sharp rise in activity for a relatively short period, as are the earlier ones (for example, there were 1,208 mergers recorded in 1899 and 1,245 in 1929), but reflects a high level of activity over a long period. No completely reliable statistics are available on the number or magnitude of corporate acquisitions and mergers during this entire period. However, the following figures have been compiled from the sources indicated for the years 1895 through June 30, 1962, on manufacturing and mining concerns "acquired." [1]

[1] *Historical Statistics of the United States,* years 1895 through 1956, Chart V30–31, p. 572; U.S. Department of Commerce, *Survey of Current Business,* 1957 through 1959; Federal Trade Commission statistics for 1960–June 30, 1962. The number of mergers for the period prior to 1919 was accumulated on a basis different from the method used subsequently, but no comparable basis is available for both periods.

Period	Number of "Acquisitions"	Rate Per Annum
1895–1904	3,012	301.2
1905–1924	4,118	205.9
1925–1931	5,846	835.1
1932–1944	1,907	146.7
1945–June 30, 1962	7,349	419.9
	22,232	

No doubt the number of corporate acquisitions and mergers of manufacturing and mining companies during this period of over sixty years greatly exceeds the above figures, considering that until recent years, companies generally have not been included unless such actions were reported by Moody's Investors Service and Standard & Poor's Corp. Such statistics would cover transactions for most companies large enough to be of interest and are reasonably indicative of relative activity and trends in the acquisitions and mergers field.

Merger movements generally parallel business activity and stock market prices. This is a natural sequence, as acquisitions of companies, in effect, are investments; and prosperous periods generate greater investment activity. The chart on page 5 compares corporate acquisitions and mergers,[2] the industrial production index,[3] and stock market prices from 1895 to June 30, 1962.[4] It will be noted that, except for the early merger movement, which was sharp and of short duration, there is a general relationship among the three indices throughout most of the period covered.

The First Merger Movement. The merger wave spanning the turn of the century, from the standpoint of the number of companies and the magnitude of their operations and net assets involved, had a vital effect on our economy. Notable among the business

---

[2] Ibid.

[3] The industrial production index for the years 1895–1918 was taken from statistics of the *National Bureau of Economic Research—Number 66,* General Series and were adjusted to 1957 series. The years 1919–1960 were obtained from the *Federal Reserve Bulletin.*

[4] The average price per share of stocks was taken from Standard & Poor's Corp. statistical summary of 425 industrial stocks using a base of 1941–1943 = 10 as reported by U.S. Department of Commerce, *Survey of Current Business.*

THE INDUSTRIAL PRODUCTION INDEX and AVERAGE STOCK MARKET PRICES

from 1895 to JUNE 30, 1962

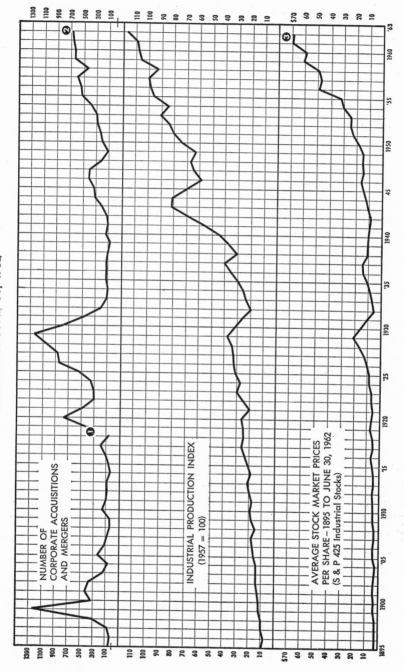

NUMBER OF
CORPORATE ACQUISITIONS
AND MERGERS

INDUSTRIAL PRODUCTION INDEX
(1957 = 100)

AVERAGE STOCK MARKET PRICES
PER SHARE – 1895 TO JUNE 30, 1962
(S & P 425 Industrial Stocks)

❶ Method of recording was revised in 1919.

❷ Recorded mergers Jan. 1 to June 30, 1962, totalling 342, were annualized to 684.

❸ The STANDARD & POOR'S INDEX for 425 INDUSTRIAL STOCKS is based on average prices for each year through December 31, 1961, and for six months to June 30, 1962. The INDEX at the latter date was 59.10 compared with average 69.62 for the first six months period.

combinations during this period, which involved multiple consolidations of companies into single business enterprises, were those that produced corporations presently among the largest in the country. These include such corporate giants as United States Steel, Bethlehem, and Republic—the three largest companies in the steel industry—and American Tobacco, E. I. du Pont, General Electric, International Harvester, Anaconda, American Can, Allis-Chalmers, American Smelting and Refining, and National Distillers.

This early merger movement was characterized by the combination of a great many companies in the same industries into single enterprises and resulted in large concentrations of industry volume in the top companies thus created. For example, the formation of United States Steel Corp. combined the six largest iron and steel companies in the country, in addition to several smaller ones. American Tobacco Co. similarly represented a combination of a number of the largest tobacco companies in the country. Another feature of the first merger movement was that invariably these consolidations were accompanied by public security issues. This is not generally so in the later merger movements.

EARLY ANTITRUST ACTION. At the close of this merger wave, the Supreme Court rendered a decision in the *Northern Securities* case in 1904,[5] in which it held that the consolidation directly of two, and indirectly of three, competing railroad lines constituted a violation of the Sherman Anti-Trust Act, enacted in 1890. This decision contravened that of the same Court in its review of the *Knight* case in 1895,[6] which involved the acquisition by the American Sugar Refining Co. of the capital stock of four independent refineries. The popular interpretation of the decision in the latter case was to the effect that a number of corporations combining by agreement would not be operating in restraint of trade and thereby creating a monopoly.

Whether or not this interpretation was justified is a moot point, but let it suffice to say that the period from 1895 to 1904, following this earlier decision, gave rise to the consolidation of

[5] Northern Securities Co. v. United States, 193 U.S. 197 (1904).
[6] United States v. E. C. Knight Co., 156 U.S. 1 (1895).

some of the most important business combines in the history of this country.

Following the *Northern Securities* decision, a number of actions were brought by the government under the Sherman Anti-Trust Act; and in 1911, the American Tobacco Co. was declared by the Supreme Court to be a monopoly in restraint of trade and ordered to disintegrate.[7] Among the separate and independent organizations divested as a result of this order were R. J. Reynolds Tobacco Co., Liggett & Meyers Tobacco Co., P. Lorillard Co., and United Cigar Stores Co.

About the same time, Standard Oil Co. (New Jersey) was ordered by the Supreme Court to distribute shares in thirty-three companies, pro rata among its stockholders.[8] Standard Oil, which incorporated in 1882, had acquired from the trustees of the Standard Oil Trust, in 1892, the stocks and assets of such companies in exchange for its stock. The companies whose stocks were divested presently constitute many of the large petroleum and pipeline companies in the country.

United States Steel Corp., in a similar action brought against it by the government in 1911, fared better than American Tobacco Co. and Standard Oil Co. (New Jersey). In this action, it was alleged that the corporation had created a combination in restraint of trade by acquiring competing companies, which together produced more than 50 per cent of the iron and steel in the United States and controlled a large proportion of available ore, coal, and other properties. The District Court, in 1915, entered a decree, later affirmed by the Supreme Court in 1920,[9] dismissing the government's petition and refused to dissolve the combination.

Federal antitrust aspects of acquisitions and mergers are discussed more fully in Chapter 13.

The Second Merger Movement. The movement from 1925 to 1931 coincided with the period of the greatest relative stock market activity in our history. For three successive years, trading on the New York Stock Exchange exceeded one billion shares—

[7] United States v. American Tobacco Co. 221 U.S. 106 (1911).
[8] Standard Oil Co. v. United States 221 U.S. 1 (1911).
[9] United States v. United States Steel Corp., 251 U.S. 417 (1920).

1928, 1,253,000,000; 1929, 1,534,000,000; and 1930, 1,108,000,000. From 1930 through 1961, we have had only two years of billion-share trading on the Exchange, when 1,038,997,071 shares were traded in 1959 and 1,292,280,196 in 1961. When you consider that the average number of shares listed on the Exchange during 1930 was 1,212,238,474 compared with 6,773,189,356 in 1961, it stamps the second merger movement period as unique in the annals of speculation.[10] This period from 1925 to 1931 covered significant mergers of such present large combines as National Steel, National Dairy Products, General Foods, Borg-Warner, Caterpillar Tractor, Owens-Illinois Glass, United Aircraft, and Bendix Aviation.

ABUSES THAT GAVE RISE TO PUBLIC UTILITY HOLDING COMPANY ACT. The second merger movement also constituted the most active period in history of the acquisition, by holding companies, of interests in public utility operating companies, resulting in the control by several holding companies of substantial utility empires. In 1935, the Public Utility Holding Company Act of 1935 was passed, causing a number of such empires to divest themselves of many operating subsidiaries.[11] This law was passed after an extensive investigation and congressional hearings, which disclosed widespread abuses resulting from holding-company control of subsidiary public utility companies.

Among the charges made at these hearings were that the holding companies were responsible for the issuance of securities "upon the basis of fictitious or unsound asset values having no fair relation to the sums invested in or the earning capacity of the properties and upon the basis of paper profits from inter-company transactions, or in anticipation of excessive revenues from subsidiary public utility companies; when such securities are issued by a subsidiary public utility company under circumstances which subject such company to the burden of supporting an overcapitalized structure and tend to prevent voluntary rate reductions." [12] It was also disclosed that subsidiary public utility companies were subjected to excessive charges for services, con-

---

[10] *New York Stock Exchange Fact Book*, 1962, pp. 41 and 44.
[11] Public Utilities Holding Company Act of 1935, August 26, 1935.
[12] *Ibid.*, Sec.1(b)(1).

struction work, equipment, and materials or otherwise were caused to enter into transactions, by the holding companies, that were not at arms' length.

It was during the course of these investigations that H. C. Hopson, of Associated Gas and Electric Properties, and Samuel Insull, of Insull Utility Investments, Inc., gained considerable notoriety for allegedly indulging in many of the abuses cited, through their control of holding companies. Hopson later was convicted on a charge of mail fraud growing out of his alleged manipulations; but Insull, although indicted on a number of charges relating to his activities as head of the Insull utilities empire, was acquitted of all of them in a series of trials.[13]

The Third Merger Movement. Post-World War II mergers have been of importance to such enterprises as General Dynamics, Sperry Rand, Burlington Industries, Olin-Mathieson Chemical, American Metal Climax Molybdenum, W. R. Grace, Minnesota Mining & Manufacturing, Campbell Soup, Textron, American-Marietta, Borden, and Foremost Dairies.

Whereas the turn of the century merger wave was characterized by horizontal acquisitions, i.e., the combining of companies in the same general lines of business, the second wave, although continuing this trend, gave rise to more vertical acquisitions, leading to integration of manufacturers, suppliers, and distributors. The latest movement, expanding the vertical acquisitions trend, is also unique in the number of conglomerate business combinations effected.

This era is also notable for the number of commercial bank mergers that took place. Among those combined during the last decade were New York City banks, which in total resources at December 31, 1961, ranked, in the order listed below, as the second to sixth largest banks in the country, from the standpoint of total resources.

The Chase Manhattan Bank
Combining The Chase National Bank of the City of New York and The Bank of the Manhattan Co. (March 31, 1955)

[13] *The New York Times:* Hopson, issues of May 10, 1940, p. 12; January 1, 1941, p. 1. Insull, issues of February 28, 1933, p. 34; November 25, 1934, p. 1; December 7, 1934, p. 19; December 22, 1934, p. 17; March 10, 1935, p. 16.

Manufacturers Hanover Trust Co.
Combining Manufacturers Trust Co. and Hanover Bank (September 8, 1961)
First National City Bank (New York)
Combining National City Bank of New York and First National Bank of the City of New York (March 30, 1955)
Chemical Bank New York Trust Co.
Successively combining Chemical Bank & Trust Co. and Corn Exchange Bank Trust Co. (October 15, 1954) and then New York Trust Co. (September 8, 1959)
Morgan Guaranty Trust Co. of New York
Combining J. P. Morgan & Co., Inc., and Guaranty Trust Co. of New York (April 24, 1959)

Merger Activities Span Several Movements. It is not intended to imply that important business combinations took place only during these merger wave periods, as this is not the case. National Dairy Products and The Borden Co. each commenced acquiring companies in the 1920's and have continued over a period of years in adding some hundreds of concerns in the processing and distribution of various dairy and miscellaneous products.

The large steel companies, over a period of fifty odd years, have acquired companies in the ore, coal, and coke fields; in many lines of steel fabricating, shipbuilding, cement, prefabricated housing; and, incidentally, became owners of several railroads.

The large textile companies, commencing shortly before World War II and continuing for several years after, entered into numerous vertical acquisitions. As a result, Burlington Mills Corp. (basically a gray-goods manufacturer), M. Lowenstein & Sons (primarily a converter), J. P. Stevens & Co. (then a leading sales agent), and Ely & Walker Dry Goods Co. (a dry goods wholesaler) all emerged with more or less integrated textile operations.

What are some of the reasons for mergers and acquisitions? In the earlier merger era, industry dominance, with its advantages of large-scale purchasing, national distribution outlets, and influence on wages and prices, was a prime reason for the many consolidations during that period. Some of these early combinations would not now be permitted under antitrust laws, as presently interpreted and enforced.

MERGERS IN RECENT YEARS

The reasons for mergers and acquisitions since World War II are more varied and, in part, may be attributed to prevailing economic conditions and our federal tax structure. It is interesting to note the increasing trend in manufacturing and mining mergers and acquisitions reported by the Federal Trade Commission during the past eleven and one-half years: [14]

Year	Number
1951	235
1952	288
1953	295
1954	387
1955	525
1956	537
1957	597
1958	457
1959	656
1960	635
1961	671
1962, to June 30	342

What are the reasons for this high level of activity? The Federal Trade Commission made a study of recorded acquisition and merger activities, within its jurisdiction, covering the period from January 1, 1951, to July 31, 1954, to ascertain the advantages gained by the acquirer. The advantages identified by the Commission, in order of frequency, were: (1) enlarge capacity to supply old markets, (2) lengthen product line, (3) diversify, (4) gain facilities in markets not previously supplied, (5) gain facilities to further process or distribute goods, and (6) other (including acquisition of plants, patents, etc.).[15]

All these advantages listed might be summarized as being in the interests of corporate growth. Many companies, some of which have been mentioned, have permanent acquisitions programs with the broad objective of expansion by such means, as well as through product development and sales promotion.

[14] *Statistical Abstract of the United States,* 1960, p. 500; Federal Trade Commission records, January 1, 1960, to June 30, 1962.

[15] Federal Trade Commission, *Report on Mergers and Acquisitions,* May, 1955, p. 7.

The following more specific reasons for acquisitions and mergers may be cited, in addition to the general one of corporate expansion:

ACQUIRING COMPANIES' REASONS FOR MERGING

1. *Diversification,* with the general objective of achieving economic protection not available in a one-product enterprise. Companies in recent years that have embarked on diversification programs include General Dynamics, which added to its nuclear submarine line, and companies producing aircraft, electronics products, guided missiles, compressed gases, concrete products, and refractory materials. Also, Textron, Inc., which started on a horizontal and vertical acquisitions program, resulting in expansion and integration in the textiles field, then went in for broad diversification. Its 1960 sales volume of $383,000,000 apportioned by product groups was 17 per cent in automotive; 24 per cent in a wide range of consumer products, including optical items and power tools and implements; 22 per cent in defense, 20 per cent in industrial items, such as rolling mills and metal working machinery; and only 17 per cent in textiles.[16]

2. *Adding new and profitable products to their line* faster than by means of research and development and consumer acceptance over a long period. Many businesses have been acquired by drug and pharmaceutical companies in order to add products that would have taken the acquirers long periods of time and substantial expenditures to develop in their own laboratories. Likewise, cosmetic and toiletry items, which have gained wide consumer acceptance, are an attractive asset for would-be acquirers in that field.

3. *Acquiring management or technical personnel.* Even during the unprecedented period of prosperity since World War II, there have been (and still are) a number of companies that have not been operating successfully. Usually the capital stocks of such companies, if they have an established market, sell at depressed prices. Where their directors become aware of the reason for poor operating results, they may endeavor to obtain the necessary management or technical skills by means of a downstream merger or acquisition.

[16] *Moody's Industrial Manual,* 1961, p. 2823.

4. *Acquiring profitable operations to absorb a tax-loss carry-over.* Prominent among companies that included this as an important factor in its acquisitions was Kaiser Frazer Corp. (now Kaiser Industries Corp.), which had a substantial tax-loss carryover when it acquired certain assets of Willys-Overland, a profitable enterprise, in 1953 and later acquired Henry J. Kaiser Co. and other interests, utilizing loss carryovers to offset $76,000,000 of consolidated taxable income during the period from 1956 to 1959.[17] Another company, Studebaker-Packard, whose tax-loss carryover was estimated to be $120,000,000 at the end of 1958, has been endeavoring to acquire profitable companies.[18]

SELLING COMPANIES' REASONS FOR MERGING

1. *Major management stockholders wishing to retire* and having no understudies capable of continuing the business profitably.

2. *Expansion of business to a point where there is need for substantial additional financing,* and major stockholders not wishing to assume such a burden.

3. *As a means of survival* for public as well as private companies, where operations have been at a depressed level for a long period.

4. *The prospects of technological or marketing changes* adversely affecting the future operations of the company.

5. *Being wooed by larger companies with attractive purchase or exchange offers,* often with the promise to principals that they will have executive positions in the combined enterprise.

During recent years, many larger companies have been seeking out desirable (and sometimes not so desirable) medium-sized and smaller companies to absorb. This has resulted in spirited bidding competition and generous purchase prices in relationship to either current earnings or net tangible assets of companies acquired. The rivalry for acquisitions was well illustrated by the bidding early in 1960 by about fifty companies attempting to acquire Honolulu Oil Co., including several companies not in the oil business.[19]

[17] *Ibid.,* p. 1894.
[18] *The Wall Street Journal,* September 6, 1960, p. 24. See also "Francis of Studebaker-Packard," *Fortune,* November, 1960, p. 83.
[19] *New York Herald Tribune,* February 16, 1961, p. 33.

FEDERAL TAX FACTORS

An overriding factor influencing companies to acquire as well as sell or merge upstream is our federal income and estate tax structure. For example, several stockholders in a closely held corporation have invested $500,000 in a company. If they were to sell out at a price of $7,500,000, or a gain of $7,000,000 over their original investment, this gain would be taxed at a maximum rate of 25 per cent (capital gains) compared with normal personal income tax rates ranging up to 91 per cent, which apply to dividend income.

As an even more attractive proposition, the same stockholders, if they exchanged their capital stock for stock having a fair market value of $7,500,000 in a listed company, would not have to recognize any taxable gain or loss when the transaction took place. If such stockholders were advanced in years, it would be advantageous for them, provided the company from whom they receive the stock continued to operate profitably, to hold such stock, ultimately to become an asset in their estates. An estate tax, even in the $5,000,000 bracket or more, would be considerably less relatively than the combination of a 25 per cent capital gains tax on a cash sale and an estate tax later on the remaining 75 per cent.

The reorganization provisions of the Revenue Code also encourage acquisitions and mergers from the standpoint of the acquiring company. This is particularly true where the acquirer buys net assets of a company or buys its capital stock with the intention of liquidating the acquired company within two years thereafter. In each of these cases, the acquirer is entitled to step up the original tax basis of the seller to the fair market value of the assets acquired.

In other words, if a company purchased net assets for $6,000,000 either directly or through the capital stock and subsequent liquidation route from a company whose tax basis for such assets was $3,000,000 and if the fair value of tangible assets such as land, buildings, machinery and equipment, and inventories, etc., could be shown to be $6,000,000 or more at the date of purchase, the acquirer could allocate his full purchase price to these assets for tax purposes. Accordingly, up to 52 per cent of the purchase price, in excess of the tax basis of the selling company, could be recovered through tax deductions on the increased values upon disposition of inventories and other assets and depreciation on fixed assets.

Although certain attributes of these provisions were in the 1939 Internal Revenue Code, the 1954 Revenue Code codified by definite rules a maze of general provisions involving conflicting interpretations followed under the former Code. In addition, the 1954 Code is helpful in providing that (1) some cash may be employed in an acquisition of assets for voting stock, and the non-taxable exchange provisions would still prevail; (2) the stock of a parent company can be used by a subsidiary in a tax-free acquisition by the latter; and (3) creeping control can be employed, so that a company owning 40 or 50 per cent of another can acquire the remainder of the stock in a tax-free reorganization, which was a doubtful procedure under the 1939 Code. Also, the revised Code permits the sale of assets and distribution to shareholders of the proceeds under a one-year plan of liquidation without also taxing the corporation on such gains.[20] Chapter 9 contains a comprehensive discussion of the federal tax aspects of acquisitions and mergers.

Business combinations of public utilities and banks have been mentioned in this chapter only to highlight their activities during certain merger periods. Mergers of these and other regulated industries are not included in the statistics quoted. Although many of the comments in this book, which relate primarily to manufacturing, mercantile, and mining companies, will have equal application to regulated industries, the special problems of the latter are not considered.

The next chapter will discuss broad aspects of business combinations and illustrate some of the problems encountered and remedies utilized in dealing with them.

[20] Int. Rev. Code of 1954, §§ 337, 354, and 368.

Chapter 2

TYPES OF BUSINESS COMBINATIONS

MERGERS AND ACQUISITIONS DEFINED

There are several terms generally used in referring to business amalgamations. The most common of these is "merger," which in its broad sense indicates the combination of two or more business entities into a single economic enterprise. To be more exact, however, the only types of business combinations that should be designated as mergers are statutory mergers or consolidations, i.e., when one or more companies are merged into another or into a new corporation in conformity with the statutes dealing with such transactions in the states of their incorporation.

Statutory Mergers. Statutory merger or consolidation agreements must be submitted to stockholders and require approval of holders of at least a majority of shares of voting stock (in many states more) of each of the merging or consolidating corporations. At present, with the exception of a few states, dissenting stockholders of any of the corporations involved in a statutory merger or consolidation have the right of appraisal of their stock and to receive cash for its value if they do not approve the terms of the merger. Should there be a substantial number of shares represented by dissenting stockholders, this could upset the tax-free status of the reorganization and also create the financing problem of raising the cash to pay off such stockholders. This subject is discussed more fully in Chapter 13 under "General or Business Corporation Laws."

Acquisitions. Thus, a number of so-called mergers involving exchanges of capital stock legally are acquisitions, particularly where there are large numbers of shareholders involved. In such non-merger cases, one company "acquires" the voting stock of another solely in exchange for its voting stock. Acquisitions, in a legal sense, may also be effected for cash or cash equivalent, such as debt securities.

Business Combinations (Accounting Term). In its discussion of the accounting aspects of mergers and acquisitions, the American Institute of Certified Public Accountants uses the term "business combinations," as a general description and further classifies them as "purchases" and "poolings of interests" according to the attendant circumstances.[1]

PURCHASES. A purchase is described as a business combination of two or more corporations in which an important part of the ownership interest in the acquired corporation or corporations is eliminated.

POOLINGS OF INTERESTS. A pooling of interests is a combination of two or more corporations in which the holders of "substantially all" of the ownership interests in the constituent corporations survive in the combined enterprise. In a pooling of interests, as contrasted with a purchase, no new basis of accountability of assets arises. The assets and liabilities of the constituent corporations are combined, and adjustments are made through capital and surplus accounts to reflect the outstanding capital stock of the combined enterprise. Accordingly, no goodwill arises in such transactions as is generally the case in purchases.

The accounting as well as tax aspects of business combinations are of such importance that they not only influence the form of a transaction, but also could adversely affect the interests of one or both parties to the transaction to the extent that negotiations might be terminated.

EXCHANGES OF VOTING STOCK

Mergers, and acquisitions involving the exchange of voting stock of the acquirer, are generally undertaken under the "tax-free" reorganization provisions of the Internal Revenue Code;

[1] Committee on Accounting Procedure, American Institute of Certified Public Accountants, *Business Combinations*, Bull. No. 48, January, 1957.

i.e., the stockholders of selling companies are not required to recognize gain or loss on the securities received from acquiring companies. Such securities have a substituted tax basis equivalent to the basis of the securities surrendered immediately or in liquidation, if received by the disappearing corporation, as a result of the business combination.[2]

Use of Preferred or Convertible Preferred Stock. Customarily, the surviving company issues its common or capital stock (if it has only one class outstanding) in exchange for the capital stock or net assets and business of the company acquired; although preferred stock or convertible preferred stock may be used in part or wholly for this purpose, provided it is voting stock. However, if such stock can be termed "Section 306 stock" under the Internal Revenue Code [3] (see page 167) and is disposed of by the recipients, the gains thereon could be subject to tax at ordinary income rather than capital gains rates.

EXCHANGES OF NON-VOTING STOCK OR DEBT SECURITIES

In a statutory merger or consolidation, if permissible under applicable state corporation laws, non-voting common or preferred stock or even debt securities may be issued by the surviving corporation. However, the issuance of non-voting stock or debt securities would preclude pooling of interests accounting treatment, which is most desirable in the majority of cases of mergers and acquisitions involving an exchange of securities.

Quite often, a company may wish to acquire another solely in exchange for its own voting stock and will acquire the net assets and business of the company rather than its capital stock. This type of transaction may have advantages when the acquirer wishes to be assured that liabilities taken over from the acquired corporation will be limited to those disclosed and assumed and it will not be subject to indeterminate or undisclosed liabilities that later come to light.

There are varying situations encountered in effecting business combinations—at times because of existing conditions, and at others because of the objectives of the parties involved. Some

---

[2] Int. Rev. Code of 1954, particularly § 358.
[3] *Ibid.,* § 306.

of the more interesting of these situations and their solutions, as carried out within the "tax-free" reorganization provisions of the Internal Revenue Code, are discussed below.

Merger and Sale of Part of Stock by Stockholders of Merged Company. There are times when certain stockholders of a company being absorbed in a business combination desire some cash but do not wish to dispose of the entire amount of capital stock received in an exchange. This may be accomplished while still preserving the pooling of interests accounting treatment on behalf of the acquirer. The general view prevails that up to 25 per cent of the number of shares received in an exchange may be disposed of without nullifying the pooling of interests accounting treatment. Care must be exercised in such circumstances so that the tax-free status of the reorganization is preserved. An example of this type of deal follows.

THE INDIANA STEEL PRODUCTS CO. AND GENERAL CERAMICS CORP. On November 16, 1959, General Ceramics Corp. was merged into The Indiana Steel Products Co. on the basis of an exchange of 0.353 of a share of Indiana Steel common for each share of General Ceramics. When the merger was consummated, former General Ceramics stockholders held 208,270 shares out of a total of 562,261 shares of Indiana General Corp. (formerly Indiana Steel) stock then outstanding. Shortly after the merger, certain former General Ceramics stockholders sold 50,000 shares of Indiana General stock (or approximately 24 per cent of the total shares received by all General Ceramics stockholders) in a public offering.[4] *In such a public offering, the selling stockholders, in most cases, bear the underwriting commissions; printing, legal, and accounting costs; and filing fees incidental to the sale of their stock, if the surviving company is not concurrently offering some stock for sale.*

Redemption of Part of the Common Stock of Merged Company Prior to Effecting the Deal. The same result as in the previous example may be accomplished by redeeming part of the stock of a company to be absorbed in a business combination prior to effecting the exchange of stock. Such a redemption will not affect the

[4] Indiana General Corp., Prospectus, December 15, 1959.

pooling of interests accounting treatment, but it generally should not exceed 25 per cent of the total outstanding shares of the absorbed company. In other words, any plan that would eliminate a substantial equity interest (customarily considered to be more than 25 per cent) of either party shortly before or after a business combination is inconsistent with the concept of a continuity of ownership interests. As in the preceding example, care must be exercised to preserve the tax-free status of the transaction. An example of a redemption prior to effecting a merger follows. Another interesting feature of this deal is the issuance of convertible preferred stock by the acquirer.

GENERAL DYNAMICS CORP. AND MATERIAL SERVICE CORP. Effective December 31, 1959, General Dynamics Corp. acquired all of the 57,532 outstanding shares of common stock of Material Service Corp. in exchange for 2,064,516 shares of its no par convertible preference stock, entitled to cumulative dividends of $2.90625 annually and $58.125 per share, plus accrued dividends, in the event of liquidation. This stock is convertible at the rate of approximately 1.057 shares of common for each share held, becoming eligible for conversion in stipulated amounts beginning in 1961. As an interesting sidelight, immediately before the merger, 19,011 shares, constituting approximately 25 per cent of 76,543 shares of Material Service Corp. then outstanding, were redeemed at the rate of $1,652 per share by the distribution of certain assets unrelated to operations taken over by General Dynamics.[5]

EXCHANGE OF COMMON AND PREFERRED STOCK FOR COMMON STOCK

At times, it is desirable from the standpoint of the acquirer to exchange voting preferred stock for common stock, particularly if the par value of such stock is substantially above the market value of the issuer's common stock. In such a case, the seller emerges with less voting power in the combination than he would have had if only common stock had been issued by the acquirer. This may be important to the acquirer if there are stockholders with substantial interests in the selling company. From the

[5] General Dynamics Corp., Annual Report to Stockholders, 1959.

standpoint of the seller, the inducement to accept preferred stock is that he will have a safer investment and higher dividend yield. An interesting example of an exchange involving the issuance of part preferred and part common stock follows.

WARNER-LAMBERT PHARMACEUTICAL CO. AND NEPERA CHEMICAL CO., INC. During 1956, Warner-Lambert Pharmaceutical Co. exchanged 70,702 shares of $4.50 cumulative $100 par value preferred stock and 175,000 shares of common stock for all of the outstanding shares of common stock of Nepera Chemical Co., Inc., and 3,079 shares of its common stock to the holder of a 25 per cent minority interest in Nepera International Corp., Inc., the remaining stock of which was owned by Nepera Chemical. At the time the exchange agreement was executed, the common stock of Warner-Lambert was selling for $45.50 per share, so that approximately 53 per cent of the acquisition was made by means of common stock and 47 per cent by preferred stock, assuming the par value of the latter to be its fair value. Each class of stock was entitled to one vote per share, so that the aggregate voting power of the Nepera stockholders exchanging their shares was approximately 25 per cent less in the combined enterprise than it would have been if Warner-Lambert had issued all common stock in the exchange. During 1959 and 1960, Warner-Lambert purchased and canceled all the $4.50 cumulative preferred stock from the holders for a total cash consideration equivalent to its aggregate par value.[6]

Acquisition of Substantially All Remaining Stock Where Prospective Acquirer Already Has an Equity Interest. There are companies that buy into others secretly, up to the point where disclosure must be made to the Securities and Exchange Commission,[7] and then engage in a proxy fight to gain control of the remaining stock. However, such two-step acquisitions are often carried out by peaceful means with the cooperation of the management of both companies involved. A company may invest in the common stock of another for various business reasons, such as where one may be a supplier or customer of the other or with the express purpose

[6] Warner-Lambert Pharmaceutical Co. Proxy Statement, November 19, 1956; Annual Reports to Stockholders, 1959 and 1960.

[7] Securities Exchange Act of 1934, Sec. 16(a), see Chapter 13, page 258.

of ultimately effecting a business combination. In the latter case, if after a period the prospects of effecting a deal look poor, the investing company may sell its holdings. On the other hand, if a compatible deal can be worked out, it is a relatively simple matter to gain the approval of stockholders. This is particularly true where the management of both companies are in accord and control a substantial amount of the capital stock of the company proposed to be acquired. An example of such a two-step business combination follows.

FEDERAL PACIFIC ELECTRIC CO. AND CORNELL-DUBILIER ELEC-TRIC CORP. In February, 1960, Federal Pacific Electric Co. offered to exchange, on a share-for-share basis, a 5½ per cent convertible $23 par value second preferred stock for the 512,390 shares of common stock of Cornell-Dubilier Electric Corp. then outstanding. At the time of the offer, Federal owned 22,800 shares, and several of its principal stockholders owned 105,300 shares, an aggregate of 24 per cent, of the shares of Cornell common stock outstanding. Under the exchange offer, the holders of Cornell had the right to indicate that the tender of their stock was conditioned upon Federal's acquiring at least 80 per cent of the combined number of shares of common stock and preferred stock (of which there were few shares outstanding) of Cornell, so that the exchange would be tax free for federal income tax purposes. The exception to this offer was that the principal Federal stockholders of 105,300 shares of Cornell indicated their intention to unconditionally tender their shares of Cornell on a "no-profit" basis. Federal's June 30, 1960, annual report to stockholders indicated that holders of over 96 per cent of the common stock of Cornell accepted the offer and exchanged their shares for Federal convertible preferred stock.[8]

Acquisition of Company for Common Stock with Concurrent Redemption and Retirement of Shares of the Acquirer. When a company proposes to acquire another whose earnings currently are depressed or non-existent, a cash deal may be desirable so that earnings per share of the acquirer are not reduced to any great

[8] Federal Pacific Electric Co., Prospectus, February 18, 1960; Annual Report to Stockholders, June 30, 1960.

extent. However, the same result may be accomplished by an exchange of capital stock for stock of the seller and a concurrent repurchase and retirement of shares of stock from existing stockholders of the acquirer. Thus, the "tax-free" aspects of the business combination are preserved for the seller. The following is a good example of such a combination of transactions.

FORD MOTOR CO. AND PHILCO CORP. Effective November 30, 1961, Ford Motor Co. exchanged 997,703 shares of its common stock for the net assets and business of Philco Corp. at the rate of 1 share for each 4½ shares of Philco common stock then outstanding, and Ford common stock having a market value of $101.50 for each of the 100,000 shares of Philco 3¾ per cent Series A preferred stock outstanding, plus cash equivalent to the accrued and unpaid dividends on such stock to the date on which distribution of Ford shares is available to holders of Philco preferred. Under the plan of reorganization, Philco agreed to distribute to all of its stockholders the Ford common stock and, in addition, the cash equivalent to the accrued and unpaid dividends to its preferred stockholders, in complete liquidation of Philco. Concurrently, Ford Motor Co. repurchased from the Ford Foundation and retired a number of its Class A non-voting shares, substantially equivalent (1,063,000 shares) to the number of voting common shares issued to Philco. Thus, the total outstanding shares of its capital stock remained virtually unchanged despite the Philco transaction. Inasmuch as Philco was operating at a loss when the agreement was entered into, Ford minimized the possible near term dilution of earnings per share resulting from the transaction by not increasing its outstanding shares of capital stock.[9]

Restricting Voting Power Through Issuance of Different Classes of Stock to Two Groups of Stockholders of Acquired Company. In a statutory merger, if permitted by the laws of the states of domicile of the two companies involved, different classes of stock may be issued to holders of common stock of the merged company. Thus, if a few stockholders hold a substantial portion of the stock of the merged company so that they would become dominant stock-

[9] Philco Corp., Proxy Statement, October 27, 1961.

holders of the surviving company, they could be issued a high par value or dividend class of stock that would be convertible, over a period of years, into common stock; and the remaining stockholders could be issued common stock. An interesting case follows that not only combined this feature of the issuance of two classes of stock, but also resulted in a disproportionate exchange ratio in favor of the smaller selling stockholders.

ATLAS CHEMICAL INDUSTRIES, INC., AND THE STUART CO. During 1961, Atlas Chemical Industries, Inc. (formerly Atlas Powder Co.) exchanged 96,690 shares of its new Class A stock, entitled to non-cumulative annual dividends of $3.75 a share, for 483,450 shares of The Stuart Co. common stock held by three principal stockholders, on a 1 for 5 basis, and 396,600 shares of its new common stock to all other Stuart stockholders (in excess of 1,200) on the basis of 1.5 shares of Atlas new common for each share of Stuart common. The Class A stock is convertible to the extent of 20 per cent on each anniversary date of the merger on the basis of 1 Class A share for 6 common shares, with a provision for acceleration of conversion in certain circumstances. This is equal to 1.2 Atlas common shares for each share of Stuart held by such principal stockholders, compared with 1.5 shares of Atlas common issued to other stockholders of Stuart.

Another interesting feature of this disproportionate exchange is that the Atlas Class A stock is entitled to only one vote per share, the same as the common stock, so that the former principal stockholders of Stuart have their voting power in the combined enterprise considerably reduced (from 580,140 shares to 96,690 shares) until they are able to convert their Class A shares into common.[10]

EXCHANGE OF SHARES OF ACQUIRER WITH AGREEMENT TO REPURCHASE FROM SELLER

On occasion, a company may wish to sell out, and its stockholders will be reluctant to accept capital stock in exchange for its net assets and business. However, advantages to both the acquirer and seller may be recognized in effecting the deal through

[10] Atlas Powder Co., Proxy Statement, March 27, 1961; Atlas Chemical Industries, Inc., Listing Application to the New York Stock Exchange, May 10, 1961.

the issuance of capital stock. In such cases, the acquirer may be willing to enter into an agreement to repurchase the capital stock issued to the seller at a stipulated price, within a period. Such arrangements are relatively rare as the seller is taking all the risks of market depreciation without any converse benefits. Also, the tax status of such transactions are not too clearly defined. One such example is of interest, in which treasury stock was issued by the acquirer, as follows:

PHILADELPHIA AND READING CORP. AND BRID CORP. Effective April 10, 1959, Philadelphia and Reading Corp., through a subsidiary, exchanged 175,000 shares (357,000 shares after reflecting a two-for-one stock split and a 2 per cent stock dividend) of Philadelphia and Reading Corp.'s common stock held in its treasury for the assets and business of Blue Ridge Manufacturers, Inc. (now BRID Corp.) including Imperial Shirt Corp.

Philadelphia and Reading and Union Underwear Company, Inc. (a subsidiary) also agreed to buy at the option of BRID Corp., or any of the shareholders of BRID Corp., 306,000 shares of common stock of Philadelphia and Reading Corp. at a price of approximately $34.31 per share (after giving effect to the stock split and stock dividend) during the period from April 10, 1960, to April 10, 1962, and under certain conditions to purchase an additional 51,000 shares of such stock at the same price during a thirty-day period commencing October 10, 1960.[11]

ACQUISITIONS FOR CASH OR CASH AND SECURITIES

Other types of business combinations that are considered acquisitions or purchases for legal and accounting as well as federal income tax purposes include the purchase of a company's capital stock or net assets for (1) cash, (2) part cash and part stock, (3) debt securities, or (4) non-voting stock, except where permitted by law in the case of a statutory merger.

Tax Factors. Such transactions are taxable to the selling stockholders, and a new tax basis is created for the acquiring company. The acquiring company allocates the purchase price, whether in cash or a combination of cash and securities, to the tangible

[11] Philadelphia and Reading Corp., Annual Report to Stockholders, 1959.

and intangible assets received. Where capital stock is purchased, the acquired corporation must be liquidated in order to obtain this "stepped-up" tax basis of assets.[12]

If the price paid for the capital stock or net assets and business is substantially above the federal income tax basis of the selling company, it is often advantageous for the purchaser to pay cash or a combination of cash and securities so that he may establish a new tax basis. From the seller's standpoint, however, it is usually better to receive payment through an exchange of capital stock, thereby deferring any federal income tax on the transaction.

In a non-taxable transaction, the federal income tax basis of assets should always be ascertained by the acquiring company. It is not safe to assume that the basis is the same as the book amounts at which assets are carried by the selling company.

If there are several commonly owned corporations involved in a sale, it is possible to arrange that cash be paid for one or more companies and securities exchanged for others, so that only part of the over-all transaction results in a taxable gain to the seller. Thus, the seller may postpone a substantial part of the tax on his gain on disposition of capital stock or net assets, while receiving some cash for investment diversification or other purposes.

Financing the Purchase. BY PUBLIC OFFERING OF SECURITIES OR LONG-TERM LOANS. Where a company is purchasing the capital stock or net assets and business of another, the transaction may be financed in various ways, assuming the acquiring company does not have cash available for such an acquisition. Some companies may raise the necessary funds by means of a public offering of capital stock, while others might do so by means of long-term loans from banks or insurance companies or by the sale of debenture bonds.

BY ISSUANCE OF DEBT SECURITIES TO THE SELLER OR BY INSTALLMENT PAYMENTS. Debt securities may be issued in whole or in part, as consideration for a purchase; or capital stock may be issued as part consideration; and the transaction will still retain its "taxable" attributes. In other cases, a company may acquire the capital stock or net assets and business of another in

---

[12] Int. Rev. Code of 1954, § 334(b)(2).

an installment purchase. Thus, the acquiring company may finance the purchase, at least in part, from income derived from operations of the acquired company over the period of the installment payments.

A few interesting variations of "taxable" acquisitions under the Internal Revenue Code follow.

PURCHASE WITH PART OF PRICE CONTINGENT UPON FUTURE EARNINGS. At times, the prospective acquirer and seller have difficulty in arriving at a price, either because of disagreement as to future earnings prospects of the company proposed to be sold or uncertainty regarding the utilization and acceptance by the Internal Revenue Service of a "tax-loss carryover." This problem may be solved by a fixed base price with an additional amount to be paid over a period contingent upon future operating results. This technique may also be used in "tax-free" reorganizations, where capital stock only is employed.[13] An interesting example of a case in a "taxable" deal involving a contingency provision follows.

STUDEBAKER-PACKARD CORP. AND D. W. ONAN & SONS, INC. Under an agreement as of September 30, 1960, Studebaker-Packard Corp. acquired all the outstanding common stock of D. W. Onan & Sons, Inc., for (1) cash equal to the closing net worth of Onan as of August 31, 1960 (estimated at approximately $6,430,000) of which $6,000,000 was paid on October 5, 1960, (2) 324,325 shares of common stock of Studebaker-Packard, and (3) contingent cash payments totaling $3,000,000 to be paid on April 15, 1961, and annually thereafter out of net earnings of the then Onan Division of the corporation at the rate of one-third of such earnings (before federal income taxes) for each period through 1963, and thereafter at the rate of one-half of such earnings (after federal income taxes). An additional feature of the agreement was that $430,000 (estimated) was withheld from the initial cash payment until the net worth of Onan at August 31, 1960, was determined as the result of a joint audit by independent public accountants.[14]

[13] See merger of Peerless Cement Corp. and Hercules Cement Corp. into American Cement Corp., Annual Report, 1957, p. 21.
[14] Studebaker-Packard Corp., Prospectus, December 22, 1960.

Acquisition of Majority of Capital Stock of Company Through Exchange, Principally of Non-Equity Securities. It is possible to obtain control of a company through a tender or offer directly to its stockholders to purchase their capital stock for cash or debt securities. Such transactions are taxable to the sellers, for federal income tax purposes. The purchase offer usually has to be at a fair premium above the market price to induce the selling stockholders to tender their shares. The desirable features of these deals, from the acquirer's standpoint, are that he eliminates the problem of having a new group of substantial and possibly controlling stockholders and he may gain some leverage for earnings on common stock. An example of such an exchange offer involving debentures and common stock purchase warrants follows.

NATIONAL THEATRES & TELEVISION, INC., AND NATIONAL TELEFILM ASSOCIATES, INC. In February, 1959, National Theatres & Television, Inc. (formerly National Theatres, Inc.) offered $11 of its 5½ per cent sinking fund subordinated debentures and a warrant for ¼ share of its common stock in exchange for each of the outstanding shares of common stock of National Telefilm Associates, Inc., which had a market value of 9⅛ at December 31, 1958. On September 29, 1959, National Theatres announced it had acquired, through this exchange offer, 1,114,636 shares representing 87.27 per cent of a total of 1,277,197 outstanding shares of National Telefilm and 79 per cent of the total of 440,955 of the latter's warrants to purchase common stock that were outstanding on that date. In its annual report for the period ended September 29, 1959, National Theatres indicated that its long-term debt had increased to $35,668,486 from $16,504,295 at the end of the preceding year, largely as a result of obligations assumed and incurred in the acquisition and operation of National Telefilm.[15]

PURCHASE OF ASSETS AND BUSINESS FOR
CONVERTIBLE DEBENTURES AND COMMON STOCK

A variation of the purchase of capital stock for debt securities is the use of convertible debentures. Such debentures have a con-

[15] National Theatres & Television, Inc., Annual Report to Stockholders, September 29, 1959.

siderable appeal to the investor because his capital is protected to a much greater degree than in an equity security; he has a virtually guaranteed income; and he has the advantage of exercising his option to convert his investment into equity shares at a fixed price, if the company prospers. From the standpoint of the acquiring company, although it may enjoy the advantage of leverage on earnings on common stock by the issuance of such securities, it is generally not desirable to have too large a part of its total capitalization in convertible debentures. If a company issuing them prospers, these bonds will tend to keep the market price of common stock depressed, because of their continued conversion and dilution of per share earnings. A case involving the use of convertible debentures in a purchase follows. An interesting feature of this deal is that substantial amounts of cash and marketable securities were included in the assets of the seller.

CERRO DE PASCO CORP. AND CONSOLIDATED COPPERMINES CORP. On March 25, 1959, Cerro de Pasco Corp. acquired all the assets of Consolidated Coppermines Corp. in exchange for 201,333 shares of its common stock, $26,311,700 of 5½ per cent subordinated debentures due 1979 (convertible into common stock at $49.43 per share until December 31, 1968, with protection against dilution), a cash adjustment of $50,333, and the assumption by Cerro of the liabilities of Consolidated. The principal assets acquired were 93.4 per cent of the capital stock of Rockbestos Products Corp. and approximately $23,000,000 in cash and marketable securities. Later in 1959, minority interests in Rockbestos and The Titan Metal Mfg. Co. were acquired by Cerro.[16]

Installment Purchase of Capital Stock. The purchase of a company on an installment basis has been mentioned as one of the methods of financing an acquisition. Customarily, the balance remaining after the down payment is covered by interest-bearing notes in favor of the seller. In order to qualify for deferred recognition of gain to the seller, for federal income tax purposes, not more than 30 per cent of the purchase price may be paid during the year of sale, with the balance being paid over any period thereafter. An example of an installment purchase follows.

[16] Cerro de Pasco Corp., Annual Report to Stockholders, 1959.

MINUTE MAID CORP. AND TENCO, INC. In September, 1959, Minute Maid Corp. acquired all the outstanding shares of Tenco, Inc., for (1) a cash consideration of $3,000,000, (2) 5 per cent promissory notes, due in 1960 and 1961, in the amount of $2,550,000, and (3) 299,996 shares of Minute Maid to be delivered on or before April 1, 1960, of which the fair market value was considered to be $5,962,400, or a total consideration of $11,512,400. When settlement was made under this transaction, former Tenco stockholders actually received 311,992 shares of Minute Maid common stock to give effect to a 4 per cent stock dividend in November, 1959. It will be noted that less than 30 per cent of the purchase price was paid in 1959, thus qualifying the transaction for installment federal tax treatment on behalf of the sellers. As a matter of further interest, Minute Maid was merged into the Coca-Cola Co. on December 30, 1960.[17]

Financial, accounting, federal income tax, and certain other considerations have been covered *very broadly* in this chapter to acquaint the reader with some of the problems and remedies inherent in corporate acquisitions and mergers. Such aspects and other matters will be discussed more fully in later chapters.

[17] Minute Maid Corp., Annual Report to Stockholders, 1959; *Moody's Industrial Manual,* 1961, p. 2518.

Chapter 3

WHAT TO GUARD AGAINST

In Chapter 1, a number of mergers (primarily consolidations) were mentioned dating back to the turn of the century, most of which are presently considered successful enterprises. However, a number of consolidations during this period did not turn out well, despite the belief of many of the bankers or promoters who underwrote their security issues that the mere act of consolidation would boost earnings beyond those of the constituent companies prior to amalgamation.

SOME IMPORTANT STUDIES

Arthur S. Dewing, in an article in 1921, reviewed a "random selection" of thirty-five industrial combinations that met the following six conditions:

(1) Must have been in existence for at least ten years before 1914, (2) must have been formed as a combination of at least five separate, independent and competing plants, (3) must have a national rather than a mere sectional or local significance, (4) must have published financial reports in which at least some degree of confidence can be placed, (5) must have available published or accessible reports covering the earnings of the separate plants prior to their consolidation and the estimates of earnings made at the time the combination was effected. Lastly, the group as a whole must represent a wide diversity of industries.[1]

In tabulations showing aggregate earnings of the separate enterprises prior to consolidation, Dewing notes that they were 18 per cent greater than for the year following consolidation and exceeded by approximately the same percentage the average annual earnings for the ten years subsequent to consolidation. He further notes that the promoters had estimated the earnings

[1] Arthur S. Dewing, "A Statistical Test of the Success of Consolidations," *Quarterly Journal of Economics,* November, 1921.

of the companies, in the aggregate, to be 50 per cent greater after consolidation than before.

It is recognized that averages may be misleading; but approximately 75 per cent of the companies shown in Dewing's tabulations had poorer earnings after consolidation, both for the year following and in the annual average for ten years, than for the period prior to consolidation.

Later and More Comprehensive Study of Early Mergers. Later, in 1934, Shaw Livermore published an article in which he made a much more comprehensive survey analyzing 409 companies participating in business combinations during the 1888 to 1905 period movement.[2] He eliminated a number of companies studied as not being involved in true mergers and classified the remaining companies into two groups—one designated as a primary group of 156 and another as a secondary group of 172 industrial mergers.

His primary list consisted of companies "with power enough to influence markedly conditions in their industry." The secondary group "possessed leadership in their respective industries only in a few cases, and in those largely as a result of their later growth rather than a consequence of consolidation."

Livermore based his judgment of the success or failure of a merger on earning power of the merged enterprises, i.e., earnings on invested capital covering a maximum period of thirty-three years subsequent to merger in his studies (less if the company had been formed later than 1901, or had since been absorbed by another successful concern). He compared the earnings on capitalization of the companies included in his studies with publications on industrial profits, in the same industries, of the Department of Commerce and the National Bureau of Economic Research.

His findings are classified in the tabulations on page 33.

Livermore's classification of companies in the "failure" category did not necessarily mean they had failed in the legal sense, but had failed to show earning power, had been reorganized, or had made severe capital adjustments.

His "limping group" were those whose earnings records were mixed, generally with poorer results in the more recent years of his review. It is interesting to note in each tabulation that the

[2] Shaw Livermore, "The Success of Industrial Mergers," *Quarterly Journal of Economics*, November, 1935.

failures and limping groups approximated 50 per cent of the totals.

Primary Group

	Number	Per Cent of Total
Early failures	53	34.0
Later failures	10	6.4
"Limping group"	17	10.9
Rejuvenations	10	6.4
Successes	56	35.9
Outstanding successes	10	6.4
Total	156	100.0

Secondary Group

	Number	Per Cent of Total
Failures	78	45.3
"Limping group"	11	6.4
Rejuvenations	3	1.8
Successes	80	46.5
Total	172	100.0

The names of the companies included in the studies of Dewing and Livermore are listed and classified in their articles.

The record of unsatisfactory mergers and acquisitions in the turn-of-the-century movement is not unique. Federal Trade Commission statistics indicate that 41 per cent of acquisitions and mergers in 1959 were undertaken by companies having assets in excess of $50,000,000 each, and an additional 32 per cent by companies whose assets ranged from $10,000,000 to $50,000,000.[3] With the managerial skills available in these large companies, one would believe that all such transactions would be consummated advantageously and skillfully. This is not necessarily so.

Results of a Recent Selective Study of Acquisitions. Booz·Allen & Hamilton, management consultants, recently made a survey of 128 acquisitions by companies in the Chicago area.[4] The appraisal by the management of the acquiring companies of the success of results in their acquisitions is summarized below.

	One to Two Acquisitions	Three to Four Acquisitions	Five to Ten Acquisitions
Results good	27%	44%	62%
Results doubtful	50	31	25
Sold or liquidated	23	25	13
Total	100%	100%	100%

[3] *Statistical Abstract of the United States*, 1960, p. 501.
[4] Booz·Allen & Hamilton, *Management of New Products*, 1960.

It is evident from this record, which generally parallels that of most companies entering into the mergers and acquisitions field, that experience teaches. Unfortunately, this is a high-stakes game and not many companies can afford to make mistakes in playing it.

MAJOR PITFALLS

Since the end of World War II, there has been a burgeoning sellers' market in acquisitions and mergers. Many large enterprises are constantly searching for companies to acquire or absorb, resulting in spirited competition for the more desirable, or seemingly desirable, medium-sized and smaller companies. For this reason, purchase prices have been generous in relationship to net tangible assets and current or realistically prospective earnings. Nevertheless, we should not lose sight of the fact that this situation may be reversed during periods of business depression, when companies have been sold for less than their net current assets.

Publication of Business Combinations That Did Not Work Out. Royal Little, chairman of the board of Textron, although he acknowledged a high average of successful acquisitions, admitted that at times he had not done so well and cautioned that the doctrine of *caveat emptor* also prevails in the acquisition of companies. During recent years, *Business Week* had several articles,[5] and *The Wall Street Journal* had at least one [6] commenting on business combinations that did not work out.

It is difficult, generally, to develop the particulars of recent acquisition or merger situations that did not work out because of the reluctance of management to admit mistakes in this area. A few are discussed below to illustrate some of the pitfalls in business combinations.

Insufficient Investigation of the Acquired Company. It is of the utmost importance, as discussed more fully in subsequent chapters, that a careful investigation be made of a company proposed to be acquired before closing the deal. This investigation normally should include an examination of the financial statements

---

[5] "Polyglots and a Touch of Babel," *Business Week*, September 21, 1957; "Mergers Boom, Buyers Choosier," *Business Week*, July 12, 1958.

[6] "Mergers' Aftermath," *The Wall Street Journal*, October 3, 1960.

of the seller by independent certified public accountants at a reasonably current date. This may be done by the seller's or by the purchaser's accountants, if the former are, in fact, independent and maintain the high standards of auditing subscribed to by the national and state professional accounting associations. An example of a case where the acquirer discovered long after closing that the assets and income of the seller were substantially overstated follows.

H. L. GREEN Co., INC., ACQUISITION OF THE OLEN Co., INC. The merger of The Olen Co., Inc., a chain of 123 variety stores with sales of $20,000,000 a year, into H. L. Green Co., Inc., a chain of 224 variety stores in the United States and Canada with a volume of $110,000,000 a year in the latter part of 1958, appeared to be an excellent deal for the larger company in acquiring management to reverse its declining earnings trend. Unfortunately, the management wizard, Maurice Olen, president of Olen, who was made president and chief executive of the H. L. Green combined enterprise, acknowledged he had "juggled his accounts" by overstating assets, principally inventories, and understating liabilities. When this discovery was made in 1959, the Olen Co., instead of having a reputed net worth in excess of $1,000,000, was found to have had an excess of some $3,000,000 of liabilities over assets. Naturally, its reported earnings for the several years prior to the merger were likewise overstated.[7]

Corporate Indigestion. It is rarely desirable to acquire too many companies in too short a time, particularly in widely diverse industries. Before acquiring a company, it should be carefully investigated and its potential determined in the hands of the purchaser. This is necessary in order to arrive at a fair price and also to determine how the company should be operated after acquisition and its place in the integrated operation of the purchaser. An interesting example of the disastrous results of an overly ambitious acquisitions program follows.

UNITED STATES HOFFMAN MACHINERY CORP. ACQUISITIONS. United States Hoffman Machinery Corp., which acquired new

---

[7] H. L. Green Co., Inc., Annual Report to Stockholders, 1958; T. A. Wise, "The Looting of H. L. Green," *Fortune,* March, 1960.

management in 1954, embarked on a program of broad diversification in 1955, acquiring seventeen companies that year and eight in 1956 in such diverse industries as tin cans and containers, books, vending machines, motion picture screens, electronic meters and devices, vacuum tubes, air frames and missile components, candy, metal furniture, filtration and vacuum systems, heating systems components, and army ordnance materials. It started to divest itself, in 1957, of its interests in some of these acquisitions or their assets via the sale or liquidation route with depressing results over the next few years, as indicated by the following reported figures:

Year	Net Income or (Loss) *
1955	$2,302,134
1956	1,052,761
1957	(1,617,876)
1958	(5,449,889)
1959	(3,156,899)
1960	(2,244,188)

* Includes "special items," primarily adjustments of investment carrying amounts of "goodwill" applicable to subsidiaries acquired.

As of December 31, 1960, the company had outstanding 2,363,414 shares of common stock with an aggregate net book equity of $2,230,708, or less than $1 a share, after adjusting for redemption value of preferred stock outstanding. This compared with 795,142 shares of common stock outstanding (adjusted for a three-for-one stock split in 1955) with an aggregate net book equity of $8,958,558, or approximately $11 a share, as of December 31, 1954. Incidentally, the company's retained earnings of $5,200,468 at December 31, 1954, had been transformed into an accumulated deficit of $12,301,589 at December 31, 1960.[8]

Loss Companies in Unrelated Fields Present Greater Acquisition Risks. Many companies that include acquisitions as part of their corporate growth plan wisely limit their prospects to companies in allied fields having similar marketing and distribution outlets. For example, a company selling industrial products would not be

[8] United States Hoffman Machinery Corp., Annual Reports to Stockholders, 1954, 1955, 1956, 1957, 1958, 1959, and 1960.

interested in acquiring another in the consumer-products field. Also, one selling to manufacturers or marketing through distributors would not wish to become involved in selling to dealers or direct to consumers. Another factor considered important is that the company proposed to be acquired should be operating on a profitable basis. Companies operating at a loss may be acquired at a bargain but prove to be a drain on the profits of the acquirer. An example of the result of an acquisition of a company operating at a loss in a depressed industry and an unrelated field follows.

AMERACE CORP. MERGER AND CONSOLIDATION. In 1957, Amerace Corp. was formed by a merger and consolidation of (1) American Hard Rubber Co., which produced rubber compounds, plastics, chemicals, fiber glass, and hose; (2) Bachmann Uxbridge Worsted Corp., producers of woolens and worsteds; and (3) Wardell Corp., which was then holding cash and securities, since it had disposed of its business in 1953. Backmann Uxbridge had suffered losses during the three years preceding the consolidation and brought, as a legacy to the merger, a tax-loss carryover of $2,900,000.

In 1960, Amerace sold the Bachmann Uxbridge Division net assets and business to Indian Head Mills, Inc., at a substantial discount, taking a loss of $10,000,000, after federal income taxes, on the transaction. The president's report to stockholders for that year tells the Bachman Uxbridge story, as follows:

The decision to sell this division was not easy. In 1957, when American Hard Rubber Company and Wardell Corporation merged into Bachmann Uxbridge to form Amerace Corporation, we held high hopes that the worst was over in our country's woolen and worsted industry. Backmann Uxbridge's textile veterans and Amerace's central management shared this view. For three years, it looked as though we were right. During those years—1957, 1958 and 1959—Bachmann Uxbridge made substantial profits, in contrast with a substantial loss in 1954 and moderate losses in 1955 and 1956.

Although Bachmann Uxbridge's earnings were high in 1959, new orders taken toward the end of the year for 1960 delivery, indicated a slowdown in business. This curtailment in the first half of 1960 produced losses instead of profits. The losses finally reached $596,585, thereby offsetting equivalent profits in other divisions. But that was not the worst of the picture.

Unmistakable signs of the deterioration of the entire woolen and worsted industry, due to factors beyond your management's control, grew as these losses were incurred. No relief was in sight. Because your Board of Directors saw these losses piling up and could not determine when they might be stopped, it decided to sell the Backmann Uxbridge Division and put the proceeds of the sale to work where they could earn, not lose, money for Amerace. We could find no buyer who was willing to pay nearly the amount for which Bachmann Uxbridge's assets were carried on our books. So we took the best offer we could get, and our books reflect the loss which we sustained in eliminating this profit drain.

As yet, we have seen no improvement in the depressed state of the domestic woolen and worsted industry. In fact, since the Bachmann Uxbridge sale was consummated, other fine, old companies have given up the discouraging battle in that industry. This tends to confirm the business wisdom of our decision to stop devoting energy and capital to woolen and worsted textiles.[9]

Do Not Overbid To Acquire Control of a Company. A mistake that has been made more than once by companies and individuals seeking to acquire control of a company is to be overeager. When they commence purchasing the capital stock of the company they propose to acquire, the price per share may be reasonable. But when their objectives become known, the stockholders hold out for higher and higher prices until the stock is greatly overpriced. An interesting example of a costly acquisition, the financing of which had a materially adverse effect on the acquirer's business, follows.

FAIRBANKS WHITNEY CORP. ACQUISITION OF CONTROL OF FAIRBANKS, MORSE & CO. Fairbanks Whitney Corp. (then Penn-Texas Corp.) in connection with a proxy contest had acquired 49.54 per cent of the common stock of Fairbanks, Morse & Co. by the spring of 1958, at a cost in excess of $28,000,000. In 1958 and 1959, under new management, it acquired additional shares from Robert H. Morse and Canadian Fairbanks-Morse Co., Ltd., to bring its total interest in Fairbanks, Morse up to 85 per cent of that company's outstanding common stock, at an additional cost of approximately $12,000,000, or an aggregate investment of some $40,000,000.

Fairbanks Whitney Corp., until 1952, was primarily engaged in coal mining and distribution, and through a series of acquisitions since that year now produces a variety of items, including machine tools, gauges, dies, controls, accessories for aircraft and missile fuel systems, etc. Fairbanks, Morse's principal products consist of diesel engines, pumps, motors, locomotives, and an extensive line of scales.

[9] Bachmann Uxbridge Worsted Corp., Proxy Statement, May 7, 1957; Amerace Corp., Annual Report to Stockholders, December 31, 1960.

Since Fairbanks Whitney's acquisition of the substantial interest in Fairbanks, Morse, the latter had a lower profit in 1959 than in some years. In 1960 and 1961, they had losses of $181,000 and $767,000, respectively; and for six months to June 30, 1962, they reported a loss of $137,000. Meantime Fairbanks Whitney, which had been selling some of its earlier acquisitions during recent years, was having trouble with its other operations, with cumulative losses for the four years ended December 31, 1961, and a small profit reported for the six months to June 30, 1962. The consolidated net income or loss figures of Fairbanks, Whitney include its interest in Fairbanks, Morse from November 1, 1958.[10]

Dangers of Too Broad Diversification Cannot Be Overemphasized. An interesting case involving an acquisition in a non-related industry is discussed below. Despite the seeming lack of similarity of the businesses of the two companies, the acquirer was ordered to divest itself of the acquired company as the result of an antitrust suit under the broad provisions of Section 7 of the Clayton Act "to prevent the possibility of potential competition."

AMERICAN RADIATOR & STANDARD SANITARY CORP. ACQUISITION OF MULLINS MANUFACTURING CORP. In its 1955 annual report to stockholders, American Radiator & Standard Sanitary Corp. reported the acquisition, effective January 30, 1956, of Mullins Manufacturing Corp., to be operated as the Youngstown Kitchens Division. This deal was effected by the issuance of 1,666,657 shares of common stock of American Radiator that had a market value, at the time of the merger, of about $36,000,000. In its report, American Radiator mentioned that the merger would permit it to extend its activities into the packaged kitchen line. The division also produced steel parts for the automotive and appliance industries, as well as military items.

In its nine months' report to stockholders for the year 1961, American Radiator announced the sale of assets of the Youngstown Kitchens Division for approximately $6,200,000, at an estimated loss of $3,600,000, after federal income taxes (about

[10] Penn-Texas Corp., Prospectuses, October 15, 1958, and April 24, 1959. Fairbanks Whitney Corp. in *Moody's Industrial Manual*, 1960, p. 2971–2974; 1961, p. 2176–2179. Annual Report, 1961, *The New York Times*, August 2, 1962, p. 33. Fairbanks, Morse & Co., Annual Report, 1961; Quarterly Report to Stockholders, June 30, 1962.

$7,500,000 before taxes). The sale was made in compliance with a court decree entered in an antitrust suit arising out of its merger with Mullins. This interim report states that "although the disposition of these assets will reduce our annual sales volume by approximately $20,000,000, the net effect on earnings should be favorable, since the division was operating at a loss." The losses of this division during the period it was owned and operated by American Radiator were probably sizable, relative to the original investment in 1956, as Mullins had net assets in excess of $30,-000,000 when it was acquired.[11]

Compared with the relatively few unsuccessful acquisitions and mergers publicized, there are many times the number of outright failures or less than satisfactory combinations that you never hear about, as indicated by the studies discussed earlier in this chapter.

REASONS FOR FAILURE OF BUSINESS COMBINATIONS

What are some of the reasons why business combinations are not successful from the standpoint of the acquirer? Included among them are the following:

1. Lack of knowledge of the history and potential of the industry of the seller
2. Failure to fully investigate all aspects of the seller's business (before signing a binding agreement), including his motives for selling and the contribution required in management and financing in order to operate the enterprise successfully
3. Failure to determine how the acquisition will fit into the combined enterprise and its expected contribution in profits, management, marketing, and other areas
4. Making sweeping changes in management, personnel, policies, and procedures after consummating the transaction but before determining what made the acquired company successful
5. Being overeager to effect the deal and accordingly paying too high a price in terms of capital stock or cash for what is obtained.

No Such Thing as a Permanent Growth Industry. Theodore Levitt has pointed out that there is no such thing as a permanent growth industry.[12] He cites the case of the railroad industry, which was

---

[11] American Radiator & Standard Sanitary Corp., Annual Reports to Stockholders, 1955 and 1956; report to stockholders for nine months ended September 30, 1961, dated November 15, 1961.
[12] Theodore Levitt, "Marketing Myopia," *Harvard Business Review,* July-August 1960.

in a seemingly impregnable position years ago, as was the motion picture, dry cleaning, coal, and oil industries, as well as individual and chain service grocery companies. He attributes the reasons for their reverses or retardation in growth to the failure to realize broad aims and being product rather than customer oriented. Had they endeavored to cater to customers' requirements rather than to conduct operations in the same old way, they would have continued to grow.

EXAMPLES OF CHANGES IN INDUSTRIES. *Railroads*. The broad aim of railroads was passenger and freight transportation, not necessarily by rail, but by whatever means appeared desirable from the customer's standpoint. These increased needs are being largely filled by airplanes, buses, trucks, and cars. Most of us, of course, remember what happened to the electric streetcar.

Textiles. The woolen textile industry has been in the doldrums for many years, partly as the result of importations from other countries, but more because it failed to adjust itself to the changing demand for lighter-weight clothing and the increasing use of synthetic fibers.

Food Chains. As late as the 1930's, the big food chains were operating service stores. From 1935 to 1945, there was a sweeping conversion to the supermarket-type operation, with a number of the medium-sized chains, which were caught napping, being absorbed in the process.

Electronics. During recent years, "electronics" has been a magic word, which, if merely included in a corporate name, meant extra dollars in the sale of companies or public offerings of their securities. However, a number of acquirers of companies in this glamour industry have found, to their regret, that it is highly competitive and requires considerable astuteness to produce reasonable profit returns.

Failure To Plan How Executive Personnel, Plant, and Facilities Fit in Before Closing. An article by Robert L. Chambers, which was written for the benefit of a prospective seller, also contains a moral for the would-be acquirer.[13] The author cites a case history

[13] Robert L. Chambers, "How Not To Sell Your Company," *Harvard Business Review*, May–June 1961.

in which the "new boss" made sweeping changes immediately after taking over in personnel, procedures, systems, and plant operations. Within two years, the company, once a leader in its industry, became a corporate skeleton.

To look at the other side of the coin, before effecting a business combination agreement, you should plan on how the executive and other personnel, plant, and facilities will fit your requirements. It makes no sense to give long-term contracts, at high compensation rates, and stock options to executives you later find you should dismiss or retire; or to assume a long-term lease or pay a high price for a plant if you will shortly be abandoning operations at that particular location.

Who Is Acquiring Whom? This is a good question to consider if there are one or several large stockholders of the company proposed to be acquired who would emerge as major stockholders of the acquirer. Management of the latter could suddenly find itself deposed, in such a situation, either through power wielded by these major stockholders as directors of the combined enterprise or by means of a proxy fight instituted by such persons.

Overpaying—A Major Cause of Disgruntlement in Acquisitions. In a number of cases, where dissatisfaction arises on the part of the acquirer after consummation of a deal, the main complaint boils down to the view that he has overpaid for what he has received; and often this is the sad truth. In some cases, in seeking to absolve himself of blame in failing to be prudent, he contends that the seller misrepresented or concealed important facts. Rarely does he have legal grounds for sustaining such a position and soon finds this out.

Concept of Professional Management of Widely Diverse Businesses Is Questionable. There is a concept with some degree of acceptance in business circles that professional management can successfully operate any type of business. This is a somewhat questionable viewpoint and is not sustained by the record. True, there are certain fundamental principles that apply in financial-accounting, sales administration, and personnel management to all businesses. However, research, production, and marketing procedures and requirements vary widely among businesses. This may be the reason that the highest ratio of unsuccessful acquisitions and mergers has resulted from broad diversification programs.

HOW TO CONSUMMATE SUCCESSFUL ACQUISITIONS AND MERGERS

What then can be done to improve the ratio of successful acquisitions and mergers? This can be accomplished by following the advice of one of the country's largest stockbrokerage houses, "Investigate—and then invest."

Whenever a company plans to acquire or merge with other companies, its first step should be to define its objectives. A company's objectives may vary greatly, ranging from expansion of capacity, product diversification, improvement of competitive position, and extension of market outlets to integration of operations, acquisition of management or technical personnel, or merely the investment of excess funds. The company's second step should be to form an acquisitions committee, or study or project group if the word "committee" has a distasteful connotation to management. If a company has a properly staffed corporate development or long-range planning group, such a unit could logically handle this activity.

Value of Committee or Group Participation in Merger Field—the Exception to the Rule. Generally, on the subject of committees, C. Northcote Parkinson, although a spoofer, is quite in order when he depicts committees as confused, bewildered, and time-wasting groups,[14] as does Clarence B. Randall, who believes that committees have flourished in number to the point where they often cause postponement of vital decision making.[15] Unquestionably, the committee approach is overdone in many, perhaps the majority, of the cases where it is utilized. However, the acquisitions and mergers field appears to be one area where a committee may operate to advantage. A wide divergence of information generally is required in such transactions, and it takes the judgment of more than one person to reach a sound conclusion as to the desirability of effecting a deal. Thus, preliminary studies of acquisition pros-

[14] C. Northcote Parkinson, "On Blahmanism, Confusionism, Etc.," *The New York Times Magazine,* January 3, 1960.
[15] Clarence B. Randall, "The Myth of the Management Committee," in *The Folklore of Management,* Chap. 3, (1961).

pects may utilize the skills of operating and marketing personnel as well as accounting and broad managerial knowledge.

FUNCTION OF AN ACQUISITIONS GROUP. The function of an acquisitions group should be to study, review, and advise, and its findings presented to management or to the Board of Directors for decision making. Depending on the size of a company and its acquisitions program, this group may include one or more full-time members; or it may consist entirely of executives who devote only a portion of their time to this activity. This aspect of form does not make much difference, as long as the members of the group are experienced and knowledgeable in their respective fields.

DESIRABILITY OF BOARD OF DIRECTORS LIAISON WITH THE GROUP. If possible, a member of the Board of Directors should serve with the acquisitions group; and, in certain cases, he should be an "outside" director. There are times when the interests of the stockholders may not coincide with the personal interests of all the management group with regard to a proposed acquisition or merger. For instance, it may be quite apparent that one or more members of a management team would be eliminated or downgraded in position if a proposed business combination were effected; yet the merger might be highly advantageous for the owners.

Directors Should Define General Objectives and Policies. When an acquisitions group is established, the company's Board of Directors should advise it of general objectives, policies, and types of mergers and acquisitions to consider. If a company intends to acquire more than one company, it is often desirable to prepare a brochure containing the following and other pertinent information.

REGARDING THE PROSPECTIVE ACQUIRER.
1. History and background.
2. Executive personnel and organization structure.
3. The extent to which the company operates on a centralized or decentralized basis.
4. Product lines and products.
5. Plant, warehouse, and office locations.
6. Marketing methods and areas served.

7. Engineering, research, and development.
8. Statement of financial position and statements of income for the latest fiscal year and one or more preceding years.

REGARDING COMPANIES BEING SOUGHT FOR ACQUISITION OR MERGER.

1. Acquisition objectives of the prospective acquirer, i.e., horizontal or vertical integration or complementary or broad diversification. Also, whether cash deals or exchanges of capital stock or both would be of interest.
2. Size of companies in which interested—indicate sales volume and profit ranges.
3. Preferable plant, warehouse, and office locations.
4. Product lines—it is desirable to indicate whether industrial- or consumer-product lines or both are sought and, if possible, to list a number of products that would be of interest to the company.
5. Engineering, research, development, patent, and copyright preferences regarding products manufactured.
6. Marketing—the method that would be preferable, such as through distributors, dealers, salesmen, or manufacturers' representatives. Also, indicate geographical areas interested in serving.
7. Management—whether the company wishes active and competent management to continue or would be willing to supply management.

ADVANTAGES OF DEFINING OBJECTIVES. Such a brochure has the dual purpose of crystallizing for management its acquisitions objectives and, when distributed to persons assisting in the search for companies, pinpointing the prospective acquiring company's requirements, obviating the necessity for reviewing data on prospects that would not be of interest.

How To Find Acquisition Prospects. Rather than limiting itself to certain companies that happen to come to the attention of the directors, an acquisitions group should study all companies that may be considered good prospects. This can be done by:

1. Reviewing *Thomas' Register of American Manufacturers*, the classified industries section of *Moody's Industrial Manual*, or similar directories.
2. Confiding in bankers, the company's independent public accountants, its legal counsel, and others who often know of companies that might be interested in a sale or merger.

3. Encouraging suggestions from officials in the sales and operating
   divisions with respect to unlisted companies.
4. Engaging investment bankers, business consultants or brokers.
   (In Chapter 8, "finders' fees and brokers' commissions" are discussed in detail.)

Systematic investigation of prospects by an acquisitions group
has often turned up one whose management had previously given
no thought to business combination possibilities.

A corporate acquisition or merger is not a routine transaction
and, in most cases, involves a substantial outlay of capital stock
or cash. It is vital that the chief executive of a company and its
directors have all the facts to enable them to reach an informed
decision on the merits of a proposed transaction. Accordingly, a
careful investigation should be made of each company proposed
to be acquired and all pertinent factors evaluated before definite
proposals are made as to purchase price or merger terms.

CHECKLISTS

It is often desirable to prepare checklists to make certain that
all major problems are considered by acquisitions groups and that
important areas of investigation are covered. A checklist, which
may be used as a guide, is included as Appendix A of this book.
The list is arranged as follows:

Section   I. Summary of Information Concerning Proposed Acqui-
               sition or Merger
                  The Proposed Transaction
                  Tax Aspects
                  Securities and Exchange Commission Aspects
                  Possible Pitfalls to Acquiring Company
                  Status and Development of the Company
                  Accounting Principles and Practices
Section   II. Corporate, Accounting, and Financial
Section III. Tax Considerations
Section   IV. Securities and Exchange Commission Considerations
Section   V. Management and Administration
Section   VI. Manufacturing
Section VII. Selling and Distribution

Areas of investigation to be undertaken are discussed in the
next two chapters; accounting, tax, and Securities and Exchange
Commission considerations are covered in later chapters.

Chapter 4

FINANCIAL AND ACCOUNTING INFORMATION NEEDED BEFORE EFFECTING THE DEAL

Examples in the previous chapter of pitfalls encountered in business combinations indicate the importance of obtaining sufficient information to insure the success of such ventures. The type and variety of data required are discussed in this and the succeeding chapter.

Whether or not information is obtained before or after overtures are made, the following areas should be covered:

Corporate, accounting, and financial
Management and personnel
Sales, marketing, and distribution
Operations, engineering, research, and development

In addition, consideration should be given to the desired form of the acquisition or merger, that is, the relative advantages of a cash or part-cash deal versus an exchange of capital stocks. Whether it is desirable to acquire the net assets and business or the capital stock of the company proposed to be acquired and the objectives of the proposed sellers also must be considered. The conventional forms of acquisitions and mergers, as well as a number of examples of unusual business combinations, are discussed in Chapter 2.

Also, legal, tax, and governmental regulatory requirements should be considered to the extent that they influence the form of the business combination and the time required to effect it. In some instances, these requirements may present insurmountable difficulties. Certain tax, legal, accounting, and other aspects of business combinations are alluded to briefly in Chapter 2 and are discussed more fully in later chapters.

A considerable amount of information required may be obtained on a number of prospects before making any overtures to them. Such information would be available in *Moody's Industrial Manual,* or similar publications; annual reports to stockholders; registration statements; Forms 10–K, or other reports and proxy statements filed with the Securities and Exchange Commission; and Dun & Bradstreet reports on unlisted companies.

Corporate, accounting, and financial information to be obtained and studied is discussed in this chapter. The primary purpose of obtaining such information is to make comparisons of the net assets and net income of the company being considered with similar data of the prospective acquiring company, to evaluate the respective companies, and to project future operations of the combined enterprise. Management and personnel; sales, marketing, and distribution; and operations, engineering, research, and development information to be obtained and studies to be undertaken are discussed in Chapter 5.

FINANCIAL STATEMENTS—BALANCE SHEET

Audited financial statements should be obtained for a period of five to ten years, or less, depending upon the significance of statements for the earlier years, if there has been a rapid growth pattern. These statements may be supplemented by particulars on the following, for the latest year or period, unless otherwise specified.

Cash.

1. Ascertain minimum and maximum cash balances at month ends for the latest fiscal year, as well as for the current interim period.
2. Amounts of cash subject to legal restrictions under agency or trustee arrangements—such arrangements are common in real estate management companies and mill agencies and also apply to cash withheld from employees for the payment of income and social security taxes. To the extent companies are acting in a trust capacity, they should not be financing their business with such restricted funds.
3. A cash forecast should be prepared covering a period of several years to ascertain if working capital will be sufficient for operating and growth requirements.

Marketable Securities and Other Investments. Details of items and their approximate market or fair value—the valuation of investments in marketable securities does not present any great problem, but investments of a substantial amount in non-marketable securities may require some investigation to ascertain their fair value. This is particularly so in the case of investments and advances applicable to unconsolidated subsidiaries and affiliates.

Accounts and Notes Receivable.
1. Credit terms
2. Aged analysis
3. Accounts with a balance exceeding 5 to 10 per cent of total receivables
4. Amount of other than normal trade debtors accounts, such as government, officers and employees, etc.
5. Apparent adequacy of reserve for bad debts
6. Amount of accounts and notes receivable discounted and whether with or without recourse

HAVE NOTES FOR DELINQUENT ACCOUNTS RECEIVABLE BEEN ACCEPTED AND RENEWED? There have been instances where companies have accepted notes from delinquent accounts receivable trade debtors and renewed the notes upon the maturity of the original notes. Thus, notes receivable may appear to be current but actually represent balances for merchandise sold months or years before.

HAS PROVISION BEEN MADE FOR DISCOUNTS? Certain companies make a practice of giving quantity discounts to customers under escalation clauses. Inquiry should be made to ascertain that provision has been made for such discounts on the basis of the quantities expected to be sold during prescribed periods to customers.

WILL THE ACQUIRER WISH TO CONTINUE TO DO BUSINESS WITH PRESENT CUSTOMERS? Considering that the combined enterprise generally will continue to transact business with customers of the acquired company, any information that will assist in planning future policy should be obtained. For example, the company proposed to be acquired may be dealing with customers who are borderline credit risks as the result of entering into a competitive field at a relatively late date. In addition to reviewing this situation, it should be determined if the company's collection terms are more liberal than those generally found in the industry and if special discounts or rebates are granted.

Inventories.

1. Summary of dollar amounts of (a) raw materials and supplies, (b) work in process, and (c) finished products
2. Methods of valuing inventories on cost or market basis, i.e., last-in, first-out; first-in, first-out; accumulated average; etc.; and the practice followed with regard to obsolete or slow-moving items—also, the method of determining market, whether replacement cost, outside or published quotations, or sales price less selling and distribution costs
3. Description of the cost system used and its adequacy
4. Amounts of inventories out on consignment and data on inventories held on consignment
5. Physical inventory-taking practices and approximate dollar amount of inventories carried at various locations; particulars of adjustments made over a period of several years to book inventories as the result of physical inventories taken

REVIEW CAREFULLY THE METHOD OF PRICING INVENTORIES. There are various methods of pricing inventories, each of which may be acceptable as long as consistency is followed in their application. Therefore, divergent practices followed by companies may result in material differences in relative inventory valuations. For example, one company may be following a very conservative policy in inventorying overhead applicable to finished goods and work in process or using low standard cost rates for inventory pricing. Similarly, such a company may follow a policy of liberal write-downs of slow-moving stock and write-offs of stock deemed to be obsolescent. Another company may be following contrary practices. Furthermore, some companies follow the practice of writing off maintenance supplies, small tools, and spare parts as purchased; whereas other companies handle such items on an inventory basis.

DOES THE COMPANY SHIP MERCHANDISE ON CONSIGNMENT? Many companies sell merchandise on consignment, and some of them follow a practice of booking such consignment shipments as sales and accounts receivable. Accordingly, they will take up a profit on such shipments; whereas the merchandise actually should be considered as inventory of the company.

A REVIEW OF WORK IN PROCESS REQUIRES PARTICULAR CARE. A review of work in process will require considerable care, particularly if a company manufactures products having a long production cycle or has long-term contracts, as in the manufacture of government defense items, custom-made heavy machinery or equipment, and in construction projects. In such cases, it is usually desirable to review engineering or other cost estimates to determine if work in process will be completed at a normal profit including, where applicable, shipping and erection costs. Long-term contracts, where work has not even been commenced, should also be considered from the standpoint of the company's ability to complete them at a normal profit.

RESTATEMENT OF INVENTORIES FOR COMPARATIVE PURPOSES. If it should appear too difficult to restate inventories of several companies involved in a business combination on a comparable cost basis, it may be practicable to restate such inventories to market values or selling prices for purposes of comparison.

ASCERTAIN LIABILITY FOR MERCHANDISE RETURNABLE IN THE FUTURE. In certain industries, there is a trade practice of accepting returned merchandise even though it may have been sold several months or years before. Inquiry should be made as to this practice in order to estimate the possible liability to be incurred upon the return of merchandise in the future applicable to sales during the period under review.

ARE PHYSICAL INVENTORIES TAKEN REGULARLY? Although the practice is to be deprecated, many closely held corporations and smaller companies do not take periodic physical inventories that are observed and tested by their independent public accountants.

DO THE INDEPENDENT PUBLIC ACCOUNTANTS DISCLAIM RESPONSIBILITY FOR THE INVENTORIES? Where independent public accountants take exception to or disclaim responsibility for such inventories, the reviewer should be wary. In these circumstances, the possibilities for inventories being overstated or understated are illimitable. In the case of overstatement, there may be substantial physical shortages; deliberate overstatement of book records; or substantial quantities of slow-moving, obsolete, or unsalable merchandise included at unrealistic values. Equally serious is the deliberate understatement of inventory values, thereby reducing profits and reported federal income tax liabilities. Although this is not a widespread practice, it unfortunately is indulged in by some closely held corporations. The fraud and other penalties for deliberate understatement of inventories may be substantial if discovered and proven by the Internal Revenue Service and could affect the financial position of a company.

ARE GOODS HELD ON CONSIGNMENT OR STORED FOR ACCOUNT OF CUSTOMERS? Often, companies have on their premises goods received on consignment and also, due to trade practices, may store for the account of their customers goods that have been sold and billed. The reviewer should make necessary inquiries to determine that inventories shown in the financial statements do not contain any goods of such a nature.

INVENTORY TURNOVER. Inventory turnover during the year, that is, the ratio of average aggregate inventory to cost of goods sold, may furnish valuable information to an analyst. Reference to published industry information may indicate that a company is carrying too large an inventory in relation to its volume of business. In such a case, its borrowing requirements will be increased beyond reasonable needs; and it will incur unnecessary expenses for interest, storage, and plant and warehouse handling costs.

Prepaid and Deferred Items.

1. Dollar amounts of major items
2. Method of write-off or amortization

Such items are generally not material in the average company's financial statements. However, there are cases where substantial amounts may be carried as assets for the following types of items:

1. Prepaid advertising supplies and expenses
2. Preproduction, research, experimental, and development expense
3. Unamortized debt expense

The reviewer should satisfy himself as to the reasonableness of deferring such costs and expenses to future operations, particularly those indicated in the (1) and (2) classifications. Also, he should determine whether and to what extent any of these items would be considered as assets in the event of a business combination.

Property, Plant, and Equipment.

1. Gross balances of assets and accumulated allowances for depreciation and amortization by major classifications of assets such as land, buildings, machinery and equipment, leasehold improvements, etc.
2. Depreciation methods and rates used and whether tax basis and book basis of fixed assets and depreciation provisions and accumulated allowances are identical
3. Particulars and approximate dollar amounts of major additions to property, plant, and equipment for the past five years
4. Maintenance and repairs for the past five years
5. Particulars of recent appraisals, if any, and amounts of insurance coverage of property, plant, and equipment.

COMPARISON OF METHODS USED FOR DEPRECIATION. Comparison should be made of the methods and rates of depreciation used by the several companies involved. For example, one company may be using accelerated methods while the other uses the straight-line method of depreciation. Also, there is considerable leeway in rates of depreciation that may be used for similar assets.

It is significant to determine if a company has expended substantial amounts for fixed assets during recent years and otherwise appears to be maintaining its plant and equipment in good order. The information obtained under this subsection will be of interest to the person reviewing manufacturing operations of the company proposed to be acquired.

Goodwill, Patents, and Other Intangibles.

1. Gross balances of such assets and accumulated amortization by major classifications, such as patents and goodwill
2. Methods of amortization used, and where such assets have a tax basis, whether it is identical to the book basis

The reviewer should be concerned about any substantial amounts carried for intangibles unless there is, paradoxically, tangible evidence to support such values. This evidence would include particulars of cost as measured by the outlay of cash, securities, or other property, and of current values as measured by gross profit or royalty income on products or processes to which the intangibles apply.

In his appraisal of such items, he should consider whether and to what extent they would be treated as assets in the event of a business combination.

Liabilities.

1. Summary of dollar amounts of current liabilities classified as to (a) notes payable to banks and to others; (b) trade accounts payable; (c) accrued liabilities, showing separately any material items; and (d) sundry liabilities such as dividends declared, amounts due directors and officers, and any other items of material amount
2. Summary of dollar amounts of non-current liabilities classified as to (a) funded debt; (b) indebtedness to affiliates; (c) other long-term debt; and (d) other liabilities or reserves, showing separately any items of material amount

POSSIBILITY OF UNRECORDED LIABILITIES. Many medium-sized and smaller companies are not too precise about reflecting all liabilities in their financial statement, other than at fiscal year-ends. Therefore, it is difficult to determine from a brief review and discussion that all liabilities of a company are reflected properly in its financial statements. However, a comparison of the operating accounts of a company for the current period with previous periods, including the latest audited statements, may give some indication as to the reasonableness of liabilities currently reflected.

STATUS OF FEDERAL AND STATE INCOME TAXES. Inquiry should be made as to the status of federal and state income tax matters; that is, up to what year the returns of a company have been examined and the result of such examinations, whether deficiency assessments have been levied in settlement, or refunds received. In many cases where there have been deficiency assessments for prior years, it is probable that similar items will appear in the returns of unsettled years, requiring consideration in determining tax liability.

POSSIBLE LIABILITY FOR REDETERMINATION OF DEFENSE CONTRACTS. A number of companies have defense contracts, some of which contain redetermination clauses requiring refunds to be made to the government if the company's costs are below the original contract estimates. Such refunds can be substantial in amount.

LIABILITIES UNDER PENSION PLANS. Pension plans should be inquired into and the unfunded amounts of past service costs ascertained, as well as the annual cost of current service. If the plan is a trusteed one, the nature of the investments in the plan should be inquired into, as well as the market value of the fund compared with the amounts paid in.

ASCERTAIN APPROVAL REQUIREMENTS UNDER INDENTURES AND LOAN AGREEMENTS. The provisions of bond indentures and long-term debt agreements relating to the merger or sale of a company should be reviewed to determine what approvals will be required from bondholders and lending institutions in order to effect a business combination. In some cases, unless advance agreement is reached with lending institutions, a merger or sale of a company places it in a position of default on its loans.

Contingent Liabilities and Commitments.

1. The nature of contingent liabilities and the possible maximum amounts thereof should be noted.
2. Major outstanding commitments should be listed other than those arising out of items covered under contingent liabilities. These would include commitments as to (a) long-term leases; (b) fixed assets; (c) raw materials, supplies, and purchased products; (d) advertising campaigns; and (e) long-term sales agreements.

Contingent liabilities may be many and varied, such as product warranties and service agreements, endorsements of discounted notes, and possible litigation and loss claims where a company is a self-insurer, or if it is not fully covered by insurance.

Commitments should be reviewed from the standpoint of losses that might be incurred in carrying them out and also whether such commitments could be canceled in the event of a business combination.

Capital Stock, Additional Capital, and Retained Earnings.

1. Particulars of various classes of capital stock, i.e., amounts authorized and issued, par values, redemption and voting rights, and conversion privileges of preferred stock
2. Amounts of stock reserved for exercise of stock options and warrants
3. A list of major stockholders and the number of shares they own directly and indirectly, as well as shares under options currently exercisable
4. Particulars of additional capital (capital surplus)
5. Summary of retained earnings for a number of years, showing income for the year, dividends declared, and other charges and credits

RIGHTS OF SECURITY HOLDERS, STOCK OPTIONS, STOCK WARRANTS, ETC. It is important to determine the rights of the various security holders of a company in the event of merger or sale. Also, the status of stock options, stock warrants, and debenture and preferred stock conversion privileges should be ascertained. This is particularly important where the business combination is to be effected by an exchange of capital stocks, so that the exchange ratio is not based on shares then outstanding without regard to later increases resulting from the conversion of bonds and preferred stock and the exercise of stock options or warrants at a fraction of the fair value of the capital stock of the company to be acquired or merged.

OBTAIN LIST OF MAJOR STOCKHOLDERS. The list of major stockholders is important from two standpoints: (1) it is sometimes desirable to contact such stockholders to see if their approval of the proposed deal will be forthcoming, and (2) it may be prudent to consider if the holdings of a single stockholder or close group of stockholders are so large that they may exercise too much control in the combined enterprise.

STATEMENTS OF INCOME

As mentioned, statements of income should be summarized for a number of years and for the latest interim period, and particulars obtained on the following:

1. Sales and cost of sales by major product lines
2. Administrative, selling, distribution, and advertising costs

3. Any other miscellaneous charges or credits to income of material amount
4. Special items, that is, items of such a material amount, generally prior years' adjustments, that they were included as charges or credits after a determination of "net income"

Sales to Affiliated Interests and Large Customers. Inquiry should be made regarding sales made to affiliated companies or interests or whether a substantial proportion of sales are made to a few customers. In the case of sales to affiliated interests, it is possible that the prices were not arrived at on an "arm's length" basis. The danger of having a substantial proportion of sales made to a few customers is quite apparent. The loss of one or several accounts may severely depress the operating results of a company.

Comparison of Sales and Cost of Goods by Product Lines. Comparisons of sales and cost of goods by product lines give a valuable insight into the operations of a company. Not only do they indicate which are the more and less profitable product lines but also the trend of such sales and profits. A study of these data may indicate that generous profits in the past may not be expected in the future due to a severe decline in sales volume of a previously profitable line or to a price squeeze resulting from competitive conditions. If possible, it should be determined if the company is a low- or high-cost producer in its industry.

Comparison of Administrative, Selling, and Other Expenses. A comparison of administrative, selling, distribution, and advertising expenses also will yield valuable results. A review of these data may indicate where expenditures are out of line for the results produced. Often, companies wishing to expand volume in a product will spread their advertising and sales effort too thinly over a large geographical area.

Be on the Alert for Evidence of a "Milking" Operation. The reviewer should be alert to the possibility that relatively substantial profits have been realized in recent years at the expense of the future welfare of the company. This is known as a "milking" operation and may be indicated by a gradual but steady loss of sales volume over a recent period, but with profits being either maintained or increased. This may be accomplished by substantially curtailing advertising and selling expenses, research and development, maintenance and repairs, and expenditures for plant and equipment.

Large Expenditures for Legal and Other Expenses Should Be Reviewed. Any large amounts expended for legal and professional expenses should be the subject of inquiry, as an indication that the company may be a party to a damaging lawsuit or patent litigation, the ultimate settlement of which may involve substantial liability. Inquiry should be made regarding premises listed by a company that involve substantial rentals to ascertain if the premises are owned by an affiliated person or interest or whether any long-term lease arrangements may prove onerous in future years in the event of a business combination.

Review Interest Expense. The particulars of interest expense incurred should be reviewed to ascertain if there are any otherwise undisclosed borrowings.

SUMMARIZATION OF ACCOUNTING AND FINANCIAL DATA

The income statements of the prospective acquirer and that of the company proposed to be acquired should be summarized on a comparable accounting basis for a period of five years or more or less depending upon relevant factors, as well as for current periods to date since the past fiscal year-end and for similar periods of the prior year. Generally, adjustments will be made to conform with the accounting practices of the acquirer, unless he contemplates changes therein, particularly as a result of the business combination. In making adjustments, the following are among the items to be considered, with due regard to the materiality of their effect on net income.

Accounting Adjustments. It makes no sense to compare assets, liabilities, income, and expenses of two parties to a merger unless the figures are based on comparable accounting policies. In examining the need for accounting adjustments, the following items should be considered.

1. DIFFERENCES IN METHODS OF VALUING INVENTORIES. For example, one company may be inventorying all overhead applicable to finished goods and work in process; while another com-

pany, because of conservative practices or low standard cost rates, is inventorying a much lesser portion of such overhead. One company may be using the LIFO method for valuing a portion of its inventory and the other company using one of the other conventional methods. Similarly, practices regarding the write-down or write-off of slow-moving and so-called obsolete stocks should be reviewed.

2. DIFFERENCES IN DEPRECIATION PRACTICES. For example, one company may be using accelerated methods, while straight-line depreciation is used by the other company. Even when both companies are using accelerated methods, if one has expended substantially more in recent periods for property, plant, and equipment than the other has, adjustment should be made to place both companies on the straight-line basis during the period under review.

3. PRACTICES WITH REGARD TO INVENTORYING SMALL TOOLS AND SUPPLIES. Many companies write off to expense small tools, maintenance supplies, and spare parts; while others inventory such items. If the amounts of such items purchased annually are significant, it would be necessary to place both companies on a comparable basis of accounting therefor.

4. DEFERRED RESEARCH AND EXPERIMENTAL EXPENSES, UNAMORTIZED DEBT EXPENSE, GOODWILL, AND TRADE-MARKS. The accounts of both companies should be conformed to reflect a common practice with regard to these items.

5. RESERVES AND OTHER LIABILITIES. Policies of companies with regard to vacation pay, pension, profit-sharing and bonus plans and commitments therefor, and other similar items should be considered in computing adjusted earnings.

6. NON-RECURRING CHARGES AND CREDITS. Any substantial charges and credits resulting from transactions that are unlikely to recur in the foreseeable future should likewise be considered in adjusting earnings.

7. CHARGES AND CREDITS RELATING TO PRIOR YEARS. Any such items, whether charged or credited to income or surplus, should be reallocated to income of the appropriate prior year or years.

8. COMMITMENTS. The effect of recent actions that may not be reflected in earnings for the full period under review should be taken into consideration in determining normal earnings. Such items would include pension plans adopted during the period, sales price changes, and increases or decreases in basic wage rates and in the cost of raw materials and supplies.

9. FEDERAL INCOME TAXES. Some companies make it a practice to be generous in their accruals for federal and other income taxes, while others provide reserves on the basis of the tax computed in returns filed. A provision for deferred federal income taxes may be recorded by many companies and not by others. Where practices vary between the companies, adjustments should be made for apparent overaccruals or for possible additional assessments, if material. Also, account should be taken of any income taxes that arise from adjusting prior earnings in the ways earlier described.

The primary consideration in reviewing operations of prior periods is to estimate future operating results. With this in view, an endeavor should be made to forecast sales, costs, and expenses to arrive at estimated income of the company proposed to be acquired for periods of one to five years.

Also, pro forma statements of income of the combined operations of the prospective acquirer and the company proposed to be acquired should be prepared for historical periods and forecasted future periods.

Statements of financial position (balance sheets) on a comparable basis should be prepared, considering adjustments similar to those listed above, for both companies involved for purposes of comparing net assets.

If the contemplated transaction is to be taxable, for federal income tax purposes, a schedule should be prepared showing, at least in rough form, the possible adjustments that may be made to fixed assets, inventories, and other assets to establish a new "stepped-up" fair value tax basis of the purchaser for at least part and perhaps all of the excess of purchase price over the seller's tax basis. The effect of increased charges to income resulting from stepping up the basis of assets should be considered in forecasting earnings for future periods.

If the capital stock of the company is traded either on a national exchange or on an over-the-counter basis, the high and low market quotations should be obtained by quarter annual periods for at least two years; the latest current quotation should also be obtained.

The use, in the evaluation of a company for purposes of acquisition or merger, of data suggested to be obtained in this and Chapter 5 will be discussed in Chapter 6.

Chapter 5

MANAGEMENT, MARKETING, AND OPERATING INFORMATION NEEDED BEFORE EFFECTING THE DEAL

Usually when a company has an interest in a corporate acquisition, it first obtains financial and accounting information on the company in which it is interested, such as that suggested in Chapter 4. This is appropriate inasmuch as such data are readily obtainable and largely susceptible of evaluation. However, this does not mean that information covering the following areas is of less importance:

Management and personnel
Sales, marketing, and distribution
Operations, engineering, research, and development

As a practical matter, many of the corporate headaches that develop from business combinations are the result of improper investigation into these non-accounting areas prior to effecting a deal. It is suggested, therefore, that information be obtained along the following lines and evaluated.

MANAGEMENT AND PERSONNEL

Management and Administration. Obtain personnel and related information on officers and key executives (i.e., the chief executive and those heading up the major divisions and areas of responsibility of the company):

1. Positions, names, ages, family relationships, and ownership interests in the company. (This should also include non-officer directors where their ownership interests are material.)

2. Compensation and benefits received in the past five years, including salary; bonus or profit-sharing; deferred compensation; stock option; pension-plan contributions; and, if material, insurance, hospital and major medical payments. Particulars of employment and deferred compensation agreements should be obtained.

3. Experience, background, and major areas of responsibility. If an organization chart is not available, a rough one should be prepared covering the duties and responsibilities of the management and key personnel.

4. The amount of time devoted to the company by management personnel should be ascertained, as well as any substantial financial interests they may have in other companies not to be acquired, particularly if these companies do business with the subject company.

PROBLEM OF INTEGRATING EXECUTIVES IN BUSINESS COMBINATIONS. It is in the area of integrating people, particularly at the management level, that many business combinations do not work out successfully. Thus, it is important not only to obtain all the above background information on the management and key executive group, but also to try to gain impressions of such persons to determine if they will fit into the combined organization.

Such impressions may be obtained by observation during the course of discussions and meetings, by discreet inquiry on the outside as to the reputation of the principal executives in banking and business circles, and by sounding out their subordinates.

A well-run organization should have a training program to provide for the orderly succession of executive personnel by competent subordinates, as well as to develop a surplus of executives for corporate growth and acquisition requirements.

PROBLEM OF COMPETENT KEY EXECUTIVES OF ACQUIRED COMPANY RETIRING AFTER BUSINESS COMBINATION. On the other side of the scale, there is the situation where management of the acquired company is able, efficient, and capable of functioning well in the combined enterprise; but one or more of the principal officers decide to become inactive after the business combination. This is not an unusual situation, particularly where management people are also principal stockholders and suddenly find themselves with considerable wealth upon selling out their interests.

UNDERSTANDING SHOULD BE REACHED AS TO THE FUTURE
ROLES OF ACQUIRED EXECUTIVES. Accordingly, an understanding
should be reached with key management people of the acquired
company in cases where their continued services are required to
assure the most successful operation of the combined enterprise.
This cannot be accomplished by the mere giving of employment
contracts but by establishing and maintaining proper relationships with such acquired management personnel so that they
grow to feel a part of the combined organization and obtain job
satisfaction from their assignments.

Accounting, Financial, and Other Administrative Employees. Obtain
personnel and related information regarding accounting, financial, and other administrative employees (excluding officers and
key executives):

1. Number of employees by departments or supervisory divisions,
   indicating approximate total numbers by sexes. Also, ascertain
   the rate of annual turnover of such work force and if the
   number of employees fluctuates as the result of seasonal requirements.
2. Ages, length of service, and general background of supervisory
   personnel.
3. Particulars of pay plans for supervisory and office personnel
   and of fringe benefits afforded, such as vacations, sick pay,
   hospitalization, major medical and pension plans.
4. The degree of mechanization of accounting and clerical operations.

CONSIDER EFFICIENCY OF ACCOUNTING AND OFFICE OPERA-
TIONS. The reviewer should endeavor to gain some impression of
the efficiency with which accounting and general office procedures
are carried out. It may be that a revision of procedures and
further mechanization could result in substantial savings in payroll costs. On the other hand, a company may be operating with
less than prudent minimal requirements in personnel and equipment so that an acquiring company would have to increase
accounting and administrative costs in order to provide adequate
internal controls and produce timely financial information and
reports.

A well-operated company will have written instructions or
manuals for office and accounting procedures and an adequate

program for training and developing clerical and office supervisory personnel.

SALES, MARKETING, AND DISTRIBUTION

Sales and Marketing Employees. Information should be obtained regarding field sales, distribution, and sales administrative personnel (excluding officers and key executives):

1. Number of employees by product divisions and by function such as field sales, distribution, and sales administration. Also, determine the rate of annual turnover by category and if the number of employees fluctuates as the result of seasonal requirements.
2. Ages, length of service, and general background of supervisory personnel.
3. Particulars of pay plans, i.e., base salaries or drawing accounts, commission and bonus bases, and fringe benefits afforded.
4. Particulars of travel and entertainment expenses, and expenses incurred attending conventions.
5. Particulars of training programs for field sales and distribution personnel.

COMPENSATION BASIS SHOULD BE DESIGNED TO STIMULATE BUSINESS. Sales compensation should be on a realistic basis—designed to encourage those who produce business. For example, in established territories, compensation should have some relation to volume quotas by product lines, taking into consideration relative profit margins. On the other hand, in order to establish a marketing position in a territory, it may be desirable to compensate under a high base salary and relatively small commission or incentive bonus arrangement.

RECORDS SHOULD BE MAINTAINED TO DETERMINE PERFORMANCE OF SALESMEN. Records should be maintained on all selling personnel showing their sales volume; the approximate profitability thereof; and compensation, travel, entertainment, and convention expenses. Such information should also be maintained by territories as a basis for marketing decisions.

General Marketing Information. The following information should be obtained:

1. The principal products manufactured or purchased for resale by the company over the past five years should be listed, and its

share of the market for such products during this period estimated as well as that of its principal competitors.

2. The company's annual sales by principal products should be
   estimated for the next five years, and the total product demand
   compared with estimated industry capacity.
3. Data should be obtained showing whether any appreciable volume of the company's sales are made to a few large customers
   or if it sells large quantities or products directly or indirectly to
   the United States government.
4. The principal method of marketing the company's products
   should be determined, i.e., whether through distributors, dealers,
   manufacturers' agents, direct consumers, or some other channel.
5. The territories in which the company markets should be defined,
   and aspects of geographically expanding such territories considered.
6. It should be determined if the company is customer or product
   oriented. That is, does it systematically carry out market research to determine customers' needs and its product acceptance,
   or does it use high-pressure methods to sell its products regardless of customer requirements.
7. If the company is distributing products manufactured by others
   or has distributors who account for an appreciable volume of its
   sales, a determination should be made of the effectiveness of
   agreements covering sales for the next several years.
8. The possible effect of technological changes in the industry, price
   changes, and foreign competition should be considered, as they
   may affect the company's future.
9. A breakdown of the company's advertising and promotion expense should be obtained by product lines and advertising media.

Sales and marketing information may be obtained from company catalogues, industry reports and publications, general business publications, and market surveys. This area of investigation
is one of the most important for the acquiring company.

Is COMPANY'S ADVERTISING PAYING OFF? It should be ascertained whether the company appears to be getting appropriate
results from its advertising and promotion expenditures and is
taking full advantage of the assistance of its advertising agencies
in planning sales campaigns.

Is PRICING INFLUENCED BY AN INDUSTRY LEADER? If the industry is one in which there is a present overcapacity, consideration should be given to the effect this may have on pricing

policies. Also, it should be determined if any one or several of the leading companies in the industry influence price changes.

IS COMPANY SELLING A SUBSTANTIAL VOLUME TO RELATIVELY FEW CUSTOMERS? A company having a substantial volume of its business with a few customers or with the United States government is in a vulnerable position. If this condition has existed for a number of years, it may be an indication of an unaggressive marketing organization.

MARKETING RESEARCH IS VERY IMPORTANT. A well-developed marketing organization should be the catalyst for research and development projects. As mentioned in Chapter 3, the lack of an enlightened and aggressive marketing approach has been responsible for the decline and demise of industries as well as companies.

COMPARE PRICE OF ACQUISITION WITH COST OF OWN DEVELOPMENT AND MARKETING OF COMPETING PRODUCT. Product development may be accomplished through research and promotion or by acquiring existing businesses. This being the case, the prospective acquirer should estimate the cost and time involved in developing and marketing a competing product line for comparison with the proposed acquisition price.

OPERATIONS

Facilities. Obtain the following information in regard to facilities:

1. Particulars of major operating facilities, including location, age, condition, productive capacity, and area of land and plant.
2. Evidences of obsolescence, such as would be indicated by relatively few purchases of equipment in recent years, partial replacement of a group of machines, machines with substantial idle time, and excessive maintenance and repair costs.
3. Facilities owned and leased and the lease terms on major facilities.
4. If a recent appraisal of the company's facilities exists, this should be studied and summarized. A "sound" or fair value appraisal would of course be much more significant than an appraisal for insurance purposes, which usually shows values considerably in excess of sound values.

DETERMINE ADEQUACY OF PHYSICAL FACILITIES FOR FUTURE
NEEDS. Some of this information may be obtained in conjunction
with the compiling of corporate, accounting, and financial information, discussed in Chapter 4. Essentially, the reviewer of the
company's facilities should satisfy himself that not only are they
adequate for present operations, but will suffice for those contemplated if the business combination is effected, without the expenditure of unreasonable amounts. Dependent factors will
include availability of space for new equipment, new buildings
and employee parking, adequate access from streets and sidings,
compliance with local zoning ordinances, and availability of
manpower.

DETERMINE EFFICIENCY OF PLANT LAYOUT AND STORAGE FA-
CILITIES. The productive facilities should be arranged to provide
for a logical flow of work from one process to the other. Also,
plant storage facilities generally should be at locations convenient for the use of raw materials and supplies in the manufacturing process, and finished products storage should be at
locations that minimize the necessity for handling subsequent
to completion of the manufacturing process. Modern devices
such as pallets, conveyors, and lift trucks should be used for
materials handling.

Plants and outside warehouse facilities should be at locations
reasonably convenient to markets for the company's goods, and
the stock in such facilities should be well balanced from a turnover standpoint.

Plant Work Force. Determine the following:

1. Particulars of the plant work force, including number of employees, approximate division by sexes and by skilled and un-
   skilled workers. Also, ascertain if the total number of employees
   fluctuates as the result of seasonal production.
2. Ages, length of service, and general background of superintend-
   ents, foremen, and other plant supervisory personnel.
3. Principal provisions of union contracts, if any, and comments on
   past and present union-management relations.
4. Particulars of various pay plans for supervisory and plant employees—whether weekly, hourly, or incentive basis, and fringe
   benefits afforded.

WHAT EFFECT WOULD BUSINESS COMBINATION HAVE ON PRESENT WORK FORCE? The possible effects of a business combination should be considered in relation to the present operating work force. These effects may include increased costs because of unionization of employees not presently in unions, increases in compensation and fringe benefits because of the acquiring company's more generous plans, and possible higher turnover of labor because some employees may believe their jobs are in jeopardy as the result of a takeover by new management.

FOREMEN AND SUPERVISORS PLAY IMPORTANT ROLE IN EMPLOYEE MORALE. The relationship of foremen and other supervisory personnel to the workers is a most important factor in employee morale and efficiency. Of course, the general tenor of policy is set at a higher level; but the carrying out of such policy depends upon the establishment of fair practices and proper communications by the supervisory personnel with the working force.

GENERAL AVAILABILITY OF LABOR IN THE AREA AND ADEQUACY OF TRAINING PROGRAMS. Inquiry should also be made as to the general availability of labor in the area and the adequacy of employee training programs of the company proposed to be acquired in the event it is planned to expand operations in a particular area. If the company is operating on a one-shift basis, consideration should be given to expanding to two or three shifts. Such expansion will require additional supervisory help either through promotion from within the ranks or outside engagement.

Materials. The following should be obtained:

1. It should be ascertained whether the company manufactures for stock or against specific orders and its system of production control.
2. The purchasing department functions should be reviewed for effectiveness in such matters as price negotiations, quality, service to other departments, and its consideration of better or substitute materials.
3. The principal raw materials and purchased parts should be listed as well as their sources of supply.
4. It should be determined if the company maintains a balanced stock of raw materials, purchased parts, and supplies, considering its production schedule.

Is Purchasing Department Efficient? An efficient purchasing department will maintain adequate records to indicate that it is on the alert to protect the company from being overcharged or delayed in receiving materials, the lack of which may interrupt production. It should also follow up to see that the company obtains full advantage of trade, quantity, and cash discounts.

ENGINEERING, RESEARCH, AND DEVELOPMENT

Engineering and Research Employees. Information should be obtained regarding engineering and research personnel:

1. Number of employees by functional division such as design, control, and plant engineering, and research
2. Ages, length of service, and general background of supervisory personnel
3. Particulars of pay plans and fringe benefits afforded

Determine Which Personnel Have Made Major Contributions in Product Development and Design. An endeavor should be made to determine which research and engineering personnel have been responsible for worthwhile product development and design in recent years. Very often the loss of one or several of such persons may have a materially adverse effect on the company's future development.

General Information. The following general information should be obtained:

1. If the company manufactures engineered products, it should be determined how effective the engineering department functions from the standpoint of quality control, preparing cost estimates, production schedules, and initiating changes in methods and plant operations from time to time.
2. Ascertain, if possible, the amounts expended for research and development over the past five years and the commercially marketable products that have resulted therefrom.
3. If research has been carried out for government projects, it should be determined if such expenditures generally have been recovered through billings.

Indication of Good Engineering Department. A well-organized engineering department will be indicated by good plant housekeeping and a logical and efficient work flow, as well as the scheduling of production and shipping to meet marketing requirements.

INDICATIONS OF GOOD RESEARCH AND DEVELOPMENT PROGRAM. It may be somewhat more difficult to gauge the effectiveness of a company's research and development program, as expenditures for so-called development of existing products may be lumped with those for pure research—that is, for future products.

If possible, an attempt should be made to estimate the sales volume and profits over the past five-year period attributable to the company's own research and development during that period and the several years prior thereto.

Another indication of effective research will be a clear definition of projects including probable cost, estimated time to complete, and estimated market potential. Obviously, a company that over the years obtains basic patents that protect its product position or produce substantial royalty income is doing a good job of research and development.

KEY POINTS TO BE CONSIDERED

A principal consideration in reviewing the areas covered in this chapter should be to ascertain that a company proposed to be acquired has (1) a competent chief executive, (2) that he has a trained successor, and (3) that the company is established along proper organization lines, with appropriate responsibilities and authorities delegated to divisional heads of marketing, sales, operations, engineering, research and development, and personnel, if the activities of each of these divisions warrant such attention.

Are Philosophies and Policies of Both Companies Compatible? Furthermore, the reviewer should determine, to the extent practicable, if the philosophies and policies of the prospective seller are compatible with those of the proposed acquirer regarding centralization or decentralization of control in the various divisions of the business.

Has Company's Recent Practices Benefited Current Earnings at the Expense of Long-Range Objectives? It might be well to find out if there have, in recent years, been organizational or procedural changes in the company proposed to be acquired designed to produce good results temporarily at the expense of long-range objectives. For example, a centralization of certain operations that would ultimately reduce service to customers or the current curtailment of expenditures for advertising, promotion, research, and development might adversely affect future operating results.

Chapter 6

HOW TO VALUE A COMPANY

A purchase price or exchange ratio for securities of two companies in a business combination is generally arrived at as the result of negotiation. In reaching an agreement on price, a number of factors should be considered, some of which are readily susceptible to evaluation, and some not. It is the purpose of this chapter to discuss many of these factors and to suggest some approaches in evaluating them.

If it were possible to precisely determine the future earnings contribution and dividend-paying capacity to the combined enterprise of a company to be acquired, return on investment should be the sole criterion of present value, and every other factor discarded. Unfortunately, one cannot foretell the future; and, therefore, historical and current data traditionally have been considered as indicative of future earnings and dividend prospects.

Nevertheless, investment bankers, professional accountants, and other experts recognize prospective earnings to be the most important factor in valuing operating companies whose worth is largely dependent on continuance as a going concern. On the other hand, for companies with substantial holdings of disposable assets, such as securities or real estate, or operating companies that have been sustaining losses for several years or more, overall valuation might be related more closely to the fair market or liquidating values of the underlying assets.

In addition to potential earnings and net assets, which are acknowledged factors, dividend-paying capacity; market prices of capital stocks, in relevant cases; and other considerations such as the acquisition of management and technical know-how are important in valuing a company.

POTENTIAL EARNINGS AS A FACTOR

Traditionally, a five-year historical period has been used in investment banking circles in averaging earnings for valuation purposes. This period also has been used for federal estate and gift tax purposes as well as for Securities and Exchange Commission registration and reporting purposes.

During recent years, this practice has been modified and investment bankers are pricing initial offerings of securities at multiples of the latest year's earnings or the annual rate of earnings of a current interim period, if an increasing trend is indicated. Although this method of valuation has acceptance for securities offerings, it may not be indicative of values based on estimates of earnings potentials. However, except in the case of cyclical industries, or where earnings have been unusually affected, the use of a more recent shorter historical period as a measure of earnings potential appears sounder than averaging a longer period.

Nevertheless, it is more meaningful to estimate the earnings potential of a company proposed to be acquired rather than accept a historical period as evidence of earning power. This should be based, if possible, on the expected earnings contribution to the combined enterprise, rather than on the continuance of operations of the seller as a separate business.

How To Estimate Potential Earnings. START WITH LATE-PERIOD HISTORICAL EARNINGS. As a start, the latest year or a lesser interim period of earnings should be used, if such period is reasonably typical of earning power. If the company being considered has well-developed sales and profit forecasts, these should also be utilized.

MAKE NECESSARY ACCOUNTING ADJUSTMENTS TO EARNINGS FIGURES. The next step would be to make accounting adjustments to such figures to place them on a basis comparable to those of the acquirer, as explained in Chapter 4. In making adjustments, materiality should govern; it is not intended that numerous inconsequential items be included in such a reconciliation.

FURTHER ADJUSTMENTS FOR SAVINGS IN PERSONNEL COSTS AS A RESULT OF COMBINATION. Further adjustments should be made, to the extent practicable, for savings in administrative, technical, sales, plant, and clerical personnel costs as the result of the combination. These savings could arise from the elimination of some personnel, where a complete duplication results, or from the substitution of executive or supervisory personnel with lower-salaried replacements. In planning the personnel reorganization, qualifications of acquired personnel should be duly considered, as in some cases they may be more competent than their counterparts with the prospective acquirer.

ADJUSTMENTS FOR OTHER SAVINGS. Other savings that may be considered would result from the possible elimination of duplicate plant, office, and warehouse facilties. Savings in freight and cartage may result from the combination by shifting production to plants more strategically located to markets. To the extent that reasonable estimates may be made, whether beneficial or adverse, adjustments should be considered of the effect of "other factors" discussed later in this chapter.

DO NOT OVERESTIMATE EXPECTED SAVINGS. A word of warning: expected savings should be conservatively estimated, as experience has shown that, in many cases, they fail to materialize or at least not to the extent predicted. Also, expected increases in costs resulting from the combination should be carefully considered, particularly if the acquisition is a taxable transaction under the Internal Revenue Code. In such a case, the value of the assets acquired generally is "stepped-up" with a resultant additional charge to income for increases in inventories and other current assets and for additional depreciation and amortization of "depreciable" assets.

EFFECT OF GOODWILL ON FUTURE EARNINGS. Furthermore, to the extent that the entire purchase price cannot be allocated to tangible assets, in a taxable transaction, goodwill arises, which is not deductible for tax purposes but generally is required to be amortized, in accordance with appropriate accounting practices, by periodic charges to income. Accounting for goodwill is discussed in some detail in Chapter 7.

DIVIDEND-PAYING CAPACITY AS A FACTOR

The fundamental principles of investing have not changed through the years, although at times they have become obscured because of speculative influences. Whether a company is acquired in a cash deal or an exchange of securities, the ultimate aim should be the same—return on the capital invested. Accordingly, the company acquired should produce future earnings and a cash throwoff to pay dividends in amounts sufficient to justify the investment.

Dividend-paying Capacity Should Be on Potential Rather Than Historical Basis. When dividend-paying capacity is a factor, it should be based on indicated potential rather than the historical record. Dividends paid in the past may have no relation to the potential in this regard, particularly in a closely held company where there is every tax incentive to hold down dividend payments. Also, a company embarked on a substantial program of capital expansion or improvement may have financed a large part of such costs by the retention of more than a normal share of current earnings.

Any student of the stock market knows that companies paying dividends proportionately greater than their competitors, assuming that they are in a financial position to justify higher payments, show better market price action.

An expert testifying in the Du Pont–General Motors divestment proceedings stated:

In the long run, however, insofar as dividends are currently earned, and not simply a distribution of accumulated surplus, it is a demonstrable fact that they are the most important single factor bearing upon the relative prices of stocks, particularly with respect to seasoned securities.[1]

It is significant, also, that companies that have been on a favorable dividend basis, when reaching terms with a proposed acquirer whose common stock is not on a comparable basis, either request a substantial premium in common stock or a preferred or convertible preferred stock, at least as part consideration.

[1] United States v. E. I. du Pont de Nemours & Co., Civil No. 49C–1071.

NET ASSETS AS A FACTOR

Although net assets are not as important a factor generally as earnings, and may not be a criterion in some cases, they should not be disregarded. For example, in industries such as steel, cement, petroleum, and paper manufacturing, large initial investment and continuing outlays are required to produce sales volume and earnings. Although companies in these industries have not performed as spectacularly as such industries as electronics, space missiles, exotic fuels, and prefabricated housing, and of late the publishing industry, they have been consistent earners and dividend-payers over the years.

Also, a company whose plant and equipment is relatively new undoubtedly is more valuable than one in the same industry that is producing comparable earnings from relatively old facilities, considering that the latter will be required to invest substantial sums in the foreseeable future in replacing or rehabilitating its facilities at higher costs and hence greater charges to earnings for depreciation.

Furthermore, a company that has been operating at a loss for several years cannot be considered worthless if it has assets that may in the future produce income or be liquidated at substantial value. Many stockholders regard book "net worth" as a minimum valuation of their company. Whether or not they are right is a moot question.

Accordingly, in applicable cases, net book equities, giving effect to accounting adjustments previously mentioned and sometimes even to investment replacements costs, should be considered in valuing a company for acquisition or merger purposes.

MARKET PRICES AS A FACTOR

Market prices of securities are sometimes a factor in the determination of values in an exchange of securities. However, they should only be considered significant in determining relative values where the capital stocks of both companies are listed on a national securities exchange, are actively traded in, and where their current prices are not unduly influenced by extraneous factors.

There is no question but that stock market prices have an influence over values of companies for acquisition purposes. Their influence, however, should be more general than specific as economic indices of high or low business activity and an industry's prospects. As illustrated in Chapter 1, there is a definite correlation between stock market prices and merger activity.

Rise and Fall of Price Earnings Ratios. During recent years, the stock market pushed to speculative heights; and the sudden drop in prices, starting on May 29, 1962, was not unlooked for by some of the more sober analysts. There have been many economic explanations offered for the stock market break; but most economic indices, some months after the event, look far from anemic, yet the market remains on a lower plateau. Although it is a simple and obvious explanation, it would appear that stocks were selling at too high price earnings ratios. Standard and Poor's Standard "500" security price index, representing about 90 per cent of the market value of common stocks listed on the New York Stock Exchange, shows this story graphically in the following tabulation of price earnings ratios of 425 industrial stocks included in their index for the period 1957 through June 30, 1962.[2]

1957	12.9
1958	17.7
1959	19.8
1960	19.6
1961	20.0
1962 *	15.6

* Tentative ratio at end of second quarter of 1962 obtained from "seasonally adjusted annual rate of earnings."

The median yield on common stocks on the New York Stock Exchange, paying cash dividends during this period, based on market prices at the end of each year dropped off from 6.1 per cent for 1957 and has been hovering around a 4.0 per cent figure since that year through 1960 and then to 3.3 per cent for 1961.[3] This indicates that dividend payments, although lower with relation to market values, remained as high as a percentage of earn-

[2] Figures obtained from Standard & Poor's Corp.
[3] *New York Stock Exchange Fact Book,* 1962, p. 47.

ings for several years and generally did help to support the market price of a stock.

Composite Price Earnings Ratios Do Not Tell the Whole Story.

SOME WITH LOW RATIOS. Composite figures do not tell the whole story. Early in 1961, an issue of Forbes magazine had a list of ninety-nine companies of which ninety-three were listed on the New York Stock Exchange and six on the American Stock Exchange. The stocks of these companies were selling at discounts of nearly 40 to over 70 per cent of their net asset values. Also, the stocks of a number of these companies were selling at ten times earnings or less.[4]

SOME WITH HIGH RATIOS. By contrast, there were, at that time and at the close of 1961, many stocks listed on national exchanges selling at from five to fifteen times net asset values and forty to eighty times earnings. The yield on some of these stocks ran from 0 to 1 per cent. It is quite evident that many such stocks had not only discounted the foreseeable future but also the hereafter.

Undoubtedly, the large amount of funds that have become available for savings and investment during the period since World War II have had an influence on market prices. Such funds have been large relative to available investments and have stimulated many initial public offerings of securities.

In the frenzied rush to buy, during recent years, people forgot the time-honored principle of investing and speculated on a continued market rise, particularly in so-called glamour stocks. *However, the oldest and soundest principle has not changed; that is, investment is the productive employment of capital, the ultimate purpose of which should be a return commensurate with the risk assumed.*

During recent years, many companies, by means of public relations programs, aided by enthusiastic market analysts' reports and public speculative fever, saw their stock soar far beyond prices warranted by prospective earnings and dividend increases. A number of these companies were in the market for mergers and acquisitions. You cannot blame them if they utilized their over-

[4] "Asset Loaded Companies," *Forbes Business and Finance,* January 15, 1961.

priced stock to buy up acquisition values, which increased their earnings and net assets per share.

On the basis of the foregoing analysis, it may reasonably be concluded that management of a company to be acquired through an exchange of stock by another whose capital stock is selling at a high earnings multiple relative to that of the seller should regard factors other than, or in addition to, market prices in arriving at an exchange ratio.

OTHER VALUATION FACTORS

There are many other factors, some favorable, some adverse, that merit consideration in evaluating a company for acquisition or merger purposes. These include but are not limited to (1) the acquisition of management or technical personnel; (2) the possible loss of such personnel who may have contributed greatly to the company's success; (3) adding new and profitable products faster and cheaper than by means of research, or through consumer acceptance, which would require advertising over a long period; (4) newly developed products whose effects on profits have not yet been realized; (5) the impending expiration of patents or the loss of hitherto exclusive manufacturing know-how; (6) gaining a sales outlet for the acquirer's products or a supplier of raw materials and component parts through the acquisition; and (7) acquiring manufacturing or warehouse facilities in strategic geographical areas.

Emoluments to Principal Management-Stockholders. If the principal sellers are to continue in executive positions with the acquirer, with attractive salaries and stock options, or if they receive royalty agreements that may provide them with substantial income for years, covering the manufacture or sale of products, this too could influence the purchase price.

Manner in Which Deal Is Consummated Could Affect the Price. Additional factors include the manner in which the acquisition or merger is to be effected—whether for cash or stock or a combination of both or for convertible preferred stock, notes, or debentures. Also, the tax aspects of the transaction to the purchaser and seller will have a bearing on the price.

ARRIVING AT A FAIR PRICE

Ideally, an acquisition or merger price in terms of cash or capital stock is fair if both acquirer and seller benefit from the transaction. As several experts have put it, in a successful business combination, two and two should add up to five or six rather than four.

A purchase price in terms of cash or cash equivalent (notes or bonds), or an exchange of securities in a business combination, is dependent upon a number of factors, some susceptible to evaluation and some not. As an illustration of the breadth of this problem, different prices could be offered for the same company, and each be fair in the following varying circumstances.

1. *A cash offer* could be higher than that proposed in an exchange of securities because the purchaser would recover part of the price paid through reductions in federal income taxes resulting from a stepped-up tax basis of assets acquired. Also, a seller generally would require a higher price in a cash deal than in an exchange of securities because of the immediate income tax consequences.

2. *An exchange of securities offer* of a company in a glamour industry whose stock was selling at a very high price earnings ratio could be much more generous than one whose stock was selling on a conservative basis relative to earnings and dividend yield.

3. *A company in the same industry as the prospective seller,* whose management knew the value and potential of a company's products, might be willing to pay a top price because of the ability to integrate operations of the seller and increase sales and profits with the combined existing manufacturing and marketing facilities.

4. *An offer of an investor solely for the purpose of putting his funds to work* without any intention of exercising influence on the management of the company would ordinarily be conservative, as he would expect a return on such an investment to be better than in a blue-chip stock or mutual fund.

General Yardsticks for Price Determination. Some companies that include acquisitions and mergers in their permanent corporate growth plan have general yardsticks for price determination. That is, in cash deals they would expect a return on their investment either equivalent to the company's present return on net worth or its customary return on an investment in a new plant complete with facilities. In exchanges of capital stock, they would endeavor not to dilute their earnings per share by reason of the acquisition or merger. The latter computation may be based, to the extent practicable, on prospective rather than historical earnings.

Further aspects of arriving at a fair price will be discussed under "Cash Deals" and "Exchanges of Securities." Fundamentally, in either type of transaction, the acquirer is looking for a return on his investment. This usually is considered in terms of a constant return rather than a period "payout."

CASH DEALS

A cash purchase of either the capital stock or net assets and business of a company is a taxable transaction, for federal income tax purposes. That is, the seller has to recognize a gain or loss on the transaction and the purchaser establishes a new tax basis for the net assets acquired. Accordingly, if the purchase price exceeds the tax basis of the seller (which is generally the case), the purchaser allocates the price paid over the tangible and intangible assets acquired in the ratio that the fair value of each bears to their total fair value. The following will serve as an illustration.

Takeover Co. acquires the net assets and business of Sellout Co. for a cash consideration of $4,000,000. The federal income tax basis of net assets of the Sellout Co. at the time of sale is $2,300,000. Assume, in allocating the purchase price, that the fixed assets were written up to current appraised sound values; that there was some excess reserve for accounts receivable; and that inventories were written up to sales or market values, less selling and distribution costs, with the result as given on page 83.

Assume further that Sellout Co., for the year prior to the time of negotiations, had sales of $6,000,000 on which it had realized $300,000 net income after taxes and that this amount of income appeared to be reasonably indicative of annual earnings prospects for the next several years, had Sellout Co. continued under its then ownership.

	Tax Basis (Sellout Co.)	Allocated Purchase Price (Takeover Co.)
Cash	$ 150,000	$ 150,000
Accounts receivable	300,000	325,000
Inventories	700,000	850,000
Deferred charges	25,000	15,000
Land	100,000	200,000
Building, machinery, and equipment	1,325,000	2,000,000
Excess of cost over value of net tangible assets acquired		760,000
Total assets	$2,600,000	$4,300,000
Less—Accounts payable and accrued liabilities	300,000	300.000
Net assets	$2,300.000	$4.000.000

On the basis of $300,000 net income, a $4,000,000 investment does not appear unreasonable, although a little on the high side. Now, let us see what will happen to the $300,000 net income when Takeover acquires Sellout.

Net income		$300,000
Adjustments		
Additional depreciation on increased value of fixed assets, an average of 6% on $675,000 (rounded figure)	$ 40,000	
Additional executive and supervisory salary costs	25,000	
Increased employee benefit costs to conform to policy of acquirer	60,000	
	$125,000	
Federal income tax effect	65,000	
	$ 60,000	
Amortization of excess of cost over net assets acquired (goodwill) over a ten-year period	76,000	136,000
Adjusted net income		$164,000

On the basis of $164,000 of expected annual net income, quite obviously a $4,000,000 cash price is far too high. The illustration above purposely has been kept simple, but the relative figures of purchase price and adjusted income indicate the care that must be exercised in determining that you are buying what you think you are.

What Return Should Be Expected on an Investment? What then are some norms to be considered in acquiring a company for cash or cash equivalent? Generally, one should expect a return on the investment at least equal to the return presently realized on net assets in the acquirer's existing operations. This is assuming that the acquirer does not have a return that is distorted because of a substantial undervaluation of net assets.

The April, 1962, monthly letter of the First National City Bank contains a compilation of net income of leading corporations for the years 1960 and 1961. The figures of 2,701 industrial and other companies, excluding railroads, utilities, and financial institutions from the total of 3,557, show a return on net assets of 10.5 per cent in 1960 and 10.1 per cent in 1961. These ranged, by industry groups, from a low of 1.4 per cent in 1960 and 4.5 per cent in 1961 to a high of 20.4 per cent in 1960 and 19.7 per cent in 1961.[5] Accordingly, it would appear that a 10 per cent return on an investment in an acquired company would be no more than a fair norm. Furthermore, in certain industries such as chemicals, drugs, and cosmetics, where a continuing contribution will be required by the acquirer in developing new products and promotional techniques, a greater than average return on investment should be expected.

Consider the Cost of an Acquisition the Same as the Investment in a New Plant. If you consider a cash outlay in the acquisition of a company in the same light as a similar expenditure in the construction of a major plant, you would expect a return of 10 per cent. In fact, some companies expect a better return on new plant construction.

Return on Investment of Common Stock Sold To Raise Funds for the Acquisition. If, in order to raise the cash to purchase a company, the acquirer sells common stock, the expected return on investment might be translated into earnings per share on the stock sold. In addition to the criteria mentioned, another might be that the earnings per share from the acquisition, applicable to the stock sold, shall not be less than that on other shares outstanding relative to the company's operations.

[5] First National City Bank, Monthly Letter, "Business and Economic Conditions," April, 1962.

Purchaser Ordinarily Should Not Pay for Profits To Be Realized as a Result of Own Efforts After Acquisition. These criteria are basic in evaluating the fairness of a cash purchase price. In many cases, other factors besides estimated return on investment are considered, a number of which have been discussed in this chapter. The purchaser ordinarily should not base his price on the prospective profits to be realized from the efforts of his own organization due to these other factors, but only on the increased value of the purchased company resulting from the compatibility of the combination. However, this is an area that may be considered in price compromise by the prospective purchaser.

At Times Price Should Be Related to Liquidating Value of Acquired Company. In an unusual situation, where a company has been operating at a loss or a small and diminishing profit and there may be doubt as to the prospects of greatly improving operating results, the purchase price might be related to liquidating values, which could be somewhat below net book assets. This is so even though the acquirer has every intention of operating the company as a going concern.

EXCHANGES OF SECURITIES

An exchange of voting stocks, whether common or preferred, or, if permissible under the laws of the states in which the companies are domiciled, an exchange of non-voting stock or other securities for voting stock in a statutory merger is normally a tax-free transaction under the reorganization provisions of the Internal Revenue Code. That is, the seller does not recognize any capital gain or loss at the time of the exchange, and the purchaser assumes the seller's tax basis for net assets.

Determination of Exchange Ratios. The following examples, although not case histories, illustrate several approaches under varying circumstances in the determination of exchange ratios of capital stocks of companies involved in business combinations. It will be assumed for purposes of these illustrations that the earnings and net assets figures of the respective companies have been adjusted to an appropriate common basis of accounting.

QUALITY PRODUCTS CO. AND SUPERIOR MERCHANDISING CO.
Quality Products Co., a manufacturer selling most of its production through a few distributors, is interested in acquiring Superior Merchandising Co., its principal marketing outlet, through an exchange of capital stocks. Quality, although a good profit-maker, has shown very little earnings growth over the recent five-year period; while Superior has increased its earnings approximately 200 per cent, mainly because of a capable and aggressive marketing organization.

Approximately 40 per cent of Superior's volume consists of Quality products and the remainder from products of a dozen other suppliers in allied lines. Superior's gross profit has been fairly comparable on all products sold.

The following pertinent figures have been compiled on the companies (neither company has an active market in its capital stock).

	Quality Products	Superior Merchandising
Net book assets	$10,000,000	$4,000,000
Latest fiscal year's earnings	$1,980,000	$1,000,000
Average annual earnings for five years	$1,900.000	$665,000
Shares of common stock outstanding	500,000	250,000
Per share statistics		
Earnings		
Latest fiscal year	$3.96	$4.00
Average for five years	$3.80	$2.66
Projected for five years	$4.20	$12.26
Annual dividends	$1.25	$2.00
Net book assets	$20.00	$16.00

From the figures above, the following ratios are developed for consideration in an exchange of common stocks (dividend-paying capacity is not considered a factor in this case).

	Shares of Quality for Superior
Based on latest per share earnings	1.01
Average of five years' earnings	0.70
Average of five years' prospective earnings	2.92
Net assets	0.80

A forecast of operations and earnings of the respective companies for the next fiscal year indicates a rate of growth of Superior at

least equal to that per annum in the previous five years, whereas
Quality's forecast shows little if any improvement over its latest
year's results. Furthermore, it is considered, by the Quality
directors, that Superior's president, who had an impressive record
in running that company, should head up the combined organization. Considering the foregoing facts and factors, an exchange
ratio of one and a half shares of Quality for each share of Superior
appears to be within the area of a fair deal.

GLAMOUR CO. AND STABLE PRODUCTS CO. Glamour Co. has
increased its sales volume from $50,000,000 to $150,000,000 during the past five years, largely as the result of the acquisition of
other companies. Its per share earnings have increased only 30
per cent during this period because of heavy expenditures for
research and development and general competitive conditions in
its major product lines.

There is no way of measuring the effect on future earnings of
the company's program as none of its completed development
projects show immediate prospects of a substantial increase in
present profit margins. However, the company's stock is considered to represent a growth situation, although acknowledged
to have speculative aspects. The management of Glamour Co.
considers corporate acquisitions to be vital to the company's
growth, particularly in view of the disappointing results, to date,
of its research and development program.

Their attention is directed to Stable Products Co., whose common stock is traded "over the counter," although more than 60
per cent of it is owned by two principals who constitute the management of the company. These principals are interested in an
upstream exchange of capital stocks in order to convert their
investment into a broadly marketable security, the future of
which will not be dependent solely upon their efforts. The pertinent figures on page 88 have been compiled on the companies.

On the basis of the market prices of their respective shares, the
Stable stockholders would receive two shares of Glamour common
for each of their shares presently held. However, Glamour stock
is selling at forty times current earnings and Stable at only twelve
times. Based on the other data to be considered, the price earnings ratio of Glamour appears unrealistically high; while that

of Stable, due to the relatively nominal trading in its stock, appears low.

	Glamour Co.	Stable Products Co.
Net book assets	$90,000,000	$10,000,000
Latest fiscal year's earnings	$15,000,000	$1,250,000
Shares of common stock outstanding	20,000,000	250,000
Per share statistics		
Earnings	$0.75	$5.00
Earnings increase in past five years	30%	100%
Average of projected earnings for five years *	$0.90	$8.90
Annual dividends	$0.35	$3.00
Net book assets	$4.50	$40.00
Market price	$30.00	$60.00

* Based on ratable annual increase equivalent to prior five years.

From the figures above, the following ratios are developed for consideration in an exchange of their common stocks.

	Shares of Glamour for Stable
Based on latest per share earnings	6.66
Average of five years' projected earnings	9.89
Dividends	8.57
Net book assets	8.89
Market price	2.00

The Glamour management recognizes that market prices cannot be the sole criterion in fixing an exchange ratio but is confident that its capital stock will continue to sell at a high price earnings ratio due to its aggressive expansion policy.

In the matter of earnings and projected earnings, if you use one or the other or average them, the Stable stockholders would receive approximately 8 shares of Glamour for each share held and, if the determination is on the basis of net assets, would receive 8.89 shares of Glamour and on dividend ratios 8.57 shares.

The principal stockholders of Stable realize, however, that they may have management and other problems if they continue to expand at their present rate and would prefer not to undertake such responsibilities. Otherwise, they would not have been interested in an upstream business combination.

At this point, it is recognized that compromises have to be made on both sides in order to effect a deal. How then should this problem be approached? Although there are a number of solutions, the following two are offered as being within a reasonable area of effecting a fair deal for both parties.

Solution I. Double the price earnings ratio of Stable so that its stockholders would receive $120 equivalent in market value of Glamour (2 × 12 × 5), which would be four shares for each share of Stable stock, or a total of 1,000,000 shares. Thus, using the latest year's figures, the combined enterprise would have 21,-000,000 shares of capital stock outstanding and $16,250,000 of earnings, or $0.774 per share. Although Glamour's over-all earnings would be improved only 3.2 per cent on this basis, it would be receiving $1.25 in earnings for each share issued, compared with its own earning rate of $0.75 per share. Also, Stable earnings show a better growth potential for the future.

As far as the Stable stockholders are concerned, the following statistics are pertinent.

	Per Share of Stable Stock	Equivalent Four Shares of Glamour
Market value	$60.00	$120.00
Earnings	$5.00	$3.10
Dividends	$3.00	$1.40
Net book assets	$40.00	$19.04

This would appear to be a fair deal to the Stable stockholders from every standpoint except dividends. However, the increase in market value of their investment should be most attractive and a more than offsetting factor.

Solution II. Issue one share of $50 par value, 4 per cent convertible preferred stock and one and one-half shares of common stock of Glamour for each share of Stable. The preferred stock would be convertible into common at any time on a share-for-share basis. On this basis, Glamour would be issuing 250,000 shares of preferred stock with earnings attributable thereto of $500,000, and 375,000 shares of common stock with earnings of $281,250, a total of $781,250, for which it would receive earnings of $1,250,000. Glamour would incur a greater dividend obligation under this solution—$500,000 on the preferred stock plus $131,250 (375,000 × $0.35) on the common, or $631,250 compared with $350,000 (1,000,000 × $0.35) under Solution I. However, ultimately upon conversion of the preferred, Glamour will have issued the equivalent of two and one-half of its shares for each share of Stable compared with four shares under the previous plan. In order to assure the conversion of the preferred stock, there could be an annual sinking fund provision whereby it would be redeemable over a period of ten or fifteen years.

The following statistics are pertinent to the Stable stockholders under this plan.

	Per Share of Stable Stock	Equivalent One Share of Preferred and One and One-Half Shares of Common of Glamour
Market value	$60.00	$95.00
Earnings	$5.00	$3.16
Dividends	$3.00	$2.525
Net book assets	$40.00	$56.44

This likewise would appear to be a fair deal to the Stable stockholders. They would have a more or less guaranteed value for part of the exchange, represented by the preferred stock, plus an opportunity for capital growth should the combined enterprise prosper and the market value of the common stock increase. Also, on this basis of exchange, they would receive dividends more comparable to their previous dividends on Stable stock.

The foregoing examples of exchanges of capital stocks have been kept relatively uncomplicated and illustrate the "give and take" on both sides in combinations involving an exchange of securities.

DIFFERENT FORMULAS THAT MAY BE CONSTRUCTED FOR STOCK DEALS. It is difficult to establish norms in stock deals, *but the main objective in arriving at an exchange ratio should be to produce an equitable result for both the acquirer and the company absorbed.* Many different exchange ratios may be established by using (1) historical earnings for the latest year; (2) an average for five or more or less years; (3) projected earnings for the ensuing year or several years on the basis of the trend during recent years; (4) a composite of any of the earnings figures in (1), (2), and (3); and (5) a combination of any of these earnings computations and net assets and dividend-paying capacity.

For example, if earnings solely are to be considered in arriving at an exchange ratio, one company might show a favorable earnings result, for the latest year, but would not fare as well, in an exchange, if figures or projected figures for other periods were considered. Bearing in mind the equitable purpose of the use of a formula, a weighted combination of earnings could be utilized, as follows:

Average annual earnings for five years	33⅓%
Latest year's earnings	33⅓
Earnings for period since beginning of current fiscal year projected for full year	33⅓
	100%

The foregoing is presented only as an example. The combinations of weighted factors that may be utilized in determining relative values of capital stock for exchange purposes are illimitable.

MAKE CERTAIN THAT ALL SHARES TO BE EXCHANGED ARE CONSIDERED IN DETERMINING RATIOS. In entering into an exchange of capital stocks, both sides should carefully determine the total number of shares that will be involved in the exchange by each company. This will include shares under stock options, stock warrants, employee stock purchase plans, and shares issuable upon conversion of debentures or preferred stock. In some instances, companies have agreed upon per share exchange ratios, based on shares presently outstanding, only to find that additional shares were to be issued before closing the transaction under one or more of the above situations, without the receipt by the company of value equivalent to that of the shares issued.

WEIGH CAREFULLY THE RELATIVE ADVANTAGES OF CASH ACQUISITIONS VERSUS EXCHANGES OF CAPITAL STOCK. Companies should always weigh carefully the advantages of cash acquisitions versus those involving the issuance of capital stock, particularly if the acquirer's stock is not selling at a high price earnings ratio. Considerable leverage in per share earnings may sometimes be gained in cash deals under such circumstances.

Suppose a company whose stock is selling at twelve times earnings could make a stock deal to buy another at a comparable price earnings ratio, whose earnings were $600,000 per annum. On this basis, the seller would require capital stock having a value of

$7,200,000; and the deal would not increase earnings per share of the acquirer. Assume further that the seller would accept $8,000,000 in cash (the higher cash price being to compensate, in part, for capital gains tax that will be payable) and that this amount may be allocated over *net tangible assets*, with an additional charge to income of $200,000 per annum, or $100,000 after federal income tax credit.

On this basis, the acquired company would have income of $500,000 per annum; and if the acquirer had to borrow the entire $8,000,000 at 6 per cent (less than 3 per cent after income tax credit), the interest would be $230,000, leaving income of $270,000 to increase earnings per share on shares presently outstanding. If the acquirer had excess cash and did not have to borrow the entire $8,000,000, this leverage factor would be increased.

ACQUIRER SHOULD RECEIVE NET ASSETS THAT ARE SUFFICIENT TO SUPPORT THE EARNINGS. Even though earnings per share may be the dominant factor in determining price, either in cash or capital stock, they normally should be supported by sufficient net assets to continue to produce such earnings. If a company is in a tight position for liquid assets, as the result of having had losses in recent years, or having paid out too much in dividends, or overextending itself otherwise, the prospective purchaser should consider that any capital he furnishes, either in the form of equities, advances, or borrowed money, beyond the price of purchasing such a company adds to the cost of his investment. *Accordingly, he should measure his expected return in future earnings against this total investment and not the purchase price alone.*

Assume that a company that had current sales of $15,000,000 and net income, after taxes, of $250,000 per annum presented the following financial position.

ASSETS

Cash	$ 30,000
Accounts and notes receivable	1,000,000
Inventories	1,500,000
Land, building, machinery, and equipment	1,500,000
Prepaid and deferred items	20,000
	$4,050,000

LIABILITIES AND CAPITAL

Notes payable to banks (secured by inventories and accounts receivable)	$1,500,000
Accounts payable and accrued liabilities	1,000,000
Notes payable on equipment (secured by equipment)	350,000
Mortgage loan payable	750,000
Capital stock	300,000
Retained earnings	150,000
	$4,050,000

It is obvious from the figures above that the company is well overextended from the standpoint of borrowed capital, which amounts to $2,600,000 ($1,500,000 + $350,000 + $750,000), and compares with stockholders' equity of only $450,000 ($300,000 + $150,000). The situation above appears farfetched but could exist in the case of a close corporation if the stockholders withdrew profits to personally invest in other businesses or to pay off former shareholders and if they had acquired the company with a relatively small down payment.

A purchaser of such a company, in determining a reasonable price, would have to consider that he would be required to invest probably at least $2,000,000 in substituted borrowed capital, or assume such obligations, or retire a large part of borrowed capital by an additional equity capital investment. These amounts should be considered in addition to whatever price he paid for the net assets or capital stock of the company. If he were to ignore this need for additional capital, he might pay from $2,500,000 to $3,000,000 for the capital stock or net assets of the company; whereas a price of probably $500,000 to $1,000,000 would be more realistic, considering that his over-all investment eventually would be some $2,500,000 to $3,000,000 or more. This is on the assumption there were no other material relevant factors that should be considered in arriving at price.

Where Parties Cannot Agree on Fixed Price, Problem May Be Solved by an Additional Contingent Price. There is another interesting problem that arises when a company has an unstable earnings history or an operating loss carryover that an acquirer wishes to utilize for purposes of tax savings. There have been several cases in the past few years where companies have paid an initial price, either in cash or stock for others, with an additional contingent price to be paid based on earnings in excess of a stipulated minimum over a period of five to ten years or based on utilization and acceptance of an operating loss carry-over by the Internal Revenue Service. See Chapter 2, page 27 for an example of an acquisition involving an additional contingent purchase price.

RESULTS OF A STUDY OF SELECTED BUSINESS COMBINATIONS

Pertinent data are shown in Tables 6–1 and 6–2 on pages 96 to 100 on a number of business combinations consummated during an approximately six-year period ending December 31, 1961. These data are in chronological order of the combinations, which are coded numerically with the names of the companies listed on pages 101 and 102 following the tables.

These data were compiled in a review that covered approximately 3,700 business combinations reported on by the Federal Trade Commission, during that period, for mining and manufacturing companies. The Commission reports, for the most part, did not indicate the amount of assets acquired in such transactions. In those cases where such information was listed, approximately 270 companies acquired had net assets in excess of $5,000,000 each. A review of data in Moody's Investors Service and Standard & Poor's Corp. industrial manuals, published annual reports to stockholders, proxy statements, and other reports filed with the Securities and Exchange Commission for these 270 larger transactions developed sufficient information for a study of the sixty-five companies listed in the tables.

This review and study disclosed that larger transactions, for the most part, involved the use of voting capital stock of the acquirer or surviving company. Of the sixty-five companies listed, fifty-eight were stock deals and only six were for cash and one for debentures.

Furthermore, it revealed that the acquiring company generally paid a premium in terms of market value to the acquired company ranging up to a high of 125 per cent, although there were some few cases where the seller's stock was acquired at a discount. As indicated, for purposes of comparison of market values, prices were used at dates approximately two months prior to the first public announcements of the combinations, as it was evident that market prices subsequent to announcements were generally influenced by the proposed transactions.

Premiums paid for earnings (based on the latest fiscal year's figures) in the combinations listed ranged up to 1,335 per cent. In the latter case, on the basis of five years' average earnings of the respective companies, the premium on earnings paid by the acquirer was only 33 per cent. However, in a number of instances, earnings were acquired at discounts ranging up to almost 1,300 per cent. In the latter case, dividends and net assets of the seller substantially exceeded the equivalent per share figures of the acquirer, although the latter paid a premium to the seller equivalent to 89 per cent in market value. In one case where a premium of 35 per cent was paid by the acquirer in terms of market values, the premiums in per share equivalents of earnings, dividends, and net assets were much more substantial.

The main inference to be drawn from a review of Table 6-1 is that per share exchange ratios in business combinations are not arrived at exclusively on the basis of one factor, such as relative market values, but that at least several pertinent factors are considered in making determinations. Also, it would appear from the statistics that the sellers, in many cases, were willing to accept dividends at reduced rates for premiums in market values.

In the purchase deals for cash or equivalent shown in Table 6-2, prices substantially exceeded net book assets of the seller in all but one case. The apparent general lack of significance of net book assets in business combinations was borne out also in many cases involving exchanges of capital stock shown in Table 6-1.

Table

STATISTICS ON SELECTED BUSINESS COMBINATIONS DURING
INVOLVING THE ISSUANCE OF VOTING CAPITAL STOCK OF THE

Acquisition or Merger	First Public Announcement		Market Price Per Share Two Months Prior to First Public Announcement		Ratio of Common Shares of Acquirer for Shares of Seller	Earnings Per Share—Latest Fiscal Year	
			Acquirer	Seller		Acquirer	Seller
1[g]*	Jan.	1955	21⅝	20¾	1⅙ for 1	2.77	2.57
2	Jan.	1955	37⅜	27⅝	1 for 1	4.37	2.63
3	Jan.	1955	26⅜	26¾	1 for 1	1.20	1.53
4	Feb.	1955	13	18⅜	1½ for 1	0.97	2.67
5	Feb.	1955	33¼	25⅞	1 for 1	3.04	2.71
6[g]	Mar.	1955	5⅛	27½	6 for 1	0.47[a]	6.63
7	Apr.	1955	55¾	36⅝	¾ for 1	3.02	2.52
8	Jun.	1955	45⅜	35	1 for 1	2.84	2.60
9	Apr.	1955	36¼	28⅞	⅘ for 1	3.27	3.10
10	Jul.	1955	41⅝	49½	1½ for 1	1.46	3.58
11	Sep.	1955	55¼	13⅞	0.286 for 1	4.28	0.77
12[g]	Aug.	1955	30½	20¾	0.67308 for 1	4.48	2.61
13	Oct.	1955	13⅛	27¾	4 for 1	(4.49)	1.53
14	Nov.	1955	45¼	52½	1½ for 1	3.40	4.71
15	Jan.	1956	22½	18⅛	1 1/10 for 1	2.22	1.09
16	Oct.	1955	36¼	16¾"A" 16¾"B"	½ for each class—"A" and "B"	3.46[b]	1.85
17	Dec.	1955	58	97	1¾ for 1	2.95	6.06
18[g]	Dec.	1955	18⅝	5½	4 for 10	0.32	0.49
19	Dec.	1955	36¼	8⅝	1 for 4	3.10	0.86
20[g]	Feb.	1956	43⅝	36½	1 for 1	2.95	3.02
21	May	1956	34	44 43½"B"	1¾ for 1 common and 1 Class "B"	8.05	2.94
22	Jun.	1956	28¼	26⅝	⅚ for 1	2.45	2.00
23[g]	May	1956	15	14½	½ for 1	1.27	0.54
24	Aug.	1956	38¼	68	2⅝ for 1	2.15[d]	4.21
25	May	1956	70¾	24¼	¼ common plus $20 4% preferred for 1	4.42	2.48
26	Sep.	1956	125⅜	39¾	1 for 2½	4.83	2.35[c]
27	Jun.	1956	43⅝	33⅜	9/10 for 1	3.22[d]	2.80
28[g]	Jan.	1957	35½	43¼	1¾ for 1	2.23	3.02
29	Feb.	1957	36¾	243	10 for 1	2.06	21.31
30	Aug.	1957	35	24	¾ for 1	4.08	2.03
31[g]	Sep.	1957	33¾	24	1.1 for 1	2.34	3.96

* For explanation, see pages 98–99.

6-1

THE PERIOD FROM JANUARY 1, 1955, TO DECEMBER 31, 1961,
ACQUIRER, OR SURVIVING COMPANY, IN THE CASE OF A MERGER

| Annual Rate of Dividends Per Share | | Net Assets Per Share—Latest Fiscal Year-End | | Per Cent of Premium or (Discount) Paid by Acquirer Per Share Relative to Equivalent Figures of Seller | | | | |
| | | | | Market Price Prior to Public Announcement | Latest Fiscal Year | | | |
Acquirer	Seller	Acquirer	Seller		Earnings	Dividends	Net Assets	Acquisition or Merger
1.50	1.20	17.18	17.20 [a]	22	26	46	17	1 [g]
2.00	2.00	44.54	15.24	35	66	–	192	2
2.10	1.00	8.70	8.29	(1)	(22)	110	5	3
0.90	1.05	21.86	14.21	6	(46)	29	131	4
1.60	1.50	16.84	18.40	29	12	7	(8)	5
–	1.75	2.14 [a]	35.16	12	(57)	(100)	(63)	6 [g]
2.00	1.40	20.71	15.47	14	(10)	7	0.4	7
1.40	1.575	19.56	19.77	30	9	(11)	(1)	8
1.67	1.52	24.85	21.17	0.4	(16)	(12)	(6)	9
0.83	2.00	13.93	32.72	26	(39)	(38)	(36)	10
2.30	0.75	41.19	13.24	14	59	(12)	(11)	11
1.50	1.10	34.49	18.92	(1)	16	(8)	23	12 [g]
–	1.25	13.76	56.37	89	(1,274)	(100)	(2)	13
2.05	2.50	22.76	35.89	29	8	23	(5)	14
1.34	1.60	18.31	20.24	37	124	(8)	(0.5)	15
1.70	1.00	19.42	9.56	8	(6)	(15)	2	16
2.00	2.00	28.85	29.15	5	(15)	75	73	17
1.30	–	11.52	7.08	35	(74)	–	(35)	18 [g]
2.40	–	30.00	5.26	5	(10)	–	43	19
1.80	1.60	24.68	33.43	20	(2)	13	(26)	20 [g]
4.00	1.50	51.84	26.48	(32)	140	133	71	21
1.20	0.75	24.44	9.22	(12)	2	33	121	22
0.75 [c]	–	18.76	26.05	(48)	18	–	(64)	23 [g]
1.00 [d]	1.40	30.05 [d]	56.78	48	34	88	39	24
2.13	0.60	28.20	15.89	55	(88)	122	70	25
3.00	0.92 [d]	25.16	10.49	26	(18)	30	(4)	26
1.50 [d]	1.50	29.80 [d]	17.24	5	(8)	(20)	38	27
1.10	1.55	13.14	23.73	44	29	24	(3)	28 [g]
1.00	14.00	14.85	164.58 [a]	51	(3)	(29)	(10)	29
2.00	1.40	36.20	32.10	9	51	7	(15)	30
1.25	1.20	36.20	29.75	55	(35)	15	34	31 [g]

Table

STATISTICS ON SELECTED BUSINESS COMBINATIONS DURING
INVOLVING THE ISSUANCE OF VOTING CAPITAL STOCK OF THE

Acquisition or Merger	First Public Announcement	Market Price Per Share Two Months Prior to First Public Announcement		Ratio of Common Shares of Acquirer for Shares of Seller	Earnings Per Share—Latest Fiscal Year	
		Acquirer	Seller		Acquirer	Seller
32	Nov. 1957	$21\frac{7}{8}$	$69\frac{5}{8}$	3 for 1	3.32	5.87
33	Jun. 1958	43	40	1 for 1	6.02	5.22
34	Sep. 1958	$46\frac{1}{2}$"A" $47\frac{1}{2}$"B"	$40\frac{1}{2}$	1 for 1	2.59	2.21
35 [g]	Oct. 1958	$89\frac{1}{4}$	55	1 for 1	7.32	0.51
36	Nov. 1958	27	$27\frac{3}{4}$	$1\frac{1}{3}$ for 1	2.41	3.84
37	Jan. 1959	$87\frac{1}{2}$	$23\frac{3}{8}$	3 for 5	1.96	1.82
38 [g]	Feb. 1959	42	$6\frac{3}{8}$	1 for $5\frac{1}{2}$	1.99	(0.13)
39	Mar. 1959	$57\frac{7}{8}$	$30\frac{1}{4}$	0.765654 for 1	3.51	1.38
40 [g]	Apr. 1959	47	$26\frac{3}{8}$	$\frac{1}{2}$ for 1	3.50	1.65
41	Jul. 1959	50	22	0.75 for 1	2.42	1.36
42 [g]	Sep. 1959	$26\frac{1}{2}$	$25\frac{3}{8}$	1 $1.10 Conv. pfd. for 1	1.28	(2.62)
43	Oct. 1959	$68\frac{1}{2}$	$42\frac{5}{8}$	$\frac{4}{7}$ for 1	4.21	(1.11)
44	Oct. 1959	$39\frac{7}{8}$	$39\frac{1}{2}$	$\frac{5}{6}$ for 1	3.09	2.05
45	Nov. 1959	$31\frac{3}{8}$	$18\frac{5}{8}$	2 for 3	1.65	0.35
46 [g]	Jan. 1960	51	$35\frac{3}{8}$	1.02 for 1	3.01	2.34
47	May 1960	$18\frac{5}{8}$	$10\frac{1}{8}$	$\frac{9}{10}$ for 1	1.60	0.99
48	Aug. 1960	$90\frac{1}{2}$	54	$\frac{2}{3}$ for 1	3.01	2.52
49	Nov. 1960	$45\frac{1}{4}$	$30\frac{1}{8}$	1 for $1\frac{1}{4}$	3.51	2.09
50	Jan. 1961	$36\frac{3}{8}$	$10\frac{1}{2}$	1 for 3	2.23	0.23
51 [g]	Jan. 1961	$31\frac{3}{4}$	$18\frac{3}{8}$	$\frac{9}{10}$ for 1	1.59	1.72
52	Feb. 1961	$51\frac{3}{4}$	17	2 for 5	4.63	(1.80)
53	Apr. 1961	100 [f]	27	1 4% preferred for 3	4.00 [f]	1.93
54	Apr. 1961	75	37	6 for 10	4.10	2.28
55	Jun. 1961	73	$24\frac{3}{8}$	1 for $2\frac{1}{4}$	3.71	1.91
56	Jun. 1961	$25\frac{1}{4}$	$7\frac{7}{8}$	1 for 3.3	0.85	0.31
57	Jun. 1961	2	$3\frac{1}{8}$	$2\frac{1}{4}$ for 1	0.14	0.16
58 [g]	Oct. 1961	$91\frac{1}{8}$	$21\frac{7}{8}$	1 for $4\frac{1}{2}$	7.80	0.30

[a] Latest fiscal year amounts not available. Amounts are shown for year previous.
[b] Amount per share is before application of special credit. Earnings per share were $3.84 after special credit.
[c] Includes $0.25 extra dividend.
[d] Adjusted for stock splits that occurred prior to the exchange of shares.
[e] Net assets per share at July 31, 1958, as reported in proxy statement of Signal Oil and Gas Co., dated October 30, 1958.

6-1—*Continued*

THE PERIOD FROM JANUARY 1, 1955, TO DECEMBER 31, 1961,
ACQUIRER, OR SURVIVING COMPANY, IN THE CASE OF A MERGER

| Annual Rate of Dividends Per Share | | Net Assets Per Share—Latest Fiscal Year-End | | Market Price Prior to Public Announcement | Per Cent of Premium or (Discount) Paid by Acquirer Per Share Relative to Equivalent Figures of Seller | | | Acquisition or Merger |
| | | | | | Latest Fiscal Year | | | |
Acquirer	Seller	Acquirer	Seller		Earnings	Dividends	Net Assets	
2.00	3.60	15.96	24.07	(6)	70	67	99	32
3.00	2.00	48.15	32.86	8	15	50	47	33
0.70	0.60	19.71 e	17.47 e	16	17	17	13	34
6.00	2.00	68.15	80.66	62	1,335	200	(16)	35 g
1.20	1.80	24.25	38.89	30	(16)	(11)	(17)	36
1.20	1.30	30.09	29.32	125	(35)	(45)	(38)	37
0.80	–	19.46	8.52	20	378	–	(58)	38 g
1.80	1.00	33.60	20.75	46	95	38	24	39
2.40	1.40	59.97	26.18	(11)	6	(14)	15	40 g
1.40	1.00	28.67	25.25	70	34	5	(15)	41
1.10	0.70	26.50	27.72	4	149	57	(5)	42 g
1.00	0.40	39.78	12.45	(8)	317	43	83	43
1.55	2.00	37.14	35.73	(16)	26	(35)	(13)	44
1.00	–	27.72	20.69	12	214	–	(11)	45
1.40	1.60	30.68	51.72	47	31	(11)	(39)	46 g
0.70	0.25	10.10	9.59	10	(3)	68	(37)	47
1.30	1.30	21.41	26.05	12	(20)	(33)	(45)	48
1.80	1.30	22.73	25.88	20	33	11	(30)	49
–	0.40 a	2.97 a	5.33 a	15	223	(100)	(81)	50
1.20	0.45	17.77	29.68	56	17	140	(46)	51 g
3.00	–	35.11	35.23	22	203	–	(60)	52
4.00 f	1.20	100.00 f	14.41	23	(31)	11	131	53
2.40	2.00	28.40	10.74	22	8	(28)	59	54
2.50	0.70	33.98	23.43	33	(14)	59	(36)	55
–	–	3.56	4.66	(3)	(17)	–	(77)	56
–	–	2.67	2.21	44	97	–	172	57
3.00	–	52.44	24.48	(7)	478	–	(52)	58 g

f Represents par value of preferred stock authorized specifically for this merger. Equivalent market value of common shares into which preferred is convertible was 83, and equivalent earnings for prior year were $5.03.

g These acquisitions were accounted for as purchases by the acquiring companies; all others were poolings of interests. See Chapter 7 for discussion of accounting aspects of business combinations.

Table 6-2

Statistics on Selected Corporate Purchases for Cash
During the Period from January 1, 1955, to December 31, 1961

Acquisition or Merger	Date	Acquirer — Earnings Per Share—Latest Fiscal Year-End Prior to Purchase	Acquirer — Net Assets Per Share—Latest Fiscal Year-End Prior to Purchase	Per Cent Return on Net Assets	Net Assets at Latest Fiscal Year-End Prior to Purchase	Seller — Price Paid for Acquisition	Net Income—Latest Fiscal Year Prior to Purchase	Per Cent of Net Income to Acquisition Price
59	Dec. 1958	(0.16)	1.12	(14)	$6,718,500	$16,892,720	$1,124,886	7
60	Feb. 1959	3.84	32.80	12	$8,096,800	$11,778,000	$1,236,795	11
61	Dec. 1955	2.98	78.91	4	$12,292,500	$20,250,000 plus assumption of certain liabilities	$1,307,141	6
62	Feb. 1961	2.56	21.27	12	$21,735,000	$25,000,000	$1,841,003	7
63	Jan. 1961	1.58	11.25	14	$5,712,700	$6,655,000	($686,119)	(10)
64	Mar. 1961	2.97	90.80	3	$15,390,900	$19,154,850	$1,264,694	7
65	Nov. 1960	1.58	11.25	14	$11,221,245	$16,135,000 principal amount of 5½% convertible debentures	$1,213,507	8

LIST OF MERGERS AND ACQUISITIONS IN TABLES 6–1 AND 6–2
WITH EFFECTIVE DATES OF THE COMBINATIONS
SHOWN PARENTHETICALLY

1. American Metal Products Co.–Allianceware, Inc. (April, 1955)
2. The Diamond Match Co.–General Package Corp. (May, 1955)
3. Hooker Electrochemical Co.–Durez Plastics & Chemicals, Inc. (April, 1955)
4. Houdaille-Hershey Corp.–Frontier Industries, Inc. (June, 1955)
5. Warner-Hudnut, Inc.–The Lambert Co. (March, 1955)
6. Sterling Precision Corp.–American-LaFrance-Foamite Corp. (April, 1955)
7. Olin-Mathieson Chemical Corp.–Blockson Chemical Co. (June 1955)
8. Crown Zellerback Corp.–Gaylord Container Corp. (November, 1955)
9. Borg-Warner Corp.–Byron Jackson Co. (September, 1955)
10. Monsanto Chemical Co.–Lion Oil Co. (September, 1955)
11. Beatrice Foods Co.–D. L. Clark Co. (October, 1955)
12. Kelsey-Hayes Wheel Co.–Steel Products Engineering Co. (November, 1955)
13. Alexander Smith, Inc.–Mohawk Carpet Mills, Inc. (Mohasco Industries, Inc.) (December, 1955)
14. Square D Co.–Electric Controller & Manufacturing Co. (December, 1955)
15. American Radiator & Standard Sanitary Corp.–Mullins Manufacturing Corp. (January, 1956)
16. Warner-Lambert Pharmaceutical Co.–Emerson Drug Co. of Baltimore City (April, 1956)
17. American Cyanamid Co.–Formica Co. (April, 1956)
18. Penn-Texas Corp.–The Hallicrafters Co. (March, 1956)
19. Rheem Manufacturing Co.–Richmond Radiator Co. (February, 1956)
20. St. Regis Paper Co.–Rhinelander Paper Co. (April, 1956)
21. Union Bag & Paper Corp.–Camp Manufacturing Co., Inc. (Union Bag-Camp Paper Corp.) (July, 1956)
22. Beech-Nut Packing Co.–Life Savers Corp. (Beech-Nut Life Savers, Inc.) (August, 1956)
23. Dan River Mills, Inc.–Alabama Mills, Inc. (August, 1956)
24. Pittsburgh Consolidation Coal Co.–Pocahontas Fuel Co., Inc. (November, 1956)
25. Owens-Illinois Glass Co.–National Container Corp. (October, 1956)
26. Union Carbide Corp.–Visking Corp. (December, 1956)
27. Continental Can Co., Inc.–Robert Gair Co., Inc. (October, 1956)
28. Lone Star Cement Corp.–Superior Portland Cement, Inc. (April, 1957)
29. Weyerhaeuser Timber Co.–Eddy Paper Corp. (April, 1956)
30. Copperweld Steel Co.–Superior Steel Corp. (November, 1957)
31. Allis-Chalmers Manufacturing Co.–S. Morgan Smith Co. (January, 1959)
32. The American Metal Co., Ltd.–Climax Molybdenum Co. (American Metal Climax, Inc.) (December, 1957)
33. Eaton Manufacturing Co.–Fuller Manufacturing Co. (July, 1958)
34. Signal Oil & Gas Co.–Hancock Oil Co. (December, 1958)
35. Kennecott Copper Corp.–The Okonite Co. (November, 1958)
36. Amphenol Electronics Corp.–George W. Borg Corp. (Amphenol-Borg Electronics Corp.) (December, 1958)
37. Aluminum Co. of America–Rome Cable Corp. (March, 1959)
38. Signal Oil & Gas Co.–Bankline Oil Co. (July, 1959)

39. Continental Can Co., Inc.-Fort Wayne Corrugated Paper Co. (June, 1959)

40. American Steel Foundries-South Bend Lathe Works (June, 1959)

41. St. Regis Paper Co.-Cornell Paperboard Products Co. (December, 1959)

42. American Manufacturing Co., Inc.-Safety Industries, Inc. (January, 1960)

43. Bell & Howell Co.-Consolidated Electrodynamics Corp. (December, 1959)

44. Kalamazoo Vegetable Parchment Co.-Sutherland Paper Co. (January, 1960)

45. Boeing Airplane Co.-Vertol Aircraft Corp. (March, 1960)

46. St. Regis Paper Co.-The Creamery Package Manufacturing Co. (January, 1960)

47. Progress Manufacturing Co., Inc.-Reading Tube Corp. (June, 1960)

48. The Dow Chemical Co.-Allied Laboratories, Inc. (December, 1960)

49. Marquette Cement Manufacturing Co.-North American Cement Corp. (January, 1961)

50. Laboratory for Electronics, Inc.-Eastern Industries, Inc. (March, 1961)

51. Weyerhaeuser Timber Co.-Hamilton Paper Co. (April, 1961)

52. Midland-Ross Corp.-Industrial Rayon Corp. (May, 1961)

53. Diamond Alkali Co.-The Bessemer Limestone & Cement Co. (September, 1961)

54. National Biscuit Co.-The Cream of Wheat Corp. (August, 1961)

55. Air Reduction Co., Inc.-Speer Carbon Co. (August, 1961)

56. Bowmar Instrument Corp.-Technology Instrument Corp. (October, 1961)

57. Great American Industries, Inc.-National Phoenix Industries, Inc. (August, 1961)

58. Ford Motor Co.-Philco Corp. (December, 1961)

59. Servel, Inc.-Burgess Battery Co. (December, 1958)

60. Blaw-Knox Co.-The Aetna-Standard Engineering Co. (February, 1959)

61. Cerro de Pasco Corp.-Circle Wire & Cable Corp. (December, 1955)

62. Standard Brands Inc.-Planters Nut & Chocolate Co. (February, 1961)

63. Kayser-Roth Corp.-Mojud Co., Inc. (January, 1961)

64. Crane Co.-Midwest Piping Co., Inc. (March, 1961)

65. Kayser-Roth Corp.-A. Stein & Co. (November, 1960)

Chapter 7

HOW TO ACCOUNT FOR A "PURCHASE"
OR A "POOLING OF INTERESTS"

As indicated in previous chapters, a business combination falls
into one of two categories for accounting purposes: a purchase
or a pooling of interests. In all cases, cash deals, or those involving other than voting securities, are "purchases." An exchange of voting stock for voting stock generally results in a
pooling of interests, provided certain other requirements are met,
but it could result in a purchase.

DISTINCTION BETWEEN A PURCHASE
AND A POOLING OF INTERESTS

The following excerpt indicates the accounting distinction between a purchase and a pooling of interests.

For accounting purposes, the distinction between a *purchase* and a *pooling
of interests* is to be found in the attendant circumstances rather than in the
designation of the transaction according to its legal form (such as a merger, an
exchange of shares, a consolidation, or an issuance of stock for assets and businesses), or in the number of corporations which survive or emerge, or in other
legal or tax considerations (such as the availability of surplus for dividends).

For accounting purposes, a *purchase* may be described as a business combination of two or more corporations in which an important part of the
ownership interests in the acquired corporation or corporations is eliminated
or in which other factors requisite to a pooling of interests are not present.

In contrast, a *pooling of interests* may be described for accounting purposes
as a business combination of two or more corporations in which the holders of
substantially all of the ownership interests in the constituent corporations
become the owners of a single corporation which owns the assets and businesses
of the constituent corporations, either directly or through one or more subsidiaries, and in which certain other factors . . . are present.[1]

[1] Committee on Accounting Procedure, American Institute of Certified Public
Accountants, *Business Combinations,* Bull. No. 48, January, 1957.

This distinction between a purchase and a pooling of interests is a relatively recent development. Prior to September, 1950, the accounting treatment followed in acquisitions was uniform in certain essential respects whether the consideration given was cash or voting stock. Where acquisitions were made for voting stock, even though such transactions were "tax free," the investment in the acquired company generally was measured by the fair market value of the stock issued. Thus, goodwill arose in such transactions as in the case of cash purchases of companies. However, it was permissible, in this prepooling era, to charge off goodwill to surplus, thereby relieving future income of any charges for this excess of purchase price (goodwill) over net tangible assets acquired. This change in concept between a purchase and a pooling of interests also led to a change in the practice of accounting for goodwill.

The American Institute of Certified Public Accountants, in its annual study of reports to stockholders of six hundred leading industrial companies for the 1961 fiscal year, noted that business combinations were disclosed representing forty-eight purchases and fifty-two poolings of interests. Although the totals of each type of combination were relatively comparable, the vast majority of those involving substantial consideration were effected by exchanges of voting capital stock and therefore classified as poolings of interests.[2]

Present Concept of a Pooling of Interests. Under the present accounting concept of a pooling of interests, the constituent companies, in effect, show a combined financial position as though they had been affiliated prior to the combination. The fair market value of the capital stock of the surviving company in the combination is ignored, and its shares issued in the acquisition or merger are generally shown at par or stated value; the capital in excess of par (capital surplus) and accumulated earnings (earned surplus) of each of the companies are respectively combined, subject to appropriate adjustments, if the par or stated value of the stock issued differs from the amount at which the capital stock of the disappearing company was carried; and the

[2] American Institute of Certified Public Accountants, *Accounting Trends and Techniques* 217 (16th ed. 1962)

net book assets of the constituent companies are combined. Since the net book assets of the disappearing company are carried forward in the combined enterprise, subject to possible adjustments for purposes of accounting uniformity, no goodwill arises in pooling transactions.

Present Concept of a Purchase. When a business combination is deemed to be a purchase, the net assets of the acquired company are recorded at cost and measured in cash or the fair value of securities or other property issued, or at the fair value of the property acquired, whichever is more clearly evident of value. Customarily, in a purchase, the consideration given is used as the measure of value and is allocated to tangible and intangible assets. Thus, a new basis of values of net assets is established by the purchaser; and to the extent that the purchased cost is not allocable to tangible assets and intangible assets, amortizable for tax purposes, there is goodwill. This excess of purchase cost (goodwill) over amounts allocable to specific assets is dealt with, generally, by periodic charges to future income, either commencing immediately upon acquisition or at a later date.

A more comprehensive discussion of accounting for purchases and poolings of interests in business combinations follows.

PURCHASES

Business combinations that qualify as purchases fall into the following general categories:

1. Acquisitions of the net assets and business or capital stock of a company for cash or a combination of cash and securities
2. Acquisitions of voting capital stock of a company in a statutory merger involving the issuance, wholly or in part, of securities other than voting stock
3. Acquisitions of the net assets and business or capital stock of a company in exchange for voting stock, where other attendant circumstances preclude "pooling of interests" accounting treatment

Acquisitions of the types classified as (2) and (3) fall under the "tax-free" reorganization provisions of the Internal Revenue Code and present no problem of revaluation of individual assets.[3]

[3] Int. Rev. Code of 1954, § 368.

The fair value of the consideration given is determined in such cases and any excess thereof over the seller's basis of net assets acquired generally is allocated to goodwill, or in some cases to fixed assets or both. In either case, the amortization of such excess amount against income is without benefit of federal income tax deductions. Acquisitions of the type classified as (1), however, are taxable exchanges and require the establishment of new values by the purchaser for book as well as tax purposes. Where capital stock is acquired rather than net assets, the purchaser must liquidate the acquired company within a specified period in order to avail himself of the privilege of stepping up the tax basis of the assets acquired.[4] Otherwise, the procedure outlined below in revaluing assets is the same as though the net assets and business were purchased.

Treatment of Assets. Ordinarily, the seller disposes of his net assets and business or capital stock for a total price that may have little or no relation to the net book equity or taxable basis of net assets of his company. The purchaser then is confronted with the problem of establishing new values for the different classes of assets involved. This must be done with great care, as the values assigned must be supportable for federal income tax purposes as current fair market values, assuming the purchase price exceeds the tax base of the seller, which generally is the case.

COMPOSITION OF NET ASSETS ACQUIRED. Assets acquired may include cash; marketable securities; accounts and notes receivable; inventories of raw materials, work in process, finished goods, and supplies; property, plant, and equipment; miscellaneous investments; prepaid and deferred charges; patents; copyrights and trade-marks; and goodwill on the books of the seller. Also, in many cases, all or certain liabilities of the seller are assumed in a "purchase."

CURRENT ASSETS OTHER THAN INVENTORIES. *Cash and Marketable Securities.* The valuation of cash requires no discussion; marketable securities should be valued at their current market prices.

---

[4] *Ibid.,* § 334(b)(2).

Accounts and Notes Receivable. Accounts and notes receivable should be valued at their indicated realizable values. In many cases, reserves against such accounts have been conservatively established and if not fully required should be reduced, thereby increasing the value of accounts and notes receivable to the purchaser. In other cases, because of the business combination, some customers may be lost, particularly those in competition with the purchaser. In such cases, it may be more difficult to collect outstanding balances taken over.

INVENTORIES. Inventories of raw materials, work in process, finished goods, and supplies ordinarily are included in the financial statements of the seller at the lower of cost or market. However, the purchaser should value inventories at their market value, which generally exceeds the seller's aggregate inventory value—often substantially. An exception to this general rule would be where the purchaser intended to discontinue the manufacture or sale of certain lines of the seller and would be required to write down inventories applicable to those lines to their realizable values.

In determining market values for these purposes, raw materials and supplies should be included at current replacement cost and finished goods at sales values, less the cost of their disposition. Work in process, depending upon its nature, should be valued at replacement cost (for material, labor, and overhead) or at its sales value, less the cost of completion and disposition, if determinable.

Although the seller may have followed the practice of charging to expense perishable tools and manufacturing supplies as they were purchased, the purchaser is entitled to inventory them at their current replacement cost.

PROPERTIES. Property, plant, and equipment, with rare exceptions, is carried by the seller at cost, less accumulated depreciation. There are various permissible methods of providing for depreciation; also, the prices of fixed assets may have increased since their dates of acquisition. Accordingly, the fair market value of property, plant, and equipment may have little relation to the net carrying amount of such assets on the books of the seller.

Desirability of a Current Appraisal. A current appraisal is desirable in sustaining a valuation to be allocated from the purchase price to property, plant, and equipment, if the value of such assets is material to the transaction. This may be accomplished by having appraisals of machinery and equipment by the purchaser's company engineers, or by having a complete appraisal undertaken by one of a number of professional firms that specialize in this activity. If a professional firm is engaged, it should be advised that the purpose of the appraisal is to establish "net sound values," as there are also appraisals for insurance purposes, on the basis of depreciated replacement cost, and other special purpose appraisals.

MISCELLANEOUS INVESTMENTS. These may include non-marketable investments in other companies or non-current advances. Needless to say, sufficient underlying data should be obtained on assets in this category to value them realistically.

PREPAID AND DEFERRED CHARGES. Deferred research and experimental expense, and unamortized debt expense, may have little or no value to a prospective purchaser. Conversely, the purchaser is entitled to inventory advertising and office supplies on hand that will be utilized, at their current replacement cost, even though they have been expensed by the seller.

PATENTS, COPYRIGHTS, AND TRADE-MARKS. Patents, copyrights, trade-marks, and franchises, which generally are written off or carried at a nominal value, may be of considerable value, on a tax basis, to the purchaser. Also, favorable contracts or leases may likewise have value. These items should be carefully investigated to determine what values may be placed on them and the period over which they should be amortized for tax and book purposes.

GOODWILL. Goodwill, in an acquisition, more appropriately termed "excess of cost over value assigned to net tangible assets acquired," theoretically should be supportable by a calculation indicating a capitalization of excess future earnings. Practically, it generally is a residual figure remaining after allocating apportionable amounts of the purchase price to tangible assets and intangible assets that have a tax basis. The amount assigned to goodwill is not amortizable for federal income tax purposes.

Liabilities. The purchaser and seller should be very clear on which liabilities of the company are to be assumed by the former. In many cases, liabilities for federal and state income taxes may not be finally determined until several years have passed. The seller should take a conservative view regarding his tax liability, particularly if the buy-sell agreement stipulates that the purchaser is only assuming liabilities disclosed or those for which reserves have been provided in the statement of financial position of the seller. In some cases, the purchaser will not assume liabilities for federal income taxes, nor for state income taxes affected by federal tax liability. This matter is discussed further in Chapters 8 and 9.

Other accruals such as for vacation and holiday pay, pension costs, royalties, and commissions should be reviewed carefully.

Example of Assigning Values in a Purchase. The following is an example of the procedure followed in assigning values to net assets in the purchase of a company for an amount exceeding the net asset basis of the seller.

	Seller's Basis	Purchaser's Basis
Current assets		
Cash	$ 130,000	$ 130,000
U. S. government securities, at cost, approximate market value $110,000	100,000	110,000 (1)
Accounts receivable, less allowance for doubtful accounts of $75,000	1,500,000	1,535,000 (2)
Inventories, at cost	2,700,000	3,200,000 (3)
Prepaid expenses	35,000	105,000 (4)
	$4,465,000	$ 5,080,000
Property, plant, and equipment at cost, less depreciation of $1,200,000	1,900,000	3,050,000 (5)
Patents and trade-marks		490,000 (6)
Deferred charges to income	60,000	— (7)
Goodwill		2,080,000 (8)
Total assets	$6,425,000	$10,700,000
Liabilities		
Federal income taxes	700,000	600,000 (9)
Other liabilities	2,100,000	2,100,000
Total liabilities	$2,800,000	$ 2,700,000
Net assets of seller	$3,625,000	
Purchase price		$ 8,000,000

The purchaser allocated the price paid for the net assets and business of the company on the following bases:

1. Marketable securities at approximate market values.
2. The reserve for doubtful accounts receivable appeared excessive by $35,000 and was accordingly reduced by this amount.
3. Inventories of raw materials and supplies, including supplies on hand that had been expensed by the seller, were valued at their current replacement cost; finished goods, at sales values less the cost of their disposition; and work in process, at percentage stages of completion of finished goods.
4. Certain prepaid expenses that had no value to the purchaser were written off, but substantial quantities of advertising materials and office supplies on hand that had been expensed by the seller were valued at replacement cost.
5. Property, plant, and equipment was reflected at the net sound values resulting from an appraisal by one of the major professional appraisal firms. This value included tools, dies, and jigs that had previously been written off the books of the seller.
6. Patents and trade-marks were valued individually by the purchaser's engineers, assisted by a member of their general legal staff familiar with such matters.
7. Deferred charges to income consisted of deferred research and experimental expense that had no value for the purchaser.
8. Goodwill was the residual balance of the purchase price, after assigning values to all other assets and liabilities.
9. Federal income tax liability was reduced because the purchaser believed that tax liability for the current and prior years would be settled on a more favorable basis than that indicated by the reserve established by the seller.

As illustrated in the foregoing example, in a purchase of the net assets of a company, either directly or through a capital stock acquisition and subsequent liquidation, a new basis is established for many of the assets and, in some instances, for liabilities.

SUBSEQUENT ACCOUNTING FOR ASSETS PURCHASED

Current Assets. Marketable securities should be accounted for on the same basis as if they had been purchased in the ordinary course.

Accounts and notes receivable should be valued from time to time, the same as any other accounts the purchaser may have had prior to the transaction, and a suitable allowance made for accounts that may become uncollectible.

INVENTORIES. Inventories should be valued on the basis of cost or market, whichever is lower. Cost should be determined on the basis that the purchaser regularly uses in computing inventory valuations, such as first-in, first-out; average; and last-in, first-out. In other words, the purchaser is in no way bound by the method of inventory costing followed by the seller. To the extent that any inventories acquired from the seller remain on hand at the close of subsequent accounting periods, cost and market may be the same. Otherwise, for periods subsequent to acquisition, market is understood to mean current replacement value, either by purchase or by reproduction.

PROPERTY, PLANT, AND EQUIPMENT. Provision for depreciation on fair values allocated to machinery and equipment should be based on the estimated remaining useful lives of the assets, in accordance with the regular accounting practice of the purchaser. The depreciation practices of the seller, as to useful lives of assets, need not be followed by the purchaser, although it may be convenient to do so.

PREPAID AND DEFERRED CHARGES. These should be apportioned over the periods benefited through their use.

INTANGIBLE ASSETS OTHER THAN GOODWILL. Any amounts capitalized by the purchaser for patents, copyrights, trade-marks, and franchises should be amortized over their useful lives or to the date of their expiry, whichever is shorter. Payments for covenants not to compete should be charged to income in the periods of payment.

Liabilities, Including Federal Income Taxes. Because of differing employee benefit plans, reserves carried by the seller may not have any relation to the liabilities assumed by the purchaser for such items, either morally or legally. However, if the purchaser is assuming liabilities of the seller, it should be ascertained that provision has been made for all such obligations.

It is generally desirable for the seller to be pessimistic in his view regarding reserves required for the final settlement of federal and state income taxes, particularly when the purchaser assumes this obligation. However, if the purchaser assumes liability for federal and state income taxes, he need not reflect in his financial statements at the time of takeover the full reserves shown by the seller, if they are overly conservative.

Goodwill. Accounting for goodwill is one of the most important considerations in acquisitions for cash or cash equivalent, or for capital stock, where attendant conditions do not justify pooling of interests accounting treatment. In the case of other assets acquired that have a tax basis, the purchaser recovers part of his purchase price in the future by means of tax deductions when assets are disposed of, and through periodic charges for depreciation and amortization.

GOODWILL NOT AMORTIZABLE FOR TAXES. For tax purposes, goodwill is considered to have no ascertainable useful life and therefore is not amortizable. Accordingly, its amortization for financial accounting purposes reduces future income on an absolute basis. Because of its effect on subsequent earnings, when amortized, the accounting treatment of goodwill has been a somewhat controversial subject among accountants, as well as business executives. It therefore merits more discussion than the other accounting aspects of purchases, which have been covered briefly.

CHANGES IN PRACTICES OF ACCOUNTING FOR GOODWILL. Accounting for purchased goodwill has gone through evolutionary stages. In the earliest, goodwill was charged to capital surplus, generally in a lump sum at the time of acquisition; in the next stage, it was charged to earned surplus on a similar basis; and currently, the preferable practice is to amortize it by charges to income.

PRONOUNCEMENT OF THE AMERICAN INSTITUTE OF CERTIFIED PUBLIC ACCOUNTANTS ON THE SUBJECT OF GOODWILL. The American Institute of Certified Public Accountants through its Committee on Accounting Procedure classified goodwill (and other intangibles with which we are not here concerned) as "(a) those having a limited term of existence . . . by their nature," and "(b) those having no such limited term of existence . . ." With regard to the accounting for such intangibles, they state as follows:

Type (a):

The cost of type (a) intangibles should be amortized by systematic charges in the income statement over the period benefited, as in the case of other assets having a limited period of usefulness. If it becomes evident that the period benefited will be longer or shorter than originally estimated, recognition thereof may take the form of an appropriate decrease or increase in the rate of amortization or, if such increased charges would result in distortion of income, a partial write-down may be made by a charge to earned surplus.

Type (b):

When it becomes reasonably evident that the term of existence of a type (b) intangible has become limited and that it has therefore become a type (a) intangible, its cost should be amortized by systematic charges in the income statement over the estimated remaining period of usefulness. If, however, the period of amortization is relatively short so that misleading inferences might be drawn as a result of inclusion of substantial charges in the income statement a partial write-down may be made by a charge to earned surplus, and the rest of the cost may be amortized over the remaining period of usefulness.[5]

GOODWILL PRACTICES FOLLOWED NOT ALWAYS DISCLOSED. The number of acquisitions involving goodwill and the variety of situations encountered continue to increase. Often, factual considerations and the underlying theory relied upon in choosing the method followed in a particular case is not disclosed in published financial statements. Some companies have been including purchased goodwill, particularly if the amount involved is not relatively material, in property, plant, and equipment. The Securities and Exchange Commission requires the policy for amortization of significant intangibles to be disclosed in notes to the financial statements. This type of information also should be included in published annual reports.

The American Institute of Certified Public Accountants' survey of published annual reports for companies with fiscal years falling within the year ended April 30, 1954 and its survey for those with fiscal years ending during 1961 reported the following

[5] American Institute of Certified Public Accountants, *Restatement and Revision of Accounting Research*, Bull. No. 43, September, 1961, Chap. 5.

for companies that disclosed goodwill in their statements of financial position.[6]

	Number of Companies	
	Fiscal 1953–1954	Fiscal 1961
Carried at amortized value		
Amortization charged to:		
Income	14	45
Not indicated	2	15
	16	60
Carried at unamortized value	25	52
Carried at nominal value	131	71
Total companies disclosing goodwill	172	183

It is assumed where the charge for amortization was not indicated that it was through income. A charge directly to retained earnings or to capital in excess of par value of capital stock would have been disclosed in the financial statements. On that basis, the number of companies in the survey reporting amortization of intangibles by charges to income may be increased to sixteen in fiscal 1953–1954 and to sixty for fiscal 1961. During the same period, companies included in the survey reporting goodwill at unamortized cost increased from twenty-five to fifty-two. These figures are not exactly comparable, as some companies, amortizing goodwill through income charges, completed the amortization cycle during this period, and goodwill no longer appeared in their financial statements. Also, as indicated, a number of companies have included purchased goodwill with fixed assets and have amortized it over the approximate composite lives of such assets.

METHOD OF ACCOUNTING FOR GOODWILL PREVIOUSLY PERMITTED. The method of writing off purchased goodwill at acquisition to surplus was once commonly followed but is now prohibited, although it still has some support among businessmen. From their point of view, such an immediate write-off clears the decks of an asset that readers find difficult to understand and preserves intact the "earnings stream" of the company acquired. Even though the proponents of this presently unacceptable method

---

[6] American Institute of Certified Public Accountants, *Accounting Trends and Techniques* 93 (8th ed. 1954); 79 (16th ed. 1962).

agree that purchased goodwill is in the nature of a premium paid for prospective earnings, they are reluctant to absorb its cost by systematic charges against such earnings.

Some accountants argue that the cost of purchased goodwill should invariably be considered a type (b) intangible and carried at cost until its value becomes impaired. They reason this way on the grounds that sound values were obtained in the acquisition equivalent to the cash paid out until subsequent events indicate otherwise. The proponents of this theory contend that the cost of goodwill should be retained because when profits are large, goodwill is a definite asset that is not diminishing in value. To write it off then is illogical. When the value of goodwill has decreased and profits are smaller, the supporters of this theory believe it would be logical to then amortize this decrease in value. However, profits at a time that goodwill shows a definite diminution in value are rarely sufficient for this treatment; and, in many such cases, lump sum write-offs are made as special items in the income or retained earnings statements.

THE REAL NATURE OF GOODWILL. The cost of goodwill included in the purchase price of a going concern is essentially the discounted value of expected future earnings. Thus, purchased goodwill represents a deferred charge for a portion of income that is expected to materialize later. When these earnings are realized, such portion represents a return of cost and not profit. To take earnings from an acquired company into net income without any reduction for the cost of goodwill, in most cases, results in an overstatement of income. To charge off the cost of such goodwill at a subsequent date in a lump sum against retained earnings similarly has the effect of overstating income.

The practice of amortizing goodwill recognizes that purchased goodwill generally does depreciate; it does not exist permanently and expires—sometimes very quickly. Management must make expenditures to maintain or increase the goodwill. If new goodwill has been built up, it should not appear as an asset, because it is non-purchased goodwill. The cost of the purchased goodwill that expires and later expenditures to maintain goodwill must ultimately be matched against income. As an analogous situation, the original cost of a building is matched against income over a period of years, through depreciation charges and current repair and maintenance costs.

METHODS OF AMORTIZING GOODWILL. The method of amortization adopted should result in an objectively determined and reasonable charge to income each year until goodwill is fully amortized. Amortization of goodwill should appear as a charge in the operating section of the income statement. The following methods of amortization are being utilized currently:

Straight-line method—equal annual charges for a given period, generally five to twenty years

Irregular methods —predetermined increasing or decreasing annual charges for a given period
—annual charges based on ratio of revenues or net income

The straight-line method of amortization is most commonly used.

An ascending predetermined annual charge may be appropriate if a company was acquired on the basis of estimated growth. Irregular annual amortization based on a ratio should preferably be related to the volume of business (sales or production) rather than to net income. If based on net income, a situation might arise where there were no profits and hence no amortization. This would not make sense, since the absence of profits would ordinarily indicate the need for greater rather than less amortization. Some of the other irregular methods found in practice are not too defensible.

OCCASIONALLY THE AMORTIZATION OF GOODWILL MAY BE DE-LAYED. Under certain circumstances, the commencement of amortization of goodwill by periodic charges to income may reasonably be delayed for a time. For example, if a company is acquired in an operating loss position or at an early stage of its development, it would be appropriate to commence amortization when profitable operations are achieved. It is assumed, in such cases, that there is reasonably clear indication a profit position will be attained in the foreseeable future.

PERIOD OF AMORTIZATION OF GOODWILL SHOULD BE REVIEWED FROM TIME TO TIME. Also, at times a company may schedule the amortization of purchased goodwill over a certain period, based on conditions that then exist. It is prudent to review this amortization schedule after the passage of a few years to ascertain if the write-off should be accelerated.

ACCOUNTING FOR SO-CALLED "NEGATIVE GOODWILL." When a company purchases another for less than the amount of its net assets, a credit arises that for many years was referred to as "negative goodwill." This term obviously is anomalous as the word "goodwill," used in a business sense, connotes something of recognized value. On rare occasions, a company may make a bargain purchase; but generally when it buys another at a substantial discount from its net assets, it is because of the low or negative earning power of the acquired company.

Accordingly, the credit balance arising from such a purchase may be accounted for under one of the following methods.

1. If it is anticipated that the low earning power of the acquired business will continue for a considerable period, the balance may be taken into income on a basis related to the depreciation charges on the fixed assets acquired in the transaction.

2. If the low earning power is estimated to be of short duration, particularly if unusual expenses are to be incurred in correcting the operating situation, the credit may be taken into income during the estimated period of readjustment of the acquired company's operations.

3. If goodwill is carried by the acquirer as a result of other acquisitions and is not being amortized, it would be acceptable to apply this credit balance in reduction of such goodwill. Certainly it would not be appropriate to amortize the credit balance to income unless goodwill carried as an asset is likewise being amortized against income.

POOLINGS OF INTERESTS

AICPA "Business Combinations" Bulletins. The Committee on Accounting Procedure of the American Institute of Certified Public Accountants issued its initial bulletin on business combinations (No. 40) in 1950.[7] This, as well as the revised bulletin (No. 48) on this subject issued in 1957, stated that substantially all the equity interests of the constituent companies involved should

[7] Committee on Accounting Procedure, American Institute of Certified Public Accountants, *Business Combinations*, Bull. No. 40, September, 1950.

survive to qualify a business combination as a pooling of interests.[8] The early bulletin contained the following statement, which was deleted in the revised bulletin: "Other things being equal, the presumption that a pooling of interests is involved would be strengthened if the activities of the businesses to be combined are either similar or complementary." Otherwise, the revised bulletin constitutes an expansion of the propositions and comments made in the earlier one.

The following factors are summarized from the discussion in Bulletin No. 48 as leading to a presumption that a business combination is a pooling of interests.

1. That the consideration given by the acquirer or dominant company in a merger or consolidation be voting capital stock.
2. That the interests of the respective shareholders of the constituent companies be substantially proportionate in the combined enterprise.
3. That where all of the capital stock of a constituent company is not being acquired, no significant minority interest remains outstanding.
4. That voting rights, as between the constituents, not be materially altered through the issuance of senior equity or debt securities having limited or no voting rights.
5. That there be no plan to retire a substantial part of the capital stock issued to owners of one or more of the constituent companies, nor a plan to substantially change ownership interests shortly before or shortly after the business combination.
6. That there be a continuity of management or the power to control management. For example, where a constituent company emerges with less than 5 to 10 per cent of the voting interest in the combined enterprise, its influence on management is presumed to be quite small.

As in the case of other bulletins issued by the Committee on Accounting Procedure, Bulletin No. 48 [9] contains the following appendix.

Accounting Research Bulletins represent the considered opinion of at least two-thirds of the members of the committee on accounting procedure, reached on a formal vote after examination of the subject matter by the committee and the research department. Except in cases in which formal adoption by the

[8] Committee on Accounting Procedure, American Institute of Certified Public Accountants, *Business Combinations*, Bull. No. 48, January, 1957.
[9] *Ibid.*

Institute membership has been asked and secured, the authority of the bulletins rests upon the general acceptability of opinions so reached.

In the light of experience since the issuance of Bulletin No. 48 in 1957, it would be well to review the practices followed by the accounting profession relative to the criteria proposed by the Committee on Accounting Procedure for pooling of interests accounting treatment. The adherence in practice to these criteria is discussed in the order they are listed above.

1. There appears to be unanimity of opinion that the issuance of voting capital stock is a requirement.
2. There is general adherence to the view that the respective interests of shareholders of constituent companies be substantially proportionate in a combined enterprise. There are instances of changes in proportionate interests but these, for the most part, are minor.
3. Where all the capital stock of a constituent company is not being acquired, it is generally considered that the minority interests outstanding should not exceed 5 to 10 per cent of the total stock outstanding at the time of the combination. This practice has been followed, generally, despite the fact that a minority interest amounting to 20 per cent would not preclude a "tax-free" reorganization under the Internal Revenue Code.
4. It is considered that the voting rights of one of the constituents to a business combination may be reduced by as much as 25 per cent through the issuance of voting senior equity securities in whole or in part in exchange for common capital stock surrendered. This reduction in voting power generally results because the senior equity securities have a higher per share value than the common stock of the issuer but only the same per share voting rights.
5. It is considered that the owners of one or more of the constituent companies may retire up to 25 per cent of their interests immediately before the business combination, or retire or sell 25 per cent of their interests immediately after the business combination, and the transaction may still qualify as a pooling of interests.
6. Bulletin No. 40 did not define the relative size of constituent companies but indicated that where one corporate party to a combination was quite minor in size in relation to the others, there was a presumption that a purchase (and not a pooling) was involved. A review of business combinations during the early 1950's discloses that, unless the smaller company involved in a business combination was reasonably related in size to the dominant company, the transaction was treated as a purchase.

However, Bulletin No. 48 indicated by percentages what was intended to indicate minimum relative size, i.e., the dominant company's interest to be not more than 90 to 95 per cent of the combined enterprise. In recent years, the matter of relative size has been almost ignored. There have been many business combinations treated as poolings of interests where the stockholders of the smaller company emerged with a 1 or 2 per cent and even less voting interest in the combined enterprise. As far as management interests or the power to control management is concerned, in combinations involving several companies of reasonably comparable size, an effort is generally made to apportion representation on the Board of Directors and among the management group. Where smaller companies are involved with larger ones in business combinations, it is not practicable to accomplish such continuity of management interests and control.

Chapter 2 contains examples of poolings of interests that illustrate some of the practices commented on above.

Perhaps the sole criterion for pooling of interests accounting treatment should be the exchange or issuance of voting stock for voting stock, regardless of the relative size of the constituent companies or the presence of other so-called relevant factors. As far as stockholders of the constituent companies are concerned, there is a continuity of interests in such a business combination. The influence exerted on management by personnel or shareholders of a relatively smaller constituent in a business combination generally will not be significant, whether its stockholders emerge with a 1 per cent, 10 per cent, or even higher interest, unless such interest is held by only one or several stockholders.

Accounting Aspects of Poolings of Interests. The accountability for a pooling of interests should be the same whether a business combination is accomplished by one company exchanging its voting capital stock (1) for the voting capital stock of another, (2) for the net assets and business of another, or (3) they each exchange their capital stocks for that of a newly formed corporation. Also, the consolidation results of a combination are the same where the company acquired continues in a subsidiary relationship, as it would be if the company acquired were dissolved and became a division, or if its net assets and business were transferred to an existing or newly formed subsidiary of the dominant company.

Fundamentally, in a pooling of interests, the new enterprise is regarded as a continuation of all the constituent corporations. Therefore, their retained earnings (earned surplus) and additional capital (capital surplus) are respectively combined and carried forward. It is not generally appropriate to offset a deficit of one company against its additional capital or that of any of the other constituent companies.

TREATMENT OF CAPITAL AND ADDITIONAL CAPITAL (CAPITAL SURPLUS). The capital of the dominant surviving corporation, in a pooling of interests, will be based on its par or stated value if, as is generally the case, its additional capital (capital surplus) is not included in the capital stock account. Such combined capital stock may be more or less than the total of the stated capitals of the constituent corporations. If the combined capital is more, the excess may be appropriated first from the combined additional capital to the extent thereof, and then from the combined retained earnings. When the combined capital is less than the total capital of the constituent companies, the difference should appear as or be added to the combined additional capital accounts.

OPERATIONS PRIOR AS WELL AS SUBSEQUENT TO COMBINATION SHOULD BE COMBINED FOR FINANCIAL STATEMENT PURPOSES. Consistent with the concept of the continuation of the combined enterprises, the operations of the constituent companies should be combined for periods prior, as well as subsequent, to the date of the combination for financial statement purposes. Disclosure that a business combination has been effected and treated as a pooling of interests should be made in financial statements issued at an interim period and at the fiscal year-end subsequent to consummation of the combination.

Illustrations of Accounting Transactions and Adjustments in Poolings of Interests. A pooling of interests may be carried out under a variety of circumstances. Illustrations of the accounting transactions and adjustments in several recent poolings follow. To clarify the accounting steps that took place, the amounts at which the capital stocks of the acquired companies were carried have been credited to additional capital (capital surplus) in the examples, and the amounts relative to capital stock issued have been charged to additional capital and credited to capital stock. In practice, the difference between the amounts attributable to the capital stock surrendered and the new capital stock issued would be charged or credited to additional capital. Of course, if additional capital were insufficient to absorb such a charge, the excess would be charged to combined retained earnings.

ISSUANCE OF PREFERRED AND COMMON STOCK FOR COMMON. Warner-Lambert Pharmaceutical Co. acquired Nepera Chemical Co., Inc., in 1956 in an interesting transaction involving the issuance of Warner-Lambert preferred and common stock and the acquisition of a minority interest that existed in a subsidiary of Nepera. Warner-Lambert issued 175,000 shares of its $1 par value common stock and 70,702 shares of its $100 par value preferred stock to the shareholders of Nepera and 3,079 shares of its $1 par value common stock to the minority shareholders of Nepera's subsidiary company. The minority interest in the Nepera subsidiary at the time of the acquisition was $140,081, of which $12,500 consisted of common stock and $127,581 represented an interest in the subsidiary's retained earnings. A summary of the pooling transactions and adjustments in this deal follows.[10]

	Capital Stock		Additional Capital	Retained Earnings
(In Thousands)	Common	Preferred		
Warner-Lambert	$2,283		$13,086	$25,647
Nepera	2,000			6,586
Totals before pooling	$4,283		$13,086	$32,233
Pooling transactions and adjustments				
Cancellation of Nepera shares	(2,000)		2,000	
Issuance of Warner-Lambert shares to Nepera shareholders	175	$7,070	(7,245)	
Issuance of Warner-Lambert shares to minority interests in Nepera	3		9	128
Totals—pooled enterprise	$2,461	$7,070	$ 7,850	$32,361

MERGER INVOLVING THREE COMPANIES. Peerless Cement Corp. and Hercules Cement Corp. were merged into Riverside Cement Co., whose name was changed to American Cement Corp. on consummation of the merger in 1957. Under the terms of the merger, the cumulative preferred stock of Riverside carried

[10] Warner-Lambert Pharmaceutical Co., Proxy Statement, November 19, 1956.

through as similar capital stock of American, and the common stocks of the constituent companies were exchanged on the following bases: 2 shares of American for each share of Riverside, 1.268 shares of American for each share of Peerless, and 1.145 shares of American for each share of Hercules. In addition, provision was made for the issuance of a portion of Hercules shares held in treasury for the exercise of options by Hercules personnel. A total of 4,113,615 shares of common stock of American was issued in this exchange. An added feature of the deal was the agreement to issue a maximum of 569,391 additional shares of common stock of American in the event that income tax cases pending with respect to percentage depletion were settled favorably to Riverside and Hercules. This question was settled early in 1961, and 60,990 shares of American common stock were issued to former shareholders of Riverside. No shares were issued to former Hercules shareholders as there was no "tax saving" involved in the ultimate settlement of their depletion question. A summary of the pooling transactions and adjustments in this deal (excluding the later issuance of the 60,990 shares) follows.[11]

(In Thousands)

	Capital Stock		Additional Capital	Retained Earnings
	Common	Preferred		
Riverside (American)	$10,350	$6,000		$ 9,533
Peerless	4,651			7,008
Hercules	776		$4,875	5,185
Hercules—treasury stock	(101)			
Totals before pooling	$15,676	$6,000	$4,875	$21,726
Pooling transactions and adjustments				
Cancellation of Peerless shares.....	(4,651)		4,651	
Cancellation of Hercules shares.....	(776)		776	
Issuance of American shares				
To Peerless shareholders	5,897		(5,897)	
To Hercules shareholders	4,321		(4,321)	
Portion of Hercules treasury shares issued under option	34 *		101 *	
Balance of Hercules treasury shares canceled	67		(67)	
Totals—pooled enterprise	$20,568	$6,000	$ 118	$21,726

* Cash of $135,000 was received for these shares.

ACQUISITION OF COMMON STOCK FOR CONVERTIBLE PREFERRED STOCK. Federal Pacific Electric Co., through an exchange offer,

[11] Peerless Cement Corp., Proxy Statement, November 8, 1957; American Cement Corp., Annual Report to Stockholders, 1961.

acquired most of the outstanding common stock of Cornell-Dubilier Electric Corp. in 1960, in consideration of the issuance of its 5½ per cent convertible preferred stock. At the time of the offer, Federal Pacific had a common stock interest in Cornell-Dubilier. If all the Cornell-Dubilier common shareholders had availed themselves of the exchange offer, Federal Pacific would have issued 484,590 shares of convertible preferred stock. However, after this transaction was consummated, there was still a minority interest in common stock of Cornell-Dubilier. This interest is ignored in the following summary of the pooling transactions and adjustments in this deal extracted from a proxy statement pro forma summary, which assumed the exchange of all outstanding shares. It will be noted that the $5.25 cumulative preferred stock of Cornell-Dubilier remained outstanding after consummation of the transaction.[12]

	Capital Stock		Additional Capital	Retained Earnings
(In Thousands)	Common	Preferred		
Federal Pacific	$2,022	$ 1,805	$15,854	$ 5,486
Federal Pacific—treasury stock ...	(22)			
Cornell-Dubilier	512	803	3,499	5,257
Cornell-Dubilier—treasury stock ...	(97)	(27)		
Totals before pooling	$2,415	$ 2,581	$19,353	$10,743
Pooling transactions and adjustments Cornell-Dubilier common stock exchanged	(512)		512	
Elimination of treasury stock, including Federal Pacific's investment of $637,568 in Cornell-Dubilier	97		(216) *	(517)
Issuance of Federal Pacific preferred shares to Cornell-Dubilier shareholders		11,146	(11,146)	
Totals—pooled enterprise	$2.000	$13.727 †	$ 8.503	$10.226

* Consists of par value of 27,800 shares of Cornell-Dubilier common stock canceled and pro rata portion of capital surplus of Cornell Dubilier allocable to such shares.

† Consists of the following:

Federal Pacific 6 per cent prior cumulative preferred..	$ 1,805,000
Federal Pacific 5½ per cent convertible preferred.......	11,146,000
Cornell-Dubilier $5.25 cumulative preferred............	776.000
Total	$13,727,000

[12] Federal Pacific Electric Co., Proxy Statement, January 12, 1960.

Other Problems Encountered in Poolings of Interests. In addition to the accounting situations illustrated in the foregoing examples, there are several others deserving comment. A company may acquire a substantial interest in another as a purchase and later through an exchange of voting stock have a pooling of interests for the latter transaction.

Also, a company may use treasury capital stock in a pooling acquisition. It should not matter whether the treasury stock has been held for a long period or if it were recently acquired. There may be an advantage in reacquiring outstanding capital stock for use in an acquisition so that per share earnings will not be affected by reason of an increase in the number of outstanding shares. On the other hand, the use of treasury stock generally will result in greater charges to additional capital, to the extent thereof, and to retained earnings, inasmuch as its reacquisition cost usually will be higher than the par or stated value of the capital stock.

EXAMPLE OF A PART PURCHASE AND A PART POOLING. Prior to December 30, 1960, Crowell-Collier Publishing Co. had purchased 174,466 shares (52.78 per cent) of the outstanding $1 par value common stock of The Macmillan Co. for a cash consideration of $8,130,025. On December 30, 1960, pursuant to a plan of merger, Crowell-Collier proposed to exchange its $1 par value common stock for the remaining 156,087 shares (47.22 per cent) of outstanding common stock of Macmillan. In the Crowell-Collier proxy statement pro forma summary, from which this information was extracted, it was assumed that all the stockholders of both companies would assent to the merger, although a few of each company did not. However, for purposes of this illustration, the proxy statement figures will be used. The interest in Macmillan acquired by Crowell-Collier for cash was treated as a purchase, and the excess of its cost over the allocable portion of $5,736,786 of the underlying net tangible assets ($10,869,242) applicable to Macmillan common stock was shown by Crowell-Collier as goodwill in the amount of $2,393,235. The exchange of Crowell-Collier common stock for the remaining shares of common stock of Macmillan was accounted for as a pooling of interests. Thus, the excess of the carrying amount of the pooled portion of Macmillan common stock over the $1 par value of the 249,739 Crowell-Collier common shares proposed to be issued was credited in the amount of $1,863,508 to the latter company's additional capital (capital surplus).[13]

EXAMPLE OF THE USE OF TREASURY CAPITAL STOCK IN A POOL-ING. An interesting merger of Worcester Paper Box Corp. into Federal Paper Board Co., Inc., which took place during 1961 and was treated for accounting purposes as a pooling of interests, involved the issuance not only of treasury common stock but also of preferred stock and notes. Federal converted 800 shares out of a total of 1,000 outstanding shares of Worcester no par common stock into 25,000 shares of Federal $5 par value common stock (of which 16,565 shares represented treasury stock) plus 69,820 shares of Federal 4.6 per cent cumulative $25 par value preferred stock. For the remaining 200 shares of Worcester common stock, Federal issued $600,000 aggregate principal amount of 4½ per cent notes. The 1,000 shares of no par common stock of Worcester were carried on its books at $52,993. Accordingly, the issuance of Federal's treasury shares, plus the additionl shares of common stock, preferred stock, and notes, resulted in a charge of $2,894,332 to retained earnings as follows: [14]

Par value of cumulative preferred stock issued	$1,745,500
Cost of treasury stock	559,650
Par value of other common stock issued	42,175
Face amount of notes issued	600.000
	$2,947,325
Less carrying amount of	
Worcester common stock	52,993
Charge to retained earnings	$2,894,332

This charge to combined retained earnings completely eliminated the $2,436,899 retained earnings of Worcester and invaded the retained earnings of Federal to the extent of $457,433.

---

[13] The Crowell-Collier Publishing Co., Proxy Statement, November 18, 1960. In the annual report of The Crowell-Collier Publishing Co. for the year ended December 31, 1960, the amount reported as being charged to goodwill was $2,074,245 and the credit to capital surplus was $1,732,902. These reduced amounts resulted because all the Macmillan stockholders did not enter into the exchange.

[14] Federal Paper Board Co., Inc., Proxy Statement, March 17, 1961.

Neither Federal nor Worcester had any capital in excess of par value (capital surplus) at the time of this transaction.

IN GENERAL

As indicated in this chapter, there is considerable flexibility in the manner in which corporate acquisitions and mergers may be carried out to accomplish accounting and economic objectives of the purchaser and the seller.

Furthermore, management appears to have a choice in accounting for business combinations where voting capital stock is issued in the acquisition of the capital stock or assets and business of another. Generally, future operations of the combined enterprise will be benefited where the transaction is treated as a pooling of interests. This is so because a pooling transaction ignores the fair value of the capital stock issued, which in the vast majority of cases exceeds the book value of the net assets acquired. In a purchase, such excess value (often including substantial amounts of goodwill) would have to be dealt with, generally by charges to future income.

On the other hand, if the book value of the net assets acquired is less than the fair value of capital stock issued, it may be advantageous to treat the transaction as a purchase. By writing down the carrying value of the net assets to the market value of the capital stock issued, future earnings would be benefited. In such a case, upon using or amortizing such assets, income tax deductions would be related to the higher tax base of the former owner; whereas charges to income would be on the reduced basis ascribed to the assets at acquisition.

An interesting article on this subject very adequately makes this point,[15] as the author analyzes a number of acquisitions of St. Regis Paper Co., primarily through the use of capital stock, that were treated variously as purchases or poolings.

The business combination of Ford Motor Co. and Philco Corp., which is mentioned in Chapter 2, although accomplished by the issuance of 997,703 shares of Ford capital stock was treated by the latter as a purchase. The fact that the net book assets of

[15] Henry R. Jaenicke, "Management's Choice to Purchase or Pool," *The Accounting Review*, October, 1962.

Philco exceeded the fair market value of the Ford stock issued no doubt influenced the form of this transaction. Also, Philco was operating at a loss in 1961 when acquired by Ford; and in a pooling, this loss would have somewhat reduced the earnings per share of the combined enterprise. In a purchase, of course, operations of the selling company are reflected in the combined enterprise only from the date of acquisition.

Chapter 8

FINANCIAL AND OTHER PROVISIONS OF BUSINESS COMBINATION AGREEMENTS

The drafting of business combination agreements is in the province of lawyers and should remain so. It is not the purpose of this chapter, therefore, to resolve the many and, at times, complex legal problems involved in drawing up such agreements but to highlight some of the financial and business aspects pertaining to them. The provisions of agreements discussed will be, for the most part, those that have a dollars and cents effect on the would-be acquirer or seller.

The prospective acquirer and seller each may be acting in good faith but have a completely different understanding about the terms of the deal, including what is being bought and what sold. It should be the objective of legal counsel preparing an agreement to set forth the intent of the several parties to the agreement in language that can have only one meaning to them, to any experts involved in the proceedings such as independent public accountants and professional appraisers, and to a court. Some of the areas that have been of concern will be discussed below.

PRELIMINARY AGREEMENT

When two parties to a proposed business combination reach an area of substantial agreement on the essential terms of a deal, such as the amount and type of consideration to be paid or issued or a formula for arriving at "price," the desired legal and tax form for the transaction, and the composition of management of the combined enterprise, legal counsel for the respective companies either undertake to draft a definitive buy-sell agreement or prepare a letter (or memorandum) of intent. Such a letter of intent sets forth the general or basic conditions of a deal and may be desirable, particularly where a delay will be encountered in completing the definitive agreement.

Object of the Letter of Intent. The letter of intent should merely express the intention of the parties and not constitute a binding agreement. It may be very brief, or quite detailed, and usually contains escape clauses, such as "The general basis and conditions recited are subject to the execution of a formal contract in form satisfactory to the attorneys for both parties" and "It is understood that neither party shall be bound to the other by this letter for damages, expenses, failure to finally agree on a formal and final contract, or in any other way."

If conditions permit the preparation of a formal contract within a reasonable period of time after an oral understanding has been reached by the parties, the letter of intent procedure may be dispensed with. The provisions of a formal business combination agreement will vary depending upon whether the deal represents (1) a purchase of assets or capital stock for cash or cash equivalent or (2) an acquisition of assets or capital stock in exchange for capital stock, or a statutory merger or consolidation. See page 221 regarding possible requirement for public release of information upon signing a letter of intent.

The provisions pertinent to accounting and economic aspects of agreements are covered variously in such documents under sections entitled "representations," "warranties," "covenants," and "conditions." Sometimes these sections are separated, and at others combined.

PURCHASE OF ASSETS OR CAPITAL STOCK FOR CASH

In a purchase of assets or capital stock for cash or cash equivalent, representations and warranties as to financial data, including the statement of financial position; statements of income and retained earnings; liabilities, direct and contingent; and title to assets customarily are made only on behalf of the seller. As explained later, this is the principal difference between such agreements and those involving the issuance of capital stock by the acquirer, or for a statutory merger.

Financial Representations of Seller Should Be Properly Documented. REPRESENTATIONS AND WARRANTIES AS TO INCOME REQUIRED EVEN IN A PURCHASE. It should be borne in mind in drafting an agreement that the buyer generally does not arrive at the purchase price on the basis of the valuation of assets, but on the basis of the earnings history and potential earnings of the selling company. It is therefore essential that representations and warranties be required of the seller regarding statements of income and retained earnings for an appropriate period, usually three to five years, as well as for the latest interim period, even in the case of a purchase of the assets and business of a company.

REPRESENTATIONS OF THE SELLER AS TO FINANCIAL STATEMENTS ESSENTIAL EVEN THOUGH THEY HAVE BEEN AUDITED. Customarily, the audited financial statements of the seller are delivered to the purchaser for periods such as those mentioned in the preceding paragraph and this is indicated in the agreement. Even though such statements bear the opinion of independent public accountants, it is important to have a representation from the seller that the statements *have been prepared in accordance with generally accepted accounting principles consistently applied throughout the periods covered.*

Audits by independent certified public accountants are carried out by a combination of techniques: a review of books and records; a selective examination of source documents, such as canceled checks, vendors' invoices, receiving and shipping reports, and payroll cards and records; physical observation and tests of inventories and fixed assets; test confirmation with third party debtors, creditors, financial institutions, and others; mathematical tests of books, records, and underlying data; *and information and explanations obtained from officials and other company personnel.*

The withholding of information or explanations by company officials or personnel regarding such matters as the existence of important contracts, commitments, claims for damages, or lawsuits, which may have a materially adverse effect on a company's future operations or working capital, may not be uncovered by other techniques employed in an examination by independent public accountants. This is particularly true in the case of closely held owner managed corporations. Also, the falsification of records and underlying documents or furnishing misleading information or explanations may not be discovered in such an examination, which is not designed for the primary purpose of detecting fraud.

Thus, the primary responsibility for the accuracy of financial statements rests with the management of a company. The opinion of independent public accountants serves as a check upon management's accounting of its stewardship and not as a substitute for it.

MAKE CERTAIN THAT PUBLIC ACCOUNTANTS REPORTING ARE, IN FACT, INDEPENDENT. If a company has not had its financial statements audited by public accountants or if the public accountants employed by the seller could not be considered as independent, the buyer normally should insist that such statements, covering a reasonable period, be audited by public accountants who are, in fact, independent. This procedure should be followed for the protection of the management, directors, and stockholders, regardless of whether or not there are regulatory filing requirements because of the business combination.

The Securities and Exchange Commission covers the matter of the independence of public accountants as follows:

. . . an accountant will be considered not independent with respect to any person or any of its parents or subsidiaries in whom he has, or had during the period of report, any direct financial interest or any material indirect financial interest; or with whom he is, or was during such period, connected as a promoter, underwriter, voting trustee, director, officer, or employee.[1]

The Commission has given a number of examples of administrative rulings in which accountants were held to be not independent *with respect to a particular client.*[2] It is not practicable to summarize the situations in which a public accountant will be considered as not independent, but a review of this release will be enlightening to companies entering into business combinations.

---

[1] Securities and Exchange Commission, Regulation S–X, Rule 2.01(b), as revised. Also American Institute of Certified Public Accountants, *Code of Professional Ethics,* Article 1.01.

[2] Securities and Exchange Commission, Accounting Series Release No. 81, December 11, 1958.

ALTERNATIVE DATES FOR CARRYING OUT EXAMINATION OF FINANCIAL STATEMENTS OF SELLER BY INDEPENDENT PUBLIC ACCOUNTANTS. Whether or not a company has had its financial statements audited annually, if the date of closing for the purchase of a company is some months after the close of its fiscal year, it is generally desirable to have an examination carried out by independent public accountants at a month-end around the date of the agreement or as of the closing date.

If the examination is made as of the earlier of these dates, a stipulation may be made, as a condition of the agreement, that the purchaser shall have received a letter from the independent public accountants performing the examination, dated as of the closing date, reporting, on the basis of their limited review of the latest available interim financial statements of the seller and consultations with its officials, for the period from the date of their examination to a date not more than five days prior to the closing date, on any matters that come to their attention that would indicate that there has been a material adverse change, if any, in the financial condition of the seller.

If the purchase price is to be affected by the net worth of the seller at closing, it is usually desirable to have an examination of the financial statements of the seller carried out by independent public accountants as of the closing date.

Provisions for Specific Assets and Liabilities May Be Required by Purchaser. In addition to representations and warranties from management officials of the seller regarding their company's results of operations and statement of financial position as a whole, a purchaser will, at times, require specific coverage in the agreement with respect to certain items, such as provisions for federal and state income taxes and other liabilities; the collectibility of accounts receivable; and the condition and salability of inventories of raw materials, supplies, work in process, and finished goods.

DIFFICULTY IN PRECISELY DETERMINING ALL LIABILITIES. A specific provision regarding the adequacy of reserves for taxes and other liabilities may be desirable from a legal standpoint, even though it does appear redundant when the seller has made representations and warranties with respect to the statement of financial position as a whole, which contains such liabilities and reserves. It is most difficult for selling company officials and independent public accountants, acting in the best of faith, to determine precisely the liabilities of a company within a month or an even longer period after the effective date of an examination of financial statements.

At times, an attempt is made in an agreement to give recognition to this difficulty of determining the adequacy of provisions for liabilities by having the seller represent that no taxes or other liabilities of "material" amount, in the aggregate, exist that have not been provided for in the statement of financial position. This provision in an agreement is not always satisfactory, as the seller and the purchaser may have different interpretations regarding what is and is not "material" at a later date when some hitherto unknown or unsuspected liability comes to light.

It would appear to be more satisfactory to safeguard the purchaser, at the same time being fair to the seller, to have a stipulation in the agreement to the effect that the purchaser will hold the seller liable for liabilities, including those for taxes, suits, and others of whatever nature not fully covered by insurance in excess of a stipulated variance amount above the aggregate provisions made for liabilities in the statement of financial position at the closing. This amount could be $25,000, $50,000, or whatever is considered reasonable, depending upon the net worth of the selling company, the specified purchase price, and other relevant circumstances.

SPECIFIC REPRESENTATIONS AS TO ACCOUNTS AND NOTES RECEIVABLE AND INVENTORIES OFTEN LEAD TO LATER CONTROVERSY. Accounts and notes receivable may be valued properly in the seller's statement of financial position used as a basis for closing, and the purchaser may later find his losses on such accounts exceed the reserves provided. This situation often arises where the customer of the seller discontinues doing business with the enterprise after the purchaser takes over. It may be caused by the purchaser's more stringent credit policies and sales terms, or the fact that the seller's customer, for competitive or other reasons, just ceases to be a customer after the closing.

Inventories may be valued properly in the seller's statement of financial position, based on the continuance of the business by the seller, but appear to be overvalued from the purchaser's standpoint when he later disposes of such inventories. This situation could be caused by the purchaser's decision to discontinue one or more products or product lines; by his additional costs for depreciation resulting from a stepped-up basis of fixed assets, particularly on long-term production contracts; or for other reasons related to actions taken by or policies of the purchaser.

PURCHASER GENERALLY CLAIMS MISREPRESENTATION ONLY IF DEAL DOES NOT TURN OUT WELL. If a deal turns out well for the purchaser, he will often ignore what he considers to be minor misrepresentations or warranties on behalf of the seller. If the deal does not work out well, the purchaser sometimes endeavors to find grounds for a claim for a refund or reduction of the purchase price, if a part of it has been placed in escrow.

In many such cases, if the purchaser had made an adequate investigation before signing the business combination agreement, he would have been aware of the effect of the acquisition on the future profitability of the business and either renegotiated the asking price or discontinued negotiations. Chapters 4 and 5 cover areas of investigation to be undertaken.

Principal Financial Representations of Buyer Relate to Purchase Price or a Method of Arriving at It. The main agreement of the buyer is that he will purchase the assets and business or capital stock at a price either fixed or variable, if he assumes liabilities, or if the price is to be based on other contingencies, or on financial statements prepared at closing or at some date subsequent to signing the agreement.

Although representations as to financial position or results of operations of the buyer may be excluded from an agreement for the purchase of a company's assets or capital stock for cash, the seller should, in appropriate cases, be presented with audited financial statements and in some cases other evidence of the ability of the buyer to produce the cash required to complete the purchase. Certainly when bonds, notes, or other consideration constitute a part or all of the purchase price, the seller is entitled to satisfy himself regarding the ability of the buyer to adequately cover interest costs of such obligations from future operations and to meet the principal maturity dates on schedule.

PURCHASE OF ASSETS RESULTS IN ESTABLISHMENT OF NEW TAX BASIS FOR BUYER. A purchase of assets, for cash or equivalent, directly or through the acquisition of capital stock and subsequent liquidation of the purchased company does not come under the "tax-free" reorganization provisions of the Internal Revenue Code. The purchaser, therefore, is entitled to allocate his purchase price to the assets acquired in accordance with their current fair value. Of course, if assets are purchased, there must be a timely liquidation of the selling company, as explained in Chapter 10, to avoid the imposition of a double federal capital gains tax, i.e., on the corporation and then on the stockholders.

In the vast majority of cases, the purchase price exceeds the federal income tax basis of the assets of the seller. It is in the interests of the buyer to have current fair values of the net assets established, to the extent practicable, to equal or exceed the purchase price. It is a frequent practice, therefore, to include in the business combination agreement a tabulation in which the purchase price is allocated to the net assets acquired or else to indicate the bases upon which such net assets are to be valued. It is believed that having the buyer and seller agree on this matter lends weight to the fair values assigned to assets and to the propriety of the allocation of the purchase price.

If the purchase price is to be allocated to the net assets acquired, this obviously cannot be done as of the closing date, as the figures for assets (other than cash) and for liabilities would not be instantly available. Therefore, the figures used may be as of a date one or two months prior to closing; and the operations for the period subsequent to such effective date, whether a profit or loss, would be for account of the purchaser.

FINAL SETTLEMENT IS DELAYED IF CLOSING DATE FIGURES ARE TO BE USED FOR ALLOCATION OF PURCHASE PRICE. Alternatively, the agreement may stipulate that the purchaser agrees to pay a certain price to the seller and assume the seller's liabilities (or liabilities other than federal and state income taxes) and apply the purchase price to the assets on bases described in the agreement. The determination of the allocation of the purchase price, in such a case, may be made as of the closing date, although the figures will not be available and final settlement not made for several months thereafter.

In such instances, a sufficient amount generally is withheld from the purchase price at the closing, so the buyer does not find at the final settlement that he has overpaid the seller, who has in turn distributed most of the proceeds to the stockholders of the selling company under a plan of liquidation. This procedure is followed particularly if there is a warranty by the seller that net assets at closing shall be not less than the amount shown in a previous statement of financial position furnished as an exhibit to the agreement.

EXAMPLE OF BASES OF ALLOCATION OF PURCHASE PRICE SET FORTH IN A BUY-SELL AGREEMENT. A typical example of bases set forth in an agreement for allocation of the purchase price follows.

1. Cash	—Value in United States currency
2. Accounts receivable	—Face amount, without allowance for bad debts
3. Marketable securities	—At market value
4. Inventories	
Raw materials and supplies	—Current replacement cost
Finished goods	—Sales value, less cost of disposition
Work in process	—Over 75 per cent processed at percentage stages of completion of finished goods, less than 75 per cent processed at raw material and labor cost, plus 125 per cent of labor for overhead
5. Prepaid expenses, including advertising materials and office supplies	—At current values

6. Fixed assets, including land, buildings, building improvements, machinery, equipment, furniture, and fixtures	—At appraised values by the XYZ Appraisal Co.
7. Patents, patent applications, and patent rights	—At appraised values by the XYZ Appraisal Co.
8. Goodwill, trade-marks, trade-names, and all other intangible assets	—The difference between the sum of items (1) through (7) and the total purchase price

In the example above, it is assumed that the accounts receivable appear to be fully collectible. Although not indicated, packaging supplies, small tools and spare parts, maintenance supplies, stationery and office supplies, and advertising materials, which have previously been expensed by the seller, may be assigned values to the extent that they are good and usable. However, if this is done, the Internal Revenue Service may endeavor to assert income tax against the seller for such items previously expensed (Rev. Rul. 61–214), notwithstanding the provisions of Section 337 of the Code discussed in Chapter 9.

Although an agreement may show merely the bases of valuing other assets for allocation of the purchase prices, appraisal values of fixed assets, and sometimes of patents and trade-marks, may be inserted in it, if available, and a stipulation made that such values will be adjusted for additions or deductions from the date of appraisal to the closing date.

ACQUISITION OF ASSETS OR CAPITAL STOCK
FOR CAPITAL STOCK

One of the important differences between agreements for cash purchases of the assets and business or capital stock of a company and those involving the issuance of voting capital stock by the surviving company is that it is important for the seller to have more extensive information as to the buyer. Accordingly, financial and other representations and warranties are made on behalf of all the companies who are a party to the business combination in such cases. These representations and warranties would be of the same nature as those discussed under "purchases" in this chapter.

In addition to such representations and warranties regarding the financial data of the constituent companies, there are several other aspects of business combinations involving (1) the issuance by the acquirer of securities solely in exchange for the net assets and business or capital stock of the seller or (2) a statutory merger, which will be commented on below.

Provisions Affecting the Ratio of Exchange of Shares of Capital Stock. In an acquisition of shares of voting capital stock in exchange for voting capital stock or in a merger, consideration must be given in the agreement not only to the shares of capital stock of the respective companies outstanding at the agreement date but also to shares that may be issued by either company from that date to the closing date. Such additional shares may be issued by reason of (1) the exercise of stock options or stock warrants, (2) employees' stock purchase plans, (3) the conversion of debentures and preferred stock, and (4) stock dividends or stock splitups.

THE PROBLEM OF OUTSTANDING BUT UNEXERCISABLE STOCK OPTIONS. Stock options of executives of a company to be acquired, which are outstanding but currently unexercisable under the option plan, often become a problem in negotiating an agreement. At times, agreement is reached to pay such optionees a lump sum bonus in consideration of the termination of their option plan. However, this bonus results in taxable income to the recipients at ordinary income rates.

In such cases, consideration should be given to a provision in the Internal Revenue Code that permits, in the case of a tax-free reorganization, the surviving company to substitute its stock options in place of the absorbed company's unexercised options, provided:

(1) the excess of the aggregate fair market value of the shares subject to the option immediately after the substitution or assumption over the aggregate option price of such shares is not more than the excess of the aggregate fair market value of all shares subject to the option immediately before such substitution or assumption over the aggregate option price of such shares, and

(2) the new option or the assumption of the old option does not give the employee additional benefits which he did not have under the old option.[3]

[3] Int. Rev. Code of 1954, § 421(g).

NECESSITY OF OBTAINING A REVENUE RULING ON THE TAX-
FREE ASPECTS OF A BUSINESS COMBINATION BEFORE CLOSING. In
an acquisition involving the exchange of voting capital stocks of
the respective companies, or the acquisition for voting capital
stock of the net assets and business of a company, or in a statutory
merger, it is generally advisable to have a condition in the business combination agreement to the effect that a favorable ruling
shall have been received from the Internal Revenue Service as
to the tax-free status of the reorganization. Needless to say, it
would be disastrous, in the case of the selling company, if the
closing were completed and an adverse ruling received, so that
its stockholders were subject to tax as a result of the transaction.
In the case of a statutory consolidation, stockholders of the several companies involved similarly might be affected by an adverse
revenue ruling. See Appendixes B and C for a request for ruling
and a reply from the Internal Revenue Service.

COMMON PROVISIONS IN BUY-SELL AGREEMENTS

Provision on "Finders' Fees." Often, upon consummation of a
business combination, finders' fees will be claimed by business
brokers, consultants, investment bankers, or others. Such fees
may be properly asserted against the purchaser or seller or both
in accordance with a prearranged understanding. However, in
many cases, finders' fees are claimed by various persons for allegedly having assisted in locating a purchaser or seller when
neither of these parties were aware that the "finder" had been
engaged by them or that he performed the service claimed.

Accordingly, a provision is often included in a business combination agreement regarding finders' fees or brokers' commissions. A simple statement to the effect that each represents and
warrants that the negotiations relative to the agreement have
been carried on without the aid or intervention of any other person
in such a manner as to give rise to a valid claim for a fee or
commission may not be specific enough. At times it is desirable,
even where both parties in good faith believe this to be so, that
the provision in the agreement go on to state who shall bear the
expense of such a fee or commission if any person should establish a right to it. This provision may state that the purchaser

and the seller will each be responsible for any such fees for which they are legally found liable; or, as is sometimes the case, the surviving corporation will agree to underwrite all such claims. Finders' fees and brokers' commission are discussed further in Chapter 13.

Provision Regarding Payment of Expenses Arising Out of Business Combination. There are usually many expenses incidental to a business combination transaction, such as legal and accounting fees, costs of property surveys and appraisals, and sundry taxes and filing fees. A provision in the business combination agreement should specify which of these costs and expenses are to be borne, in a purchase transaction, by the respective parties. In an acquisition for voting capital stock or in a statutory merger, the surviving corporation, of necessity, often will bear these costs. An exception to this general practice may be made where the disappearing company in a stock deal or statutory merger is closely held and when the principals involved could personally pay their company's share of such costs. Care should be exercised in the allocation of expenses so that the status of a tax-free reorganization is preserved.

Survival of Representations and Warranties. Practices with regard to the time limit for the survival of representations and warranties of the several parties to a business combination agreement showed considerable variation in a number of contracts reviewed. These practices ranged all the way from having the representations and warranties expire with the closing to having them survive indefinitely.

In an exchange of voting capital stocks, or in a statutory merger or consolidation in which a large number of shareholders are involved in the disappearing corporation, the survival of representations and warranties after the closing generally serves no practical purpose, as the securities issued by the surviving corporation are widely dispersed. This situation points up the importance of making a careful investigation of all financial and other pertinent matters prior to closing.

Where a small number, principally management stockholders, are involved in a sale of the net assets and business of a company for cash or cash equivalent, it is reasonable to have representations and warranties survive for a period. This is particularly so where federal and state income taxes and other liabilities assumed may not be ultimately determined for some time.

THE PROBLEM OF LIQUIDATING THE SELLING COMPANY WITHIN TWELVE MONTHS. On the other hand, bearing in mind that in a non-taxable sale of the net assets and business (Internal Revenue Code, Section 337) of a company the seller has to liquidate within twelve months after the adoption of a plan of liquidation, the period for survival of representations and warranties, except in unusual cases, should not extend beyond the liquidation termination date. If there is a possibility that federal, state, or foreign taxes may not be ultimately determined and settled within this period, an exception may be made with regard to the survival of representations and warranties for such possible liabilities.[4]

Provision Regarding a Closing Date. In fixing a closing date for a business combination, sufficient time should be allowed for various actions that must take place prior to closing. Aside from the time required for legal investigation of (1) title to assets and surveys of properties; (2) patents, patent rights, and royalties; (3) the assumption of contracts; and (4) pending claims and suits, there are various other factors that require consideration. In many cases, the initiation of action for these requirements may be carried out concurrently.

TIME REQUIRED FOR AN EXAMINATION OF FINANCIAL STATEMENTS. The examination of financial statements by independent public accountants generally requires a minimum of a month to a month and a half to complete in the case of a fair-sized company that has had regular annual examinations. This time would be increased if the company has not had regular examinations by certified public accountants; or the examining accountants are not, in fact, independent; or its foreign subsidiaries or branches are substantial enough to require a concurrent examination.

If an appraisal of fixed assets and patents and patent rights is needed or a geological survey of petroleum, gas, or mineral reserves, a month or more may be required to obtain reports from the professionals engaged for these purposes. Although the formal

---

[4] *Ibid.*, § 337(b).

reports on their findings may not be required, preliminary estimates of such figures should be obtained prior to closing.

TIME REQUIRED FOR APPROVAL OF TAX-FREE STATUS BY INTERNAL REVENUE SERVICE. In a business combination where a request for ruling from the Internal Revenue Service is required that the transaction is "tax free" under the reorganization provisions of the Internal Revenue Code, it generally takes a minimum period of a month and a half to receive a reply. This period may even be extended beyond two months if there are complicated problems to be considered. Furthermore, as pointed out in Chapter 10, a request for a ruling customarily is not made until the buy-sell agreement has been signed and a copy thereof is submitted with the request.

TIME REQUIRED FOR STOCKHOLDER APPROVAL AND OTHER MATTERS. Where stockholder approval is required of a business combination, the time entailed in the preparation of a proxy statement with its pertinent financial data should be considered. Also, the period of advance notice to stockholders, as required by a company's by-laws, before holding a meeting must be added to the time of preparation of the proxy statement. If a company is subject to the filing requirements of the Securities and Exchange Commission, additional time should be estimated for submission of the proxy material to that body for approval before mailing it to stockholders.

In a statutory merger or consolidation, or where stockholders of a selling company who are offered capital stock of the acquirer have the right of appraisal under state law, a further delay may be necessary before closing, in some instances, to permit dissenting stockholders to submit their demand for appraisal and cash payment for their shares.

Where new securities are to be issued as the result of a business combination, it may be necessary to file a registration statement under the Securities Act of 1933 or an application for registration of securities under the Securities Exchange Act of 1934. Also, stock list or additional list applications may be required to list such securities on a national exchange. The time needed to prepare and process such material through the respective regulatory bodies may be substantial. See Chapters 10, 11, and 12 for a further discussion of Securities and Exchange Commission and stock listing aspects of business combinations.

In applicable cases, consideration should be given to the time required for clearance by other regulatory bodies, such as the Federal Power Commission, the Federal Communications Commission, the Interstate Commerce Commission, and the counterpart state authorities having jurisdiction. Also, clearance under state blue sky laws, which are discussed briefly in Chapter 13, may require time.

Provisions for Terminating the Agreement. Customarily, in a business combination agreement, there are provisions whereby the agreement may be terminated and abandoned for material breaches in representations and warranties, or for loss of property by casualty, so as to materially adversely affect the conduct of business. In addition, where there is a possibility that the holders of a substantial number of shares of stock may dissent and demand appraisal and payment for their shares in cash, a provision should be included giving the respective Boards of Directors the privilege of terminating the agreement.

Chapter 9

FEDERAL TAX ASPECTS

As noted in Chapters 1 and 2, tax aspects play a leading role in determining the advisability of business combinations, as well as the manner and form in which they are to be consummated. Broadly speaking, an acquisition may be "tax free" or "taxable," depending upon the form the transaction follows and the type of consideration received by the seller. All transactions are considered taxable except those that qualify under specific provisions of the Internal Revenue Code for non-recognition of gain or loss. These provisions generally relate to the tax position of the seller, since ordinarily no tax arises on the acquisition of property. This chapter indicates the choices available under the many different taxable or tax-free forms of business combinations.

TAX CONSIDERATIONS

"Tax-Free" Exchange Defers Tax. When gain or loss is not recognized for tax purposes (though perhaps realized in an economic sense), the seller's basis for the stock or other property received is the same as his tax cost for the property exchanged. Thus, a "tax-free" exchange may be thought of as a means of deferring tax until the seller disposes of the acquirer's securities in a subsequent transaction, at a time chosen by the seller in the light of particular tax consequences and for other reasons.

EXAMPLE OF "TAX-FREE" DEFERMENT. Assume, for example, a taxpayer exchanges tax free his stock in Company A, which cost $10,000, for stock in Company B with a value of $100,000. Though no gain is recognized on the exchange, when the taxpayer eventually sells all or a portion of Company B stock, gain will be recognized if the proceeds exceed the substituted basis of $10,000 allocable to the B company shares sold.

Seller's Basis Assumed in "Tax-Free" Transaction. The tax status of the transaction also affects the purchaser's basis. In general, in a tax-free transaction where stock is issued for the seller's business, the purchaser assumes the seller's tax basis and, in effect, the tax basis of all the assets acquired with the seller's business. If the value of the assets of the seller is substantially above their tax basis (as is generally the case), the purchaser cannot recognize this increment for tax purposes but must continue to use the seller's tax basis in future transactions, as for instance in computing depreciation on fixed assets. In substance, the tax accounting treatment under tax-free reorganizations, which is discussed in more detail in this chapter under "Carryover Provisions," conforms with the "pooling-of-interests" concept explained in Chapter 7.

On the other hand, in a taxable transaction, the purchaser acquires a new tax basis. If assets are acquired, an allocation of the purchase price is made among the assets purchased. See pages 109 to 116 for a discussion and illustration of a method of allocating the purchase price to net assets acquired in a taxable transaction.

In a taxable transaction, the seller exchanges stock or assets for cash or obligations of the purchaser and has a gain or loss measured by the difference between the tax basis for the stock or assets surrendered and the amount of cash and market value of the obligations received. If assets are sold, the seller usually has the alternative of keeping his selling corporation intact and having the corporation assume the tax liability on the sale or liquidating his company and paying a capital gains tax on the gain realized on liquidation.

Acquisitions in Which Seller's Cash and Capital Stock Are Utilized. If, in a stock-for-stock type of reorganization, the buyer exchanges some stock plus some cash for the stock of the seller, it is the position of the Internal Revenue Service that the entire gain on the transaction (the excess of the value of the stock, plus the cash received, over the basis of the stock surrendered) is taxable.

The Supreme Court, in *Turnbow*,[1] seems to uphold this general rule (where the selling shareholders receive *both* cash and stock) but distinguishes *Howard*,[2] where (controlling) individuals owning 80.19 per cent of the acquired company's shares received only *stock* in the exchange while the remaining shareholders received *cash* for their minority interest. The differences in approach, particularly as to the "control" requirements in reorganizations, are discussed in more detail under "Tax-Free Exchanges."

TAXABLE TRANSACTIONS

There are six possible methods of arranging a transfer of ownership of corporate assets and business in a *taxable* transaction, each with potentially different tax consequences. These methods are:

1. The shareholders of the selling corporation sell their stock to the purchaser.
2. The selling corporation completely liquidates in one calendar month, after which the shareholders sell the business assets.
3. The selling corporation adopts a plan of complete liquidation, sells its assets, and completely liquidates within a twelve-month period.
4. The selling corporation completely liquidates over a period longer than one month, after which the shareholders sell the business assets.
5. The selling corporation sells its assets, recognizes gain or loss, and continues in existence. Perhaps by means of a Subchapter S election, the capital gain may be channeled through to the shareholders and reported by them rather than by the corporation.
6. The selling corporation sells its assets, recognizes gain or loss, and then completely liquidates.

Outright Sale of Stock. The first alternative, an outright sale of stock (for cash or equivalent including debt securities), is by far the simplest taxable method for a shareholder to dispose of his corporate business holdings. A single tax is assured, if the stock is sold at a gain, and the selling shareholders will be relieved of all contingencies and future expenses of the corporation, except

---

[1] United States v. Turnbow, 338 U.S. 337, *affirming* C.A. 9, 286 F.2d, 669 (1962).
[2] United States v. Howard, C.A. 7, 238 F.2d 943 (1957).

for any specific warranties made by them to the purchasers. The ability of a corporate buyer to liquidate a company in which it has purchased 80 per cent of the outstanding stock so that it may allocate the cost of the stock to the underlying assets received is discussed later under "Liquidations."

Incidentally, an outright sale of stock is readily adaptable to the installment method of reporting gain, if not more than 30 per cent of the selling price is received in the year of sale. Under this installment method, the gross profit on a sale is prorated over the period in which payments are received. The amount reported as gross profit in any year is the amount determined by applying the gross profit percentage on the sale to the payments received in that year. The election must be made in a return for the year of the sale, and the return must be filed on the due date (usually April 15 of the year following the year of the sale by an individual) or within an approved extension of time.[3]

ILLUSTRATION OF INSTALLMENT METHOD OF SALE OF STOCK. Capital stock costing $16,000 is sold for $24,000, a down payment is made of 25 per cent of the purchase price, and the balance is to be paid in monthly installments of $300 each. Gross profit to be realized is $8,000 (33⅓ per cent). If $6,900 (less than 30 per cent of $24,000) including the down payment is collected during the year of the sale, the gross profit includable in that year's income would be $2,300 ($6,900 × $8,000/$24,000). The same result is obtained by applying the gross profit percentage to the year's collections: 33⅓ per cent × $6,900 = $2,300. The gross profit includable in the second and succeeding years is determined in the same manner, i.e., second-year collections of $3,600, gross profit $1,200 (33⅓ per cent of $3,600), etc.

One-Month Liquidation. The second alternative, a one-month liquidation and sale of assets, permits non-corporate and non-controlling corporate shareholders, whose stock has appreciated in value, to liquidate their corporation completely without recognition of gain, and to substitute their stock basis for the corporate tax basis of the property received. With certain limitations, adjustments must be made to recognize the portion of gain repre-

[3] Int. Rev. Code of 1954, § 453(b).

sented by earnings accumulated after February 28, 1913, cash received in liquidation, and security investments received that were acquired by the corporation after 1953.

For non-corporate taxpayers, all or part of the gain to be recognized may be taxed as an ordinary dividend. The tax-saving provisions of this method cannot be utilized by a liquidating collapsible corporation. The tax basis of the corporate property in the hands of the shareholder is the same as the basis of the stock turned in for cancellation, decreased by cash received and increased by gain recognized. This method, which is extremely rare today except for the later sale by the shareholders of a segment of a business, requires that certain elections must be made in order to qualify for special liquidation treatment.[4]

Sale Following Adoption of Plan of Liquidation. The third alternative, which requires an adopted plan of liquidation, a subsequent sale of assets, and a complete liquidation within twelve months after adoption of the plan of liquidation, makes it possible that no gain or loss will be recognized to the *corporation* on the sale of certain properties within the twelve-month period.[5] Those properties that *do* require recognition of gain or loss are as follows:

1. Inventory or stock in trade and installment obligations acquired in connection with their sale, unless substantially all the inventory or stock in trade is sold to *one* purchaser in *one* transaction
2. Installment obligations acquired as a result of selling inventory or stock in trade other than as described in (1) above
3. All installment obligations acquired in respect to property sold prior to the adoption of the plan of complete liquidation

In a sale of assets under this method, it is obviously advantageous to minimize the amount of gain recognized on any of the foregoing assets. Therefore, to the extent feasible, the amount of selling price allocated to these assets should be as close to tax basis as possible. Collapsible corporations are not entitled to the benefits of this twelve-month liquidation. This alternative will be discussed in greater detail under "Liquidations—Buyer vs.

[4] *Ibid.*, § 333.
[5] *Ibid.*, § 337.

Seller" where a seller's liquidation after sale of assets [6] is compared with a buyer's liquidation after acquisition of stock.[7]

Sale by Shareholders Following Corporate Liquidation. The fourth alternative, a liquidating distribution of the corporation assets in kind to the shareholders followed by a sale of the assets by the latter, will also avoid double taxation to both the corporation and its shareholders.[8]

Example of a Distribution in Kind. A closely held company with net assets having a fair market value of $100,000 is dissolved and the net assets are assigned to the shareholders, whose basis for all the stock is $10,000. The shareholders report a capital gain of $90,000 on liquidation ($100,000 less $10,000). If the former shareholders then sell such assets for $100,000, no further gain is realized since their basis for the net assets is also $100,000, representing the fair market value on the date of the liquidation. A sale for $95,000 within six months would result in a $5,000 short-term capital loss, as long as the previous fair market value of $100,000 could be supported and the items sold were considered capital assets.

Sale by Corporation That Continues. The fifth alternative, a sale of assets and continuation of the corporation, requires a recognition of gain or loss by the corporation. Because the corporation will continue in existence, gain may be deferred under the installment method if the required conditions are met. A potential double tax exists on appreciation under this method. When the shareholder subsequently disposes of his stock, whether by liquidation or sale, the previously taxed gain will be reflected in his proceeds, but not in his tax base. When the selling corporation is a subsidiary and therefore not owned by individuals, the double tax situation does not exist since no gain or loss is recognized to the parent corporation upon liquidation of an 80 per cent owned subsidiary, even though the liquidated subsidiary's only asset is cash, as long as the parent receives some distribution with respect to its stock.[9]

[6] *Ibid.*
[7] *Ibid.*, § 334(b)(2).
[8] *Ibid.*, § 331(a).
[9] *Ibid.*, § 332.

This method could be utilized if only a part of the total business of a corporation were being sold. It could also be used when a corporation had a substantial loss carryover that might offset gain from the sale of assets or future income from reinvested proceeds. Care should be exercised to ascertain that the corporation would not become a personal holding company requiring the payment of dividends to avoid a harsh tax at the corporate level.[10]

Potential Benefits of "Subchapter S." Often a corporation may sell certain assets and, if a "Subchapter S" election is in effect, the corporation's capital gain (together with the corporation's other net taxable income or loss) is attributed to and reported by the corporation's shareholders as individuals. This type of corporation (sometimes termed "pseudo" or "tax-option" corporation) is treated in many tax respects like a partnership, if the shareholders unanimously so elect by the last day of the first month of the corporation's taxable year. The advantages, disadvantages, and administrative requirements of "Subchapter S" corporations cannot be adequately covered in this study on acquisitions and mergers. However, because of the potential ("one-shot") advantages of this election in connection with the taxable sale of a business, reference should be made to "Subchapter S" of the Internal Revenue Code [11] and regulations thereunder if the selling corporation does or could meet the following requirements:

1. Is a domestic corporation (one organized or created under the laws of the United States or a state or territory, or a similar association taxed as a corporation)
2. Has ten or less shareholders
3. All shareholders are individuals or estates (but not trusts)
4. Has only one class of stock
5. Has no non-resident aliens as shareholders
6. Is not a member of an affiliated group eligible to file a consolidated return.

Sale Followed by Corporate Liquidation. The sixth and final alternative, a sale of assets and complete liquidation of the corpo-

---

[10] *Ibid.*, §§ 541–547.
[11] *Ibid.*, §§ 1371–1377.

ration, is the same as the third alternative except that the plan of liquidation is *not* adopted *before* the sale of assets, and the liquidation is not completed for other reasons within the prescribed twelve-month period. Since this method results in double taxation to both the corporation and to individual shareholders, it should normally be avoided if possible. It may be advantageous if a sale of the corporate assets will be made at a loss, and if the loss can be utilized by carryback against prior years' income. In this situation, the purchaser is losing tax basis by making a taxable acquisition, since the tax-free exchange would result in tax basis of the assets acquired in excess of their market values.

1962 TAX CODE AFFECTS FUTURE TAXABLE TRANSACTIONS

A provision, Section 1245, added to the Internal Revenue Code by the Revenue Act of 1962 may present serious tax impediments to the consummation of future *taxable* acquisitions by a company of the assets or stock of another. Most tax-free reorganizations, however, will not be affected immediately.

Depreciation "Recapture." Section 1245 is commonly referred to as the depreciation "recapture" section, since it provides for taxing gains on the sale of depreciable property (other than buildings) as ordinary income to the extent of depreciation deductions allowed *for years subsequent to 1961*. The section is initially applicable, however, only to sales made in taxable years beginning after December 31, 1962.

To ILLUSTRATE. Assume that in 1965 a company sells for $10,000 a machine having an adjusted basis at the date of sale of $6,000. Its gain on the sale is $4,000. During the years 1962 through 1965, however, it claimed $3,000 of depreciation on the machine. Under Section 1245, $3,000 of the gain will be taxed as ordinary income and only $1,000 will be eligible for capital gains treatment under Section 1231.

The future problem presented for taxable business combinations is that Section 1245 is equally as applicable to eligible property sold as part of the assets of a going business as to isolated sales of such property. Moreover, it operates to tax, as ordinary income, gains that heretofore would have been completely exempted from tax at the corporate level under Section 337.

Thus, if the machine referred to in the illustration above is sold as part of the assets of a going business in a twelve-month liquidation qualifying for exemption from tax on gains at the corporate level under Section 337, $3,000 of gain will nonetheless be taxable to the selling corporation as ordinary income. The balance of the gain, $1,000, would be exempted from tax as heretofore.

It is obvious that Section 1245 will operate to reduce greatly the tax advantages of a twelve-month liquidation to a company with a substantial investment in machinery and equipment. In addition, to an ordinary income tax on most of that portion of the gain on the sale attributable to the depreciable assets other than buildings, the capital gains tax on the liquidation distribution at the shareholder level will continue to apply.

This problem cannot be avoided by first liquidating the corporation, having the shareholders receive the depreciable property as a liquidation distribution, and then selling it to the acquiring corporation in their individual capacities. The new section provides for the recognition of ordinary income to a liquidating corporation, with respect to "Section 1245" property distributed to its shareholders, to substantially the same extent as if the corporation had sold the property for its fair market value. Thus, in the illustration above, the corporation would realize $3,000 of ordinary income whether it sold the machine to a third party itself or distributed the machine to a stockholder as a liquidating distribution, who in turn sold it to the third party.

If the acquiring corporation purchases the stock rather than the assets of the acquired corporation, Section 1245 has no immediate effect and the stockholders of the acquired corporation are eligible for capital gains treatment for their gain on the sale, as heretofore. If, however, the acquiring corporation liquidates the acquired corporation within two years from the date of acquisition, in order to step up the basis of its assets pursuant to Section 334(b)(2), then Section 1245 will apply to cause ordinary income to be recognized to the acquired corporation on the liquidating distribution, in the manner explained above. If the liquidation of the acquiring corporation is delayed until the two-year period has elapsed, then Section 1245 will not apply to the liquidating distribution if the other conditions prescribed by Section 332 for the tax-free liquidation of a subsidiary are met. But there will also be no stepup in the basis of the acquired corporation's assets.

Section 1245 Generally Not Applicable to Tax-Free Reorganizations. Although Section 1245 has no application to a completely tax-free reorganization, it can apply in the case of a reorganization in which a limited amount of gain is recognized to the extent of "boot" received. For example, if one corporation acquires substantially all the assets of another corporation in exchange for stock, but in addition pays a limited amount of cash for certain assets of the acquired corporation, then gain on the transaction is recognized to the acquired corporation to the extent of the cash (boot) received. The effect of Section 1245 in this case is to treat all or a part of the recognized gain as ordinary income. The amount treated as ordinary income will be determined by reference to that portion of the *total* gain (both recognized and unrecognized) that is attributable to the depreciable property (other than buildings) transferred, and by reference to the depreciation deductions claimed on such assets in years subsequent to 1961.

TAX-FREE EXCHANGES

Generally, acquisitions that are tax free take the form of reorganizations described in Section 368(a)(1) as follows:

1. A statutory merger or consolidation
2. An exchange of voting stock, after which the purchaser owns the controlling (at least 80 per cent) *stock* of the seller
3. An exchange of voting stock of the purchaser for substantially all the *assets* of the seller.

Statutory Mergers. When both the selling corporation and the purchasing corporation are combined into one corporate entity (i.e., into the buyer or the seller or an entirely new entity) in accordance with the merger or consolidation provisions of the statutes of the state or states in which they are incorporated, the combination is termed a "statutory" merger.

The principal advantage of a statutory merger over a stock-for-stock (B) or stock-for-assets (C) transaction is the fact that non-voting common and preferred stock may be transferred to the stockholders of the selling corporation without affecting the tax-free nature of the basic transaction. As a matter of fact, cash or debt securities may even be transferred if permitted by state statutes, as long as the selling shareholders maintain a "continuity of interest" in the surviving corporation.[12] This continuity of interest or "proprietary" interest concept may not be satisfied unless the *selling shareholders retain an "equity" (stock) interest equivalent to at least 50 per cent* [13] *of their premerger equity interest.*

DETERMINATION OF BASIS OF CONSIDERATION RECEIVED IN A STATUTORY MERGER. No gain or loss is recognized to the security holders of the various corporations in the exchange of their securities, except when they receive cash in addition to new securities, or when they receive new debt securities with a greater principal value than those surrendered. When such exceptions occur, the gain will be taxable to the extent of cash and excess principal value received and may constitute ordinary income. The tax basis of securities received will be the same as the basis of those surrendered, decreased by the amount of cash received and increased by the amount of gain recognized on the transaction.[14]

As noted in Chapter 2, because stockholder approval is usually required by both companies and because administrative rules under certain state laws involve complications, the statutory merger route is often bypassed, and one of the other reorganization plans is adopted to achieve the same results, if the receipt solely of voting stock by the sellers is acceptable.

Stock for Stock. Under this alternative, an exchange of stock for stock, the shareholders of the selling corporation merely exchange their stock *solely* for voting stock of the purchasing corporation. For qualification as a tax-free transaction, the purchaser

[12] *Ibid.,* Reg. § 1.368–1(b).
[13] Informal rule of thumb presently followed by Treasury Department but subject to revision or adjustment in particular circumstances.
[14] Int. Rev. Code of 1954, §§ 356 and 358.

must own at least 80 per cent of the voting power (a percentage of the combined number of votes for all voting stock) of the selling corporation and must own at least 80 per cent of all other outstanding stock immediately after the transaction. The Internal Revenue Service takes the view that any transfer of cash or other property to the shareholders of the selling corporation will destroy the tax-free privilege and make the entire transaction taxable.[15]

The tax basis of the new stock in the hands of the seller will be the same as the old stock exchanged. Unless indemnification warranties are given to the purchaser, the seller is relieved of responsibility for liabilities of the corporation (except for misrepresentation or willful concealment), which now becomes a subsidiary of the purchaser. The seller has also avoided incurring costs and expenses of a possible liquidation of the company.

ACQUIRER MAY RETAIN NET ASSETS IN THE CORPORATION OR OPERATE IT AS A DIVISION. The acquiring corporation may either maintain the acquired corporation as a subsidiary or liquidate it, so that its assets become commingled, or it may be operated as a division of the acquirer. This decision usually depends upon operating factors including employee problems and trade relations but can be affected by tax considerations such as the following:

1. Additional surtax saving (tax rate of 30 per cent instead of 52 per cent) on first $25,000 of income of separate company
2. Possible state franchise tax increases or decreases
3. Pension or profit-sharing plan complications
4. Accounting methods or tax elections of the acquired company that would not be appropriate for the parent
5. Unusual composition of operating loss deductions, capital gains, and similar tax attributes requiring analysis (see subsequent section "Carryover Provisions")
6. Favorable or unfavorable excise tax rulings, unemployment tax ratings, etc.

Assets for Stock. Under this alternative, an exchange of assets for stock, the selling corporation must transfer substantially all its assets in exchange for voting stock of the purchaser. The term

[15] See discussion on page 147 of *Turnbow* and *Howard* cases.

"substantially all" has never been precisely defined, although 86 per cent [16] and 90 per cent [17] have been accepted by the courts. However, it is understood that the Internal Revenue Service generally will not issue a favorable ruling on this type of transaction unless at least 90 per cent of the assets are transferred.

VOTING STOCK MUST BE ISSUED FOR AT LEAST 80 PER CENT OF FAIR MARKET VALUE OF TOTAL PROPERTY, WHETHER OR NOT TRANSFERRED. It is to be noted, in an exchange of assets for stock, that the seller may receive something other than voting stock of the purchaser. However, in order to preserve the tax-free nature of the exchange, voting stock must be issued for at least 80 per cent of the fair market value of the *total property* of the "selling" corporation, whether or not transferred. This means that the value of cash and other property given by the purchaser, plus liabilities assumed by the purchaser, may not exceed 20 per cent of the fair market value of all the assets of the seller. If the exchange is *solely* for voting stock, any amount of liabilities may be assumed by the seller without destroying the tax-free nature of the exchange.

EXAMPLE OF A STOCK FOR NET ASSETS TRANSACTION. "A" Corporation's condensed balance sheet includes the following:

	Book	Market
Cash	$ 10,000	$ 10,000
Current assets	40,000	40,000
Fixed and other assets	100,000	200,000
	$150,000	$250,000
Trade payables	(20,000)	(20,000)
Long-term debt	(50,000)	(50,000)
Net	$ 80,000	$180.000

If all the assets, except cash (over 90 per cent of total assets), were exchanged solely for voting stock, the transaction would be tax free whether or not any or all of the liabilities were assumed. If voting stock worth $150,000 plus cash of $20,000 were exchanged for the net assets except cash, the transaction would not qualify since the cash consideration ($20,000) plus liabilities

[16] First Nat'l Bank of Altoona v. United States, C.A. 3, 104 F.2d 865 (1939).
[17] Southland Ice Co., 5 T.C. 842 (1945).

assumed ($70,000) would exceed $50,000 representing 20 per cent of the total assets of $250,000.

If the proceeds to the selling corporation include assets other than voting stock, gain is recognized by the corporation to the extent of cash or other property received, if the corporation is not liquidated. Normally, in this type of transaction, the selling corporation will liquidate after the transaction—to avoid tax on cash and other property under Section 361(b)—distributing the stock of the purchasing corporation and all other remaining assets to its shareholders. If the selling corporation is *not* liquidated, the tax basis of the purchaser's stock acquired is the same as the basis of the property transferred to the purchaser, decreased by cash and other property received and increased by any gain recognized.

BASIS OF PURCHASER'S STOCK UPON LIQUIDATION. If the selling corporation *is* liquidated as a part of the transaction, the basis of the purchaser's stock in the hands of the selling shareholders is the same as the basis of their stock surrendered for cancellation, decreased by cash or other property received by them and increased by any gain recognized. The basis of the seller's assets to the purchaser is the same as in the hands of the seller, increased by the amount of gain recognized to the seller. The gain recognized to the selling stockholders for that purpose includes that part of the gain, if any, that is treated as a dividend.

FORMATION OF NEW TAX ENTITY

A tax-free acquisition or merger also may be consummated effectively through the *formation* of a new company rather than the *reorganization* of an existing company. No gain or loss is recognized if property (tangible or intangible, including securities for this purpose) is transferred to a corporation by one or more entities solely in exchange for its stock or "securities" if immediately after the exchange such entities as a *group* are in "control" of the corporation. "Control" for this purpose means ownership of stock of the corporation possessing at least 80 per cent of the total combined voting power of the voting stock and at least 80 per cent of the shares of non-voting stock.

Securities, in addition to capital stock, include long-term (usually at least five years) bonds and debentures but not notes of a short-term nature. If a transferring entity also receives cash or other property, a gain is recognized (but not a loss) to the extent of cash and market value of the "other property" received, often referred to as "boot." Furthermore, the receipt of stock for services (compensation) and even stock rights or warrants (according to Internal Revenue Service interpretation) [18] are all construed as "other property" and therefore subject to recognition of any realized gain. The assumption of liabilities does not affect the tax-free nature of these transactions except to the extent that liabilities assumed exceed tax basis of the assets transferred, in which case such excess is treated as "other property."

Existing as Well as Newly Formed Corporation May Be Utilized. This provision (Transfer to Corporation Controlled by Transferor) [19] may be availed of in combining whole enterprises or divisions of several enterprises. As a matter of fact, an existing rather than a new corporation may be utilized as long as the requisite 80 per cent control is obtained immediately after a transfer or joint transfers. However, in most situations, the individual shareholders of the corporations contributing (transferring) net assets cannot receive the new (transferee) company's stock tax free except where they transfer their stock to a holding company that becomes the common parent of a number of operating subsidiaries.

"Step," "Form vs. Substance," and "Business Purpose" Considerations. The timing of transfers must be carefully planned, particularly when a public offering is anticipated, to avoid a contention by the Internal Revenue Service that the public offering is an integral part of the basic transfer plan, thus violating the 80 per cent control requirement by the original contributing group. This illustrates the problem of "step" transactions or the "form vs. substance" concept, which must be recognized in all dealings of tax significance.

[18] Int. Rev. Code of 1954, Reg. § 1.351-1.
[19] Ibid., § 351.

Broadly speaking, the Service often looks to the end result of a series of transactions rather than the individual steps. If the result could not be accomplished tax free normally in a direct manner, the Service attempts to ignore the form or individual order of the various, separate transactions that, standing alone, would appear to meet the technical provisions of particular Code sections. Moreover, this endeavor to look to the substance of a reorganization also gains support from the "business purpose" rule, which requires that a transaction to be tax free must have a legitimate business purpose rather than merely be a device to avoid taxation.[20] The fact that shareholders benefit as a result of a transaction does not, per se, disqualify it, if it meets the test of being undertaken for sound business reasons.

LIQUIDATIONS—BUYER VS. SELLER

In alternatives 1 (outright sale of stock) and 3 (sale of assets within twelve months under planned liquidation) of the taxable transfers discussed previously, reference was made to the liquidation of the acquired corporation by the buyer and seller, respec-

---

[20] United States v. Gregory, 293 U.S. 465, 55 Sup. Ct. 266 (1935):

"When subdivision (B) speaks of a transfer of assets by one corporation to another, it means a transfer made 'in pursuance of a plan or reorganization' (Sec. 112(g)) of corporate business; and not a transfer of assets by one corporation to another in pursuance of a plan having no relation to the business of either, as plainly is the case here. Putting aside, then, the question of motive in respect of taxation altogether, and fixing the character of the proceeding by what actually occurred, what do we find? Simply an operation having no business or corporate purpose—a mere device which put on the form of a corporate reorganization as a disguise for concealing its real character, and the sole object and accomplishment of which was the consummation of a preconceived plan, not to reorganize a business or any part of a business, but to transfer a parcel of corporate shares to the petitioner. No doubt, a new and valid corporation was created. But that corporation was nothing more than a contrivance to the end last described. It was brought into existence for no other purpose; it performed, as it was intended from the beginning it should perform, no other function. When that limited function had been exercised, it immediately was put to death.

"In these circumstances, the facts speak for themselves and are susceptible of but one interpretation. The whole undertaking, though conducted according to the terms of subdivision (B), was in fact an elaborate and devious form of conveyance masquerading as a corporate reorganization, and nothing else. The rule which excludes from consideration the motive of tax avoidance is not pertinent to the situation, because the transaction upon its face lies outside the plain intent of the statute. To hold otherwise would be to exalt artifice above reality and to deprive the statutory provision in question of all serious purpose."

tively. Theoretically, the same over-all tax results should obtain under either form in that the seller will avoid a tax at the corporate level, and the buyer's (stepped-up) basis for the assets received will reflect his purchase price with certain adjustments. However, in practice the seller normally would prefer to sell stock and have the buyer liquidate the company for the following reasons:

1. Avoidance of expense and administrative problems of liquidation
2. Avoidance of potential tax deficiencies in open years (particularly depreciation disallowances caused by sale of assets at a gain [21] and other unknown or contingent liabilities unless covered by an indemnification provision in the sale contract)

Purchaser Usually Prefers To Buy Assets. On the other hand, the purchaser usually prefers to buy assets to avoid the above issues and expenses as well as to improve his position with respect to the allocation of the purchase price (in accordance with an arm's length contract with an unrelated party), particularly to minimize the amount, if any, apportioned to goodwill or other intangible assets, which are not amortizable for federal income tax purposes.

TIMELY PLAN OF LIQUIDATION MUST BE ADOPTED. Although a similar allocation question prevails, when the acquiring corporation purchases at least 80 per cent of the seller's stock within a one-year period and proceeds to *adopt* a plan to liquidate the subsidiary within two years of such purchase,[22] the practical problem of determining tax basis and supporting an appropriate apportionment of such basis to the assets when received becomes more acute. It is well to note that the plan of liquidation must

[21] United States v. Cohn, C.A. 6, 259 F.2d 371 (1958) (Also Rev. Rul. 62–92 IRB—1962—26, 9):
"Taxpayer sold property for prices exceeding the remaining cost basis shown on their books at the time of the sale. In rejecting taxpayer's argument that when salvage value is estimated at the time property is acquired it cannot thereafter be redetermined, the Court held that when actual sales, made before the end of a year for which depreciation is going to be taken, show that the actual value of the property is greater than what was estimated, it is both possible and necessary to redetermine the salvage value in accordance with such facts in order to arrive at the proper amount of depreciation allowable."
[22] Int. Rev. Code of 1954, § 334(b)(2).

be *adopted* but not necessarily *executed* within two years from the date that 80 per cent ownership is effected.

Thus, the purchase price of a business must be negotiated to reflect both the out-of-pocket expenses of a liquidation and the inherent but difficult-to-measure tax issues that follow a liquidation. In this respect, the interests of the buyer and seller are often in conflict.

POSSIBLE ASSUMPTION OF TAX LIABILITIES. A purchaser, in particular, should be aware of potential tax deficiencies of the predecessor company arising from such items as unreasonably accumulated earnings, possibly questionable write-offs of capital items, alleged excessive depreciation or depletion deductions, excessive officers' compensation or entertainment expenses, incorrect accounting methods, and significant understatement of inventory values. Incidentally, any tax deficiency assumed by the purchaser becomes additional tax basis, which should be allocated to the assets received, in accordance with the relatively complex regulations under Section 334(b)(2).

CARRYOVER PROVISIONS

In order to analyze properly the financial and tax aspects of a business to be acquired, the selling corporation should be considered in the light of three elements: its assets, its liabilities, and its tax attributes. The importance of separate consideration of these elements results from the fact that the purchaser can decide to acquire any of the following groupings:

1. Assets, liabilities, and tax attributes (tax free or taxable, if subsidiary continued)
2. Assets and tax attributes without assumption of liabilities ("C"-type reorganization)
3. Assets and liabilities without tax attributes (taxable transactions and Section 351 transfers)
4. Assets without assumption of liabilities or tax attributes (taxable transactions and Section 351 transfers)

Obviously, the price may be quite different to the purchaser under each of these alternatives, and the purchaser should be aware of the advantages and disadvantages of each in order to negotiate intelligently.

Tax Attributes of the Business To Be Acquired. The more important tax attributes of the seller with which the purchaser should be concerned are the following: [23]

1. Net operating loss carryover
2. Accumulated earnings and profits
3. Capital loss carryover
4. Methods of accounting, i.e., completed contract versus progress reporting and the treatment of bad debts, property taxes, research and development expenses, organization expenses, trademark and trade-name expenses, deferred subscription income, vacation pay, etc.
5. Methods of computing inventories, i.e., first-in, first-out (cost, lower of cost or market on basis of average, moving average, etc.); last-in, first-out (quantity or "dollar value"); other special (retail, farm-price, by-product, market, etc.)
6. Methods of computing depreciation, i.e., straight-line, declining balance, sum-of-the-years' digits, machine hours, etc.
7. Installment method of reporting income
8. Amortization of bond discount or premium
9. Methods of reporting exploration and development expenditures
10. Contributions to employees' deferred compensation plans
11. Charitable contributions carryover
12. Investment credit for certain depreciable property

Tax Attributes in Addition to Those Enumerated. There are ten other specific attributes enumerated in Section 381 of the Internal Revenue Code dealing with special situations, but those above are the ones most frequently encountered. In addition to the tax attributes enumerated, it is essential that the purchaser have a complete "tax basis balance sheet" of the seller in order to consider the effects of a taxable versus non-taxable transaction. As previously noted, in a non-taxable transaction, the purchaser will take over the assets at their *tax* basis to the seller. If there is a conflict between the buyer's and seller's tax treatment of a single carryover item, an accounting method for example, usually the buyer's treatment takes precedence after a merger or "C"-type reorganization. Of course, if a corporation is maintained as a separate entity, its tax attributes will continue, if it does not come within the provisions of Section 269 or Section

---

[23] *Ibid.,* § 381.

382(a), whether or not new ownership was acquired in a taxable or a tax-free transaction.

Special Rules for Net Operating Loss Carryover. If the seller has a net operating loss carryover and the purchaser desires to utilize the carryover "promptly" against *future* income of the combined enterprise, certain rules are applicable. The net operating loss carryover can only be utilized promptly in a *non-taxable acquisition.* For each 1 per cent equity in the purchaser that the selling stockholders receive in the acquisition, the purchaser will succeed to 5 per cent of the seller's loss carryover. Therefore, if the selling stockholders receive a 20 per cent or greater equity in the value of the purchaser's stock (except non-voting preferred stock) after issuance of the new stock, the purchaser will succeed to all of the seller's loss carryover.[24]

EXAMPLE OF THE APPLICATION OF THIS RULE. Assume the stockholders of XYZ Company obtain in a tax-free asset acquisition ("A"- or "C"-type reorganization) transaction 2,000 shares of 10,000 then issued shares of ABC Company stock representing a 20 per cent equity in the value of the latter's stock. ABC Company can proceed to utilize a $100,000 loss carryover. If the stockholders of XYZ Company obtained only 1,000 shares or a 10 per cent equity, ABC Company would be entitled to utilize only $50,000 of the loss carryover, and the remainder would go unused.

If the purchaser acquired the seller's stock in a non-taxable ("B"-type reorganization) transaction and caused the seller to be liquidated or merged thereafter, the Internal Revenue Service probably would take the position that these two steps were in reality only a single transaction whereby the purchaser acquired assets for stock. It would accordingly contend that the special limitation illustrated above should apply.

If the purchaser acquires the seller's stock by purchase (a taxable acquisition), it would be necessary for the purchaser to operate the acquired company as a subsidiary for at least two years following the purchase in order to acquire the tax attributes of the seller upon liquidation. This results from a special rule

[24] *Ibid.,* § 382(b).

previously discussed,[25] which governs the treatment of liquidation of subsidiaries within two years following a purchase of stock. Even if the seller were to continue as a subsidiary, the seller would lose its own loss carryover if it ceases to carry on a business "substantially" the same as it conducted before the acquisition. The term "substantially" in this context is difficult to define and care must be exercised within the framework of the existing facts and prospective plans.[26]

ACQUISITIONS TO AVOID OR EVADE TAX

Even if the 20 per cent test and other limitations on utilizing loss carryovers of acquired corporations, as outlined above, are carefully observed and met, the Commissioner of Internal Revenue is nevertheless empowered to deny deductions for those carryovers "if the principal purpose for which such acquisition was made is evasion or avoidance of Federal income tax." This prohibition applies not only to net operating loss carryovers, but also to any other "deduction, credit or allowance" the benefit of which the acquiring corporation wishes to obtain, if tax avoidance is in fact the principal motive. In addition, similar disallowance rules can apply to certain transfers of assets by one corporation to another in tax-free transactions, if tax avoidance is a principal motive.[27]

---

[25] *Ibid.*, § 334(b)(2).

[26] United States v. Goodwyn Crockery Co., 37 T.C. 38 (1961). (Note: Government has appeal pending in C.A. 6):

"Taxpayer corporation, a wholesaler of housewares, reported net operating loss carryovers for the years 1951 through 1955. In 1956 the capital stock of taxpayer was purchased by another corporation. After the change in ownership the taxpayer continued to wholesale housewares, absorbed a dry goods wholesaler, moved its center of operations twice, lost most of its old customers and gained different ones, and started retail sales outlets. The Commissioner disallowed deductions for net operating loss carryovers on taxpayer's 1956, 1957, and 1958 returns on the ground that the deduction was eliminated either (1) under Sec. 382 because there was a change in ownership and a change in the business or (2) under Sec. 269 because the principal purpose of acquisition was tax avoidance. The court held that the business continued substantially the same because it operated under the same business name in the same area to the same type of customers. The court viewed the changes merely as expansion. Since the court found that taxpayer corporation had been acquired for a bona fide business purpose and not for tax avoidance, it rejected the Commissioner's alternative argument."

[27] Int. Rev. Code of 1954, § 269.

Provision in Code Designed To Discourage Acquisition of "Loss Corporations." This particular section of the Internal Revenue Code was designed principally to discourage the practice of acquiring loss corporations for their favorable tax attributes, rather than for any real business motive. The regulations under this section, however, which were not adopted until 1962, are rather sweeping in scope.

EXAMPLE IS DESCRIBED IN THE REGULATIONS. The regulations describe an example along the following lines:

> Corporation A acquires all of the stock of Corporation B by a taxable purchase. Corporation B has been sustaining net operating losses for a number of years. The purpose of the acquisition is to continue and improve the operation of Corporation B's business.
> In the year following the year of acquisition, Corporation A transfers to Corporation B one of Corporation A's profitable divisions. The purpose of this transfer is to absorb the net operating loss carryover of Corporation B.[28]

In this case, although the original acquisition of B was not made for tax-avoidance purposes, and although B continued to operate its regular business, the regulations indicate that the net operating loss carryover deduction would be disallowed to B.

All indications are that the Internal Revenue Service has been making intensive use of this section of the Code in recent years in attempts to deny operating loss carryovers and other tax benefits in connection with the acquisition of loss corporations. In fact, in a recent case, the Service was upheld in disallowing deductions for operating losses sustained by an acquired loss corporation *subsequent* to the date of its acquisition. The acquiring corporation had attempted to deduct these postacquisition operating expenses, sustained prior to winding up the business of the acquired corporation, in a consolidated tax return that it filed with the acquired corporation. The court had found a principal motive of tax avoidance for the acquisition.[29]

The acquisition of a company having loss carryovers thus involves highly technical and often significant tax problems for which competent professional tax advice should be sought.

[28] *Ibid.*, Reg. § 1.269–6, Example (3).
[29] R. P. Collins & Co., C.A.–1, 303 F.2d 142 (1962).

Section 306 Stock. Preferred stock received as a distribution on common stock ("Section 306 stock") may result in ordinary income to the recipient upon disposition by sale or redemption under many circumstances. Thus, in reorganizations involving the receipt of preferred stock (in a statutory merger, or voting preferred in "B"- or "C"-type reorganizations), care must be exercised that such stock does not have a Section 306 taint by a showing that the exchange did not have the effect "substantially the same as a stock dividend." Normally, the Treasury Department will rule (see "Request for Ruling") that preferred stock will not be subject to the ordinary income provisions usually applied to "Section 306 stock" if its issuance is not based on a tax-avoidance motive.[30]

If Section 306 stock is given up in a sale or exchange *in which gain is recognized,* the proceeds (cash or other property) attributable to Section 306 stock may be treated as ordinary income to the extent of accumulated earnings and profits of the company that issued the Section 306 stock.

REQUEST FOR RULING

In almost every case involving reorganizations, it is prudent to request a ruling from the Commissioner of Internal Revenue that the contemplated transactions are tax free, as well as to be assured of the treatment of various other items such as the following:

1. Tax basis of assets or securities received by both buyer and seller
2. Absence of Section 306 "taint" to preferred securities received in transaction
3. Treatment of "boot" (money or other property received) in a transaction that would otherwise be non-taxable
4. Qualification of "substantially all the properties" in a "C"-type reorganization (stock for assets)
5. Qualification of the term "securities" in a Section 351 transfer or statutory merger
6. Qualification of voting stock, where voting rights are limited in degree or by a voting trust under state law
7. Consequences of a liquidating company transferring acquired assets to another corporation following initial transaction

[30] Int. Rev. Code of 1954, § 306.

A request for ruling should be filed in duplicate and contain a complete statement of the facts regarding the transaction, a full and precise statement of the business reasons for the transaction, and usually the particular determination expected to be made. If a particular contention is unusual, the request for ruling should support the contention through reference to the Code, regulations, rulings, or cases.

Documents To Be Attached to a Request for Ruling. In most cases, the plan of reorganization and related agreements, stockholder resolutions, and similar documents are submitted as part of the ruling request. The parties to the reorganization are occasionally asked to submit additional information regarding the allocation of expenses, prior agreements as to disposition of stock, financial statements, and even statements bearing on intent before the Rulings Division of the National Office will release the ruling. A conference procedure has also been established for cases where it will be helpful to either the Internal Revenue Service or the taxpayer. In unusual circumstances, where a clear need is demonstrated, requests for special processing of the ruling will be considered within reason.

SAMPLES OF A REQUEST FOR RULING AND A REPLY. Included as Appendixes B and C are sample forms of a request for ruling in a "C"-type reorganization and a reply from the Internal Revenue Service, which illustrate some of the points discussed above.

ESTATE PLANNING CONSIDERATIONS

Many acquisitions or mergers result from or affect the estate plans of the selling shareholders or proprietors. Although many personal objectives are involved, the following general factors should be considered by both the buyer and the seller.

1. The beneficiaries of an estate take as their tax basis the market value of securities as of the decedent's date of death (or alternatively, a date one year later, if elected, for federal estate tax valuation purposes).
2. One of the principal objectives in selling out may be to diversify holdings—to avoid a position of "too many eggs in one basket."
3. Often the founder of a business desires that his family will continue to enjoy, after his death, the fruits of the business' financial

progress in the form of salaries, fringe benefits, dividends, interest, or a combination of these.

Estate Tax Consideration. To an elderly owner, the required "stepup" in basis to market value at death seems to make a tax-free exchange advisable in a business combination so as to avoid an unnecessary capital gains tax. This same reasoning also underlies the arrangement of certain taxable transactions at the corporate rather than the stockholder level (in cases where the corporate basis of net assets to be sold exceeds the shareholder's tax basis for his stock) so as to result in a lower immediate capital gains tax. In this event, the company is continued in existence, the sales proceeds are reinvested, and the company is not liquidated until after the owner's death, thereby limiting the larger gain at the shareholder level.

DIVERSIFICATION AS THE OBJECTIVE. If diversification, on the other hand, is the principal and immediate goal of the owner, he may not be quite so interested in a tax-free disposition. However, depending upon his other capital and income requirements, the amount of stock involved, the period available for conversion into other securities, and the Securities and Exchange Commission registration aspects (discussed in Chapter 10), the reorganization provisions of the Internal Revenue Code [31] initially may be used to advantage as the first step of a planned program of gradual diversification.

PROTECTION OF FAMILY BENEFITS. The third factor, protection of the family usually through the income from senior securities, is similar to the second but becomes accentuated when the reorganization results in the receipt of speculative or unproved securities, particularly when the recipient has little capital besides his business investment.

Some income protection for the seller's family may be accomplished by the following means:

1. Employment contracts independent of the exchange (to avoid the receipt of something more than voting stock in "B" and "C" types of reorganization) that would also cover pension and life insurance benefits

[31] *Ibid.,* § 368.

2. Voting securities preferred as to dividends (considered in the light of a possible Section 306 "taint," which is eliminated when passed through an estate to a beneficiary as provided by Internal Revenue Code Section 1014)

Nevertheless, it should be appreciated, if family income protection is considered the most important factor by the seller, that taxable transactions involving cash or a mixture of cash and prime debt securities may be required, as a practical matter. In this event, a sale on the installment basis may be beneficial to both the seller (spread gain to lower bracket years plus receipt of interest on installment obligations) and to the buyer (deferred payout while amortizing "stepped-up" basis of net assets acquired).

Chapter 10

S.E.C. FILING REQUIREMENTS

A series of statutes generally referred to as the "Securities Laws" were enacted by Congress in the early 1930's to provide full and fair disclosure in securities transactions and to maintain fair and orderly security markets. The most important of these laws and the principal ones having a bearing on business combinations are the Securities Act of 1933 and the Securities Exchange Act of 1934. The 1934 Act created the Securities and Exchange Commission, an independent regulatory agency having executive and quasi-judicial powers, for the express purpose of administering the security laws.

FEDERAL SECURITIES LAWS

The Securities Act of 1933. The Securities Act of 1933 is commonly referred to as the "truth in securities" act. Its basic objectives are to provide investors with financial and other information of material importance concerning securities offered for sale to the public in interstate commerce or by use of the mail and to prohibit misrepresentation, deceit, and other fraudulent practices in the offer and sale of securities generally.

The Securities Exchange Act of 1934. The Securities Exchange Act of 1934 is more a regulatory statute than the Securities Act of 1933 and is concerned with trading in securities, both on the organized exchanges and in the over-the-counter markets. It provides for the registration of securities exchanges and the securities listed on each such exchange. Issuers of securities listed and registered on national securities exchanges are subjected to certain financial and other reporting requirements, including the preclearance of proxy soliciting material. The Act also establishes certain restrictions with respect to trading in such securities by directors, officers, and principal security holders and contains provisions designed to prevent the unfair use of inside information.

The federal securities laws are complex and provide for civil liability of the issuer, its directors and certain officers and controlling stockholders, any underwriter, and any expert involved, including accountants, where there have been materially false or inadequate representations. Any company contemplating an acquisition or merger accordingly should consult with its legal counsel and independent public accountants at an early stage in the negotiations for guidance on possible compliance requirements under the Securities Act of 1933 and the Securities Exchange Act of 1934.

COMPANIES SUBJECT TO FILING AND REPORTING REQUIREMENTS

Companies subject to the filing and reporting requirements of the Securities and Exchange Commission include (1) those whose securities are listed on a national securities exchange, and (2) those who by reason of having filed a registration statement with the Commission for a previous public offering of securities are obligated to continue to file certain current reports and other information. The latter group will include a substantial segment of companies trading in the over-the-counter market. Also, a company that previously had no reason to file information or documents with the Securities and Exchange Commission may become subject to its filing requirements as a result of the issuance of securities pursuant to a merger or acquisition plan.

Reports and Data That May Be Required. A corporate acquisition or merger may require the filing of (1) a proxy statement under Regulation X–14 of the Securities Exchange Act of 1934, or (2) a registration statement under the Securities Act of 1933. Even though a proxy statement or a registration statement may not be required, a current report (generally Form 8–K) under the Securities Exchange Act of 1934 may be needed.

The general requirements of these forms in corporate acquisitions and mergers (other than requirements for financial statements and related data) will be outlined in this chapter after a discussion of exemptions from filing available under certain circumstances. Requirements for financial statements and related data in filings under the 1933 and 1934 Acts will be discussed in Chapter 11.

The staff of the Commission has consistently expressed its willingness to discuss problems of a particular case in a preliminary meeting or meetings. This will include discussion of possible exemption from filing or the type of form required for filing or reporting. These conferences should be arranged only after consultation with counsel and limited to well-prepared questions; and the Commission appreciates being informed, in advance of a conference, of the facts to be considered. *The Commission's staff cannot devote any great amount of time to assisting anyone in constructing a proxy or registration statement, if either or both are required.*

ISSUANCE OF SECURITIES TECHNICALLY CONSIDERED A "SALE"

The offer or exchange of securities in a business combination has been interpreted as a "sale" within the meaning of the 1933 Act, which reads in part as follows:

> The term "sale" or "sell" shall include every contract of sale or disposition of a security or interest in a security, for value. The term "offer to sell", "offer for sale", or "offer" shall include every attempt or offer to dispose of, or solicitation of an offer to buy, a security or interest in a security, for value. . . .[1]

Although an exchange of securities of an issuer for securities or assets of another company is technically a sale or offer to sell, as defined above, the majority of such transactions have not been subject to the registration provisions of the Securities Act of 1933. For the most part, the only transactions requiring compliance with the registration provisions of the Act are (1) voluntary exchange offers made by one person or corporation directly to the security holders of another company, and (2) those where securities are sold to the public for cash and the proceeds are to be employed to acquire another business or significant assets.

[1] Securities Act of 1933, Sec. 2(3), as amended to October 9, 1954.

The two exemptions from the registration requirements of the 1933 Act most frequently relied upon are (1) Rule 133, known as the "no sale" rule; and (2) Section 4(1) of the Securities Act, which exempts "private" sales.

Background of "No Sale" Aspects of Certain Business Combinations. The Securities and Exchange Commission decided a number of years ago, as a matter of administrative policy, that no sale was involved when a plan of consolidation or merger or for a transfer of corporate assets to another corporation for securities of the latter was submitted to security holders and the affirmative vote of the majority bound the minority holders. The reasoning behind this "no sale" interpretation was well presented in a brief filed on behalf of the Commission in 1947, an excerpt of which follows:

In such consolidations and mergers the alteration of the stockholder's security occurs not because he consents to an exchange, but because the corporation by authorized action converts his security from one form to another. The essence of the Commission's construction is that in such cases a proposed corporate act is submitted to the stockholders to be accepted or rejected by them as a class, in their capacity as members of the corporate body. Even though the stockholder may participate in the vote which results in changing his rights as a stockholder, his action in so doing is the action of a member of the corporation exercising his franchise, rather than the action of a security holder choosing to accept an offer of exchange made to him as an individual. He is functioning precisely as he would be if he were voting on a charter amendment which would, for example, change the corporate purposes.[2]

RULE 133. To afford companies relying on its administrative policy the protection embodied in a rule, the Securities and Exchange Commission in 1951 adopted Rule 133 under the Securities Act of 1933. Section (a) of this rule, which describes the conditions where no sale is deemed to be involved, reads as follows:

Rule 133. (a) For purposes only of Section 5 of the Act, no "sale," "offer," "offer to sell," or "offer for sale" shall be deemed to be involved so far as the stockholders of a corporation are concerned where, pursuant to statutory provisions in the State of incorporation or provisions contained in the certificate of incorporation, there is submitted to the vote of such stockholders a plan or agreement for a statutory merger or consolidation or reclassification of securities,

[2] Nat'l Supply Co. v. Leland Stanford Jr. University, 134 F.2d 689 (9th Cir. 1943), *cert. denied*, 320 U.S. 773.

or a proposal for the transfer of assets of such corporation to another person in consideration of the issuance of securities of such other person or voting stock of a corporation which is in control, as defined in Section 368(c) of the Internal Revenue Code of 1954, of such other person, under such circumstances that the vote of a required favorable majority (1) will operate to authorize the proposed transaction so far as concerns the corporation whose stockholders are voting (except for the taking of action by the directors of the corporation involved and for compliance with such statutory provisions as the filing of the plan or agreement with the appropriate State authority), and (2) will bind all stockholders of such corporation except to the extent that dissenting stockholders may be entitled, under statutory provisions or provisions contained in the certificate of incorporation, to receive the appraised or fair value of their holdings.[3]

The fact that a business combination fulfills the conditions of Section (a) of Rule 133 and therefore does not require the filing of a registration statement under the Securities Act of 1933 does not mean that the recipients of such securities may, without exception, dispose of them at will. The remaining Sections (b) to (f) of this rule deal with the applicability of registration requirements where recipients of securities in such a transaction receive them with a view to offering them publicly or later to dispose of them under circumstances that would constitute a public offering. Thus, Rule 133 should be read in entirety and is reproduced as Appendix D. It should be noted, in announcing Rule 133, the Commission specifically stated that the Rule was restricted to Section 5 and did not relate to the antifraud provisions of the Securities Act of 1933 or the Securities Exchange Act of 1934, even though such provisions were also based on the occurrence of a "sale."

PRIVATE SALE EXEMPTION

Another type of transaction not requiring the filing of a registration statement in a business combination is one exempted under Section 4(1) of the Securities Act of 1933, which relates to "private" offerings and transactions. A "private" offering excludes a transaction involving an issuer, underwriter, or dealer.[4]

The factors considered by the Securities and Exchange Commission in deciding whether a business combination transaction

---

[3] Securities Exchange Act of 1934, Rule 133, as amended to July 16, 1959.
[4] Securities Act of 1933, Sec. 4(1), as amended to October 9, 1954.

or other issuance of securities qualifies as a "private" sale are as follows:

1. The number of offerees and their relationship to each other and to the issuer
2. The number of units offered
3. The size of the offering
4. The manner of offering [5]

It is important to recognize that the determination as to whether or not a transaction involves any public offering is essentially a question of fact in which all surrounding circumstances must be given consideration and no one factor is in itself conclusive.

Limited Number of Offerees an Important Consideration. One of the most important considerations in determining if a transaction is a public offering is the number of offerees involved. At one time, the view was widely held that as a rule of thumb an offering to not more than twenty-five persons would probably not involve a public offering. More recently, however, the Securities and Exchange Commission has noted that the number of persons to whom the offering is extended is relevant only to the question whether they have the requisite association with and knowledge of the issuer that makes the exemption available.[6]

The relationship of the recipients of securities to the issuer has taken on greater significance since the *Ralston Purina* case, in which the Supreme Court stated that the basic test of the availability of the exemption was "whether the particular class of persons affected needs the protection of the Act." [7] Thus, if the offerees because of their relationship as officers, directors, controlling stockholders, etc., of the company to be acquired have access to the same type of information that would be available in a registration statement under the Act, they need not be regarded as members of the investing public. This decision tended to establish the Commission's contention that the burden of proof

---

[5] Securities Act Release No. 4552. November 6, 1962 (reproduced as Appendix J).
[6] *Ibid.*
[7] Securities and Exchange Commission v. Ralston Purina Co., 346 U.S. 119 (1953).

as to the availability of an exemption rests upon the person claiming it.

It is good practice for a company or its legal counsel to consult with the staff of the Commission where there is question as to the availability of the exemption under Section 4(1), although neither the staff nor the Commission itself can or will rule authoritatively on the question. The staff of the Commission will, however, in these circumstances, issue what is referred to as a "no-action" letter. If the staff of the Commission agrees with the interpretation of company counsel, the letter would probably state that on the basis of the facts presented, no action would be taken if the terms of the proposed transaction were carried out.

Possibility That Recipient of Securities Will Make Secondary Distribution. Another consideration in determining the availability of the exemption under Section 4(1) is the risk that a recipient of securities in a business combination transaction will make a secondary distribution of the securities and become an underwriter, as defined in the Act, as follows, thereby rendering the exemption unavailable:

> The term "underwriter" means any person who has purchased from an issuer with a view to, or offers or sells for an issuer in connection with, the distribution of any security, or participates or has a direct or indirect participation in any such undertaking, or participates or has a participation in the direct or indirect underwriting of any such undertaking. . . . As used in this paragraph the term "issuer" shall include, in addition to an issuer, any person directly or indirectly controlling or controlled by the issuer, or any person under direct or indirect common control with the issuer.[8]

To afford some measure of protection against a secondary distribution nullifying the exemption relied upon, it has become standard practice for issuers to request so-called "investment letters" from recipient stockholders. It should be understood, however, that the receipt of an "investment letter" does not, per se, transform a public offering into a private placement or otherwise grant relief from compliance with the Securities Act.

INVESTMENT LETTERS. The form of investment letters requested from recipient stockholders may vary depending upon

[8] Securities Act of 1933, Sec. 2(11), as amended to October 9, 1954.

the situation and the preferences of legal counsel. A typical form
of investment letter follows:

Takeover Company
Dear Sirs:
The agreement between the Takeover Company and Absorbed Corporation dated December 15, 1961, provides that Takeover shall issue
and deliver to Absorbed certain shares of Takeover common stock in
consideration of the transfer of the business and assets of Absorbed,
and thereafter that Absorbed shall distribute such shares of common
stock of Takeover to shareholders of Absorbed in liquidation.

The undersigned, as a holder and owner of shares of common stock
of Absorbed, hereby advises you and represents that he will acquire
the shares of common stock of Takeover, which will be distributable
to him upon consummation of the said agreement, for purposes of
investment and without a view to any public distribution thereof.

Yours very truly,

_____

(Signed by stockholder)

In some instances, the investment letter may contain exceptions that recognize the right of the recipient of securities to
dispose of shares within the limits of Rule 133(d), under the so-
called "dribble out" provisions, and also to transfer shares by gift
or sale to persons agreeing to acquire such shares for "investment
purposes."

It was made clear in the *Crowell-Collier* case that an investment letter is of little value, as a defense, if it is not lived up to
by the offerees.[9] In this case, Crowell-Collier entered into a "best
efforts" deal [10] for a private placement of convertible debentures
through a broker-dealer, who in turn obtained subscription commitments for such securities from customers, business associates,
and other broker-dealers. The securities thus were distributed to
a number of purchasers, some of whom converted their debentures into common stock, portions of which were sold. The Commission found, in May 1958, that there had been a public offering

[9] Securities Exchange Act of 1934, Releases Nos. 5688, 5689, and 5690, May 7,
1958. Also, Gilligan, Will & Co. v. Securities and Exchange Commission, 267 F.2d
461 (1959), *Cert. denied,* 361 U.S. 896 (1960).

[10] A "best-efforts" deal is a form of agreement whereby the underwriters use
their best efforts to sell the securities being offered, but have no obligation to
purchase any unsold securities.

of the Crowell-Collier securities in violation of the Securities Act of 1933. Disciplinary action was taken against three broker-dealers as the result of investigation and hearings, and such action was affirmed by the court in an appeal by one of them.

REQUIRED HOLDING PERIOD OF STOCK RECEIVED IN BUSINESS COMBINATION. One question that has never been satisfactorily answered is how long the securities must be held so that their resale will not lead to an inference that they were acquired with a view toward distribution. There is no rule prescribing a holding period, and the courts have yet to resolve the matter. A possible indication of the thinking of the Commission in this area is found in Form S–14, used to register securities issued in a Rule 133 transaction, which requires that an up-to-date prospectus be available for sales of such securities for a period of two years. The more important test of the exemption is still the intent of the purchaser at the time of purchase, although the length of holding may be regarded as an indication of such intent. Even if a purchaser lives up to his investment covenant, he may find himself with "hot stock" if other purchasers in the same transaction distribute their stock publicly.

OTHER MEANS OF PROTECTING AN ISSUER OF SECURITIES. Some suggested methods of guarding against a subsequent sale of securities by offerees, which would nullify or violate the private placement exemption, are:

1. Provide for registration of the securities by the issuer upon request if the purchaser ever wants to make a public offering. Limitations as to the number of such requests and the bearing of the expenses involved would ordinarily be included in a business combination agreement.
2. Provide for restrictions on transfers of the securities, such as affixing a stamped legend on the securities indicating that they are unregistered, and request that the transfer agent not transfer them without instructions from the issuer.

GENERAL FILING REQUIREMENTS UNDER THE SECURITIES ACTS

Where a filing with the Securities and Exchange Commission is required, other than a current report form, it is most frequently a proxy statement. Accordingly, the requirements, other than for financial data, will be discussed in this chapter in the following order:

1. Proxy statements under Regulation X–14 of the 1934 Act
2. Forms S–14, under the 1933 Act, that are in effect proxy statements with certain supplementary information
3. Forms S–1 under the 1933 Act
4. Current reports, Form 8–K, under the 1934 Act

Financial Filings. Under the extensive authority granted to it by Congress, the Securities and Exchange Commission by use of its rule-making powers has constructed a network of reporting requirements, all designed to provide full disclosure of material facts about publicly held companies to their investors. All these reporting requirements follow the same basic pattern of filing material with the Commission either prior to or concurrently with its issuance to the public. All registration (including S–1 and S–14) and proxy statements must be filed with the Commission sufficiently prior to their use to permit review by the staff of the Commission. Current reports on Form 8–K, although subject to review and occasionally a request for amendment by the Commission, are considered to be "effective" when filed.

SECURITIES AND EXCHANGE COMMISSION REVIEW PROCEDURE. The review procedure of proxy and registration statements by the Commission is somewhat similar, although it will generally require a longer period, sometimes substantially, to clear a registration statement. Upon receipt of a proxy or registration statement, the staff of the Commission examines it to determine if it complies with the standards of accurate and fair disclosure established by the Acts and usually notifies the registrant by an informal letter of comment of any material respects in which the statement fails to conform to such requirements. The registrant is thereby afforded an opportunity to file an amended proxy statement or registration statement.

Failure by the staff of the Commission to cite a deficiency may not always be indicative of its agreement with the material filed but could result from a lack of information. The examination taff is not in the position of the company or its experts; it does not have available the details known to them. The absence of deficiencies does not condone the inclusion in the prospectus of information subsequently found to be misleading when the true facts come to light. Furthermore, to rebut specifically any inference that its review constitutes approval of the contents of a prospectus, the Commission, pursuant to Rule 425, requires the following legend to appear in capital letters on the cover of every prospectus:

THESE SECURITIES HAVE NOT BEEN APPROVED OR DISAPPROVED BY THE SECURITIES AND EXCHANGE COMMISSION NOR HAS THE COMMISSION PASSED UPON THE ACCURACY OR ADEQUACY OF THIS PROSPECTUS. ANY REPRESENTATION TO THE CONTRARY IS A CRIMINAL OFFENSE.

PROXY SOLICITATIONS

Regulation X–14 of the Securities Exchange Act of 1934. The Securities Exchange Act of 1934 provides as follows:

t shall be unlawful for any person, by the use of the mails or by any means or instrumentality of interstate commerce or of any facility of any national securities exchange or otherwise to solicit or to permit the use of his name to solicit any proxy or consent or authorization in respect of any security (other than an exempted security) registered on any national securities exchange in contravention of such rules and regulations as the Commission may prescribe as necessary or appropriate in the public interest or for the protection of investors.[11]

Although the statute delegates to the Commission the authority to prescribe rules and regulations for the solicitation of proxies, neither the federal securities laws nor the regulations *require* corporate management to solicit proxies from its shareholders. *If proxies are not solicited or if the securities are not registered on a national securities exchange, the rules have no application.*

THE NEW YORK AND AMERICAN STOCK EXCHANGES REQUIRE PROXY SOLICITATION (CHAPTER 12). Although a proxy may not otherwise be required under Regulation X–14, the New York and American Stock Exchanges, as a condition of listing additional

[11] Securities Exchange Act of 1934, Sec. 14(a), as amended to August 27, 1954.

securities for any acquisition of a company or property, require stockholder approval through the solicitation of proxies where:

1. The amount of stock to be so issued represents an increase in outstanding shares of 20 per cent or more.
2. The combined value of stock (including securities converted into common stock) and all other consideration approximates 20 per cent or more of the market value of the outstanding common stock.
3. An officer, director, or substantial security holder of the acquirer has a substantial interest in the business proposed to be acquired.[12]

Requirements of other national exchanges should also be checked if a company listed other than on the New York and American Stock Exchanges is involved.

Regulation X–14 of the Securities Exchange Act of 1934, adopted in 1938 and amended several times thereafter, contains rules regulating the solicitation of proxies. The purpose of the proxy rules is to provide sufficient information to enable a stockholder to intelligently exercise his right to vote upon the corporate matters presented to him for approval.

Included in Regulation X–14 is Schedule 14A, which specifies, in twenty-one items, the information required in a proxy statement. A solicitation subject to the proxy rules may not be made unless each shareholder is furnished with a written proxy statement containing such information. Schedule 14A is included as Appendix E.

Contested Proxy Solicitations. As mentioned in Chapter 13, an attempt to gain control of a company without the cooperation of its board of directors will often result in a proxy contest between the incumbent management and the opposition shareholders group. When faced with an increasing number of such proxy contests in the early 1950's, the Securities and Exchange Commission, in 1956, issued a new rule governing proxy contests for the election of directors.[13] This rule was designed to "aid public

---

[12] *New York Stock Exchange Company Manual,* October 19, 1961, p. A–284; American Stock Exchange, *Listing Standards, Policies and Requirements,* April 5, 1962.

[13] Securities Exchange Act of 1934, Rule X–14A–11.

investors in the exercise of their voting rights"[14] by furnishing them with a proxy statement containing the information called for by Schedule 14B of Regulation X–14, which has been reproduced as Appendix F.

INFORMATION REQUIRED BY SCHEDULE 14B. The data in schedule 14B to be included in the proxy statement furnished to the shareholders falls into three general categories: The first requires information as to the identity and background of each participant (as defined in the Act[15]), the second requires information as to each participant's interest in the securities of the issuer, and the third requires information as to the circumstances surrounding the individual participant's becoming involved in the contest.

TIMELY FILING REQUIREMENTS FOR PROXY MATERIAL. Three preliminary copies of the proxy material must be filed with the Commission at least ten days before the final material is used. After review by the staff of the Commission, when any necessary revisions are made, four copies of the material in definitive form must be mailed to the Commission concurrently with its distribution to stockholders and three copies to each exchange on which *any* security of the issuer is listed. It is generally inadvisable to distribute the proxy statement to stockholders, brokers, or others until the issuer receives the comments of the Commission. Similar caution should be exercised regarding press releases and other written communications that constitute a "solicitation" within the broad definition of Rule 14a–1.

Although there is no requirement to submit preliminary proxy material to the stock exchange upon which a company is listed, as a precautionary measure, it is advisable to do so and thereby avoid the possibility of having basic requirements of the exchange overlooked in the material prepared.

Form S–14 of the Securities Act of 1933. In an effort to facilitate compliance with Rule 133, the Securities and Exchange Commission, in 1959, adopted a simplified registration statement, Form S–14, to be used for securities acquired in acquisitions and

[14] *Ibid.*, Release No. 5276, January 17, 1956.
[15] *Ibid.*, Rule X–14A–11 (b).

mergers. This form may be used only where the issuer was subject to and solicited proxies from its stockholders with respect to the transaction pursuant to the Commission's proxy rules.

In substance, Form S–14 requires that a prospectus include the same information contained in the proxy statement of the successor corporation and permits it to be in the form of the proxy statement if supplemented by certain additional information, as follows:

1. The form states that "the information . . . shall be current in terms of the requirements of the appropriate registration form, other than Form S–14, at the time the registration statement is filed." [16] This means, in effect, that the financial statements must be as timely as if they were to be included in a filing by the registrant on Form S–1. However, the Commission may, upon showing of good cause, permit the furnishing of other financial statements in a particular case.

2. If not contained in the proxy statement, the prospectus must contain the information called for by item 7 of Schedule 14A of Regulation 14 under the Securities Exhange Act of 1934. Item 7 calls for information regarding remuneration and other transactions with officers, directors, and other specified persons.

3. The prospectus must contain the required information as to (a) the persons on whose behalf the securities are to be offered, and (b) the underwriting and distribution of such securities, which would be required in a filing by the registrant on Form S–1.

4. The prospectus must contain information with respect to the consummation of the Rule 133 transaction and any material developments in the business or affairs of the registrant subsequent thereto that would be required in a filing by the registrant on Form S–1.

5. Certain other matters in compliance with rules and regulations, under the Securities Act of 1933, relating to the form and content of prospectuses must be complied with.

THERE HAVE BEEN RELATIVELY FEW FILINGS UNDER FORM S–14. Although Form S–14 (consisting of the proxy statement with certain additional limited information) provides a simplified means of registering securities received in a corporate acquisition or other business combination, only a limited number of filings have been made with this form to date. Although the

[16] Securities Act of 1933, Form S–14, Part I, item 1(a), July 23, 1959.

reasons for this are not entirely clear, certain factors may play a role in the decision as to the use of the form, viz.:

1. Use of the form is restricted only to companies listed on national securities exchanges.
2. The undertakings for filing post-effective amendments required by the form are so extensive that they may place an unreasonable burden on the registrant.[17]

PRINCIPAL REGISTRATION STATEMENT

The principal registration form under the Securities Act of 1933 is Form S–1, which is used most frequently in public offerings of securities. However, in many business combinations, no public offering is deemed to be involved [18] (or the simpler Form S–14 may be used for registration), so that Form S–1 is not required in the majority of such transactions.

As mentioned previously, Form S–1 generally would be required in business combination transactions only where (1) voluntary exchange offers are made by one person or corporation directly to the security holders of another company, and (2) securities are sold to the public for cash and proceeds are to be employed to acquire another business or significant assets. With these general exceptions, Form S–14 will meet the requirements of the Securities and Exchange Commission, if it is desired to place securities issued in an acquisition or merger transaction in registration.

Form S–1 is not a "form" in the sense that one merely fills information in the blank spaces. It is rather a set of instructions regarding information to be supplied by the securities issuer in the registration statement. Whereas in a proxy statement under

---

[17] *Ibid.,* Form S–14, Part II, item 6:
"the registrant undertakes . . . to file a post-effective amendment or amendments to the registration statement so that there will continuously be available a prospectus containing certified financial statements and other information meeting the requirements of section 10(a)(3) of the Securities Act of 1933 for a period of 24 months after the effective date of the registration statement, and that for the purpose of determining liabilities under such Act, the effective date of each such amendment shall be deemed the effective date of the registration statement with respect to securities sold after such amendment shall have become effective. . . ."
[18] See comments on pages 174 and 175 regarding "no sale" Rule 133 and "private sale" exemption Section 4(1).

Regulation X–14, and in an S–14 registration statement, which embodies the proxy statement as a prospectus, much of the information furnished is a matter of administrative policy by the Commission, a Form S–1 specifically requires most of such data by its instructions.

Prospectus. In addition to registration with the Securities and Exchange Commission, before securities may be offered publicly, the Act requires that a prospectus be prepared for the information of prospective investors.[19] A Form S–1 registration statement thus consists of two parts: the first (and greater part) that will eventually become the prospectus, once the registration is effective; and the second that contains additional information such as estimated expenses of issue, exhibits of various legal documents and agreements, schedules in support of financial statements, consents of experts to the use of their opinions, undertakings for future reporting, and other miscellaneous data.

The prospectus portion of the registration statement describes the terms of the offering and gives such information as history and description of business, location of principal plants, capital structure, description of outstanding securities and the securities being offered, summary of earnings, financial statements, remuneration of directors and officers, and shareholdings of larger shareholders.

Disclosure is required of the amount of direct remuneration paid by the registrant and its subsidiaries during the last fiscal year to (1) each director, and each of the three highest paid officers of the registrant, whose aggregate direct remuneration exceeded $30,000; and (2) all directors and officers of the registrant as a group (without naming them). If there is a bonus or profit-sharing plan, a brief description of the plan must be given and the basis upon which directors and officers participate in it. Also, details must be given of amounts set aside or accrued for the persons named above under a pension or retirement plan and the estimated annual benefit to be received on retirement.

Where any person owns more than 10 per cent of any class of voting securities, the name, address, and holdings of such person

[19] Securities Act of 1933, Sec. 5, as amended to October 9, 1954.

(including any corporation) must be disclosed. Details must also be given of any material transactions the company has had with these principal shareholders.

Special Requirements of Form S–1. Form S–1 contains certain requirements for additional information to be provided in a prospectus when it is being used to register securities to be offered in an exchange offer. The most important of these requirements is general instruction F to the form that reads as follows:

F. *Exchange Offers*—

If any of the securities being registered are to be offered in exchange for securities of any other issuer, the prospectus shall also include the information which would be required by Items 6 to 10 inclusive and Item 12 if the securities of such other issuer were being registered on this form. Item 11 should be included if any promoter of such other issuer is a promoter, officer or director of the registrant or a security holder named in answer to Item 19(a). There shall also be included the information concerning such securities of such other issuer which would be called for by Item 13, 14 or 15 if such securities were being registered. In connection with this instruction, reference is made to Rule 409.[20]

The Items 6 through 15 inclusive referred to above deal with the following subjects:

Item 6. Summary of earnings
Item 7. Organization of registrant
Item 8. Parents of registrant
Item 9. Description of business
Item 10. Description of property
Item 11. Organization within five years
Item 12. Pending legal proceedings
Item 13. Capital stock being registered

[20] *Ibid.*, Rule 409, January 17, 1949:

"Information required need be given only insofar as it is known or reasonably available to the registrant. If any required information is unknown and not reasonably available to the registrant, either because the obtaining thereof would involve unreasonable effort or expense, or because it rests peculiarly within the knowledge of another person not affiliated with the registrant, the information may be omitted, subject to the following conditions:

"(a) The registrant shall give such information on the subject as it possesses or can acquire without unreasonable effort or expense, together with the sources thereof.

"(b) The registrant shall include a statement either showing that unreasonable effort or expense would be involved or indicating the absence of any affiliation with the person within whose knowledge the information rests and stating the result of a request made to such person for the information."

Item 14. Long-term debt being registered
Item 15. Other securities being registered

The last sentence of general instruction F refers to Rule 409. This rule is intended, among other things, to deal with the situation, which occasionally confronts a registrant, when the management of the company to whose shareholders the exchange offer is made does not approve of the terms of the offer and, accordingly, declines to cooperate in the preparation of the registration statement. In situations such as these, the Commission has permitted the registration statement to become effective containing only that information regarding the offeree corporation that is available from public sources.

INFORMATION OBTAINED FROM ANNUAL REPORTS TO SHAREHOLDERS. An interesting case of an exchange offer where the only information available to the prospective acquirer (Buckeye Corp.) was from annual reports to shareholders of the company to be acquired (King Bros. Productions, Inc.) follows:

The information contained in this Prospectus with respect to King Productions has, to a large extent, being assembled by the Corporation from published reports of King Productions or by its management. The financial statements of King Productions (including the "Statement of Earnings of King Productions") included herein have been taken from said Company's annual reports to its stockholders, which indicate that such financial statements have been certified by independent public accountants, and reliance is placed upon the certificates of said accountants in including said financial statements herein. The Corporation has not, however, obtained the consent of said accountants to the inclusion of such financial statements in this Prospectus. The Corporation has no means of independently determining the accuracy or completeness of such information and financial statements and makes no representations with respect thereto. The Corporation has requested the management of King Productions to cooperate in providing appropriate information for inclusion in this Prospectus, but such request has been refused upon the basis that such cooperation might create the impression that management of King Productions is joining in the Corporation's proposal. The most recent published report of King Productions was its annual report for the fiscal year ended August 31, 1959. The Corporation has had no means of determining whether there has been any change in the business or financial condition of King Productions since that date which would affect the information contained herein. However, to the best of the Corporation's knowledge and belief, the information with respect to King Productions included herein contains no misstatements or deficiencies.[21]

[21] Buckeye Corp., Prospectus, May 20, 1960.

INFORMATION OBTAINED FROM REPORTS FILED WITH THE SE-
CURITIES AND EXCHANGE COMMISSION. Another case where the
prospective acquirer (Lynch Corp.) prepared a prospectus from
public information on the company proposed to be acquired
(Peninsular Metal Products Corp.) in an exchange offer to its
shareholders follows:

Lynch and Peninsular are not affiliated, and, as is set forth under the caption
"Reasons for the Exchange Offer" herein, the Board of Directors of Peninsular
on July 27, 1961 rejected a request by Lynch for cooperation in the furnishing, at Lynch's expense, of information, including financial data, and other
material requisite for the preparation of the Registration Statement and related
material for use in connection with the proposed Exchange Offer. Accordingly,
the information with respect to Peninsular set forth herein has been taken from
various reports (on Forms 8-K, 9-K and 10-K) filed by Peninsular with the
Securities and Exchange Commission for periods ending December 31, 1957
through July 30, 1961, from Peninsular Annual Reports to Stockholders for
the years 1957 to 1960, from a registration statement (Form S-1) filed by
Peninsular with the Securities and Exchange Commission, from additional
reports and material filed by Peninsular with the American Stock Exchange,
from published information in statistical services, from certain statistical data
prepared for use at the Peninsular 1961 annual stockholders meeting and from
a list of Peninsular stockholders as of November 10, 1961.[22]

CURRENT REPORTS

A company entering into a business combination may or may
not be required to register the shares to be issued under the
Securities Act of 1933 or to solicit proxies from its shareholders
in accordance with the proxy regulations of the Securities Exchange Act of 1934, depending, to some extent, upon applicable
state law and provisions of the corporate charter. However, if
the company has previously registered securities under either
Act, it may nonetheless be required to file a "current report" with
a stock exchange or the Securities and Exchange Commission.

Requirements of the Securities Exchange Act of 1934. The Securities Exchange Act of 1934 requires that every issuer of a security
registered on a national securities exchange shall file with the
exchange:

1. Such information and documents as the Commission may require
   to keep reasonably current the information and documents filed
   pursuant to Section 12

[22] Lynch Corp., Prospectus, February 14, 1962.

2. Such annual reports, certified if required by the rules and regulations of the Commission by independent public accountants, and such quarterly reports as the Commission may prescribe [23]

The Act also requires that each registration filed pursuant to the Securities Act of 1933 contain an undertaking by the issuer to file with the Commission "such supplementary and periodic information, documents, and reports as may be required pursuant to section 13 of this title in respect of a security listed and registered on a national securities exchange. . . ." [24] Section 15(d) goes on to state that this undertaking becomes operative only if ". . . the aggregate offering price of such issue of securities, plus the aggregate value of all other securities of such issuer of the same class outstanding, computed upon the basis of such offering price, amounts to $2,000,000 or more" and that the undertaking is automatically suspended if ". . . the aggregate value of all outstanding securities of the class to which such issue belongs is reduced to less than $1,000,000 computed upon the basis of the offering price of the last issue of securities of said class offered to the public." [25]

Thus, a substantial segment of the larger companies trading only in the over-the-counter market is subject to the periodic reporting requirements of the Commission. The objective of these provisions of the 1934 Act is to provide continuing disclosure to investors by keeping up-to-date much of the information contained in the original registration statement. To provide a vehicle for such reporting requirements, the Commission has adopted a number of forms for use in filing periodic reports, chief among these being Form 8-K.

Form 8–K of the Securities Exchange Act of 1934. Upon the occurrence of certain specified events, a company subject to the reporting requirements of Sections 13 or 15(d) of the Securities Exchange Act of 1934 must file a report on Form 8-K within ten days after the close of the month in which the specified event occurs. The form itself specifies the events that are to be reported

[23] Securities Exchange Act of 1934, Sec. 13, June 6, 1934.
[24] *Ibid.,* Sec. 15(d), as amended to June 25, 1938.
[25] *Ibid.*

on and provides relief from filing in the event the same information has previously been reported by the issuer. There is also provision for incorporating by reference material contained in proxy statements filed with the Commission or annual reports to shareholders.[26]

ITEM 2 OF FORM 8–K: ACQUISITION OR DISPOSITION OF ASSETS. Item 2 of the form requires that a report be filed if the issuer or any of its majority owned subsidiaries ". . . has acquired or disposed of a significant amount of assets, otherwise than in the ordinary course of business. . . ." [27] This applies not only to an individual transaction of this type, but also to any series of related transactions that in the aggregate would be significant. The measure of significance in determining the necessity for filing the form is stated in instruction 4 of item 2 as follows:

An acquisition or disposition shall be deemed to involve a significant amount of assets (i) if the net book value of such assets or the amount paid or received therefor upon such acquisition or disposition exceeded 15 per cent of the total assets of the registrant and its consolidated subsidiaries, or (ii) if it involved the acquisition or disposition of a business whose gross revenues for its last fiscal year exceeded 15 per cent of the aggregate gross revenues of the registrant and its consolidated subsidiaries for the registrant's last ficsal year.[28]

The question frequently arises as to what constitutes the total assets or gross revenues of the "registrant and its consolidated subsidiaries." Although occasionally a point of dispute, the Commission has taken the position that the total assets and gross revenues of an issuer are as shown by its consolidated financial statements filed with the Commission and not on a constructed consolidated basis including the company to be acquired or any other adjustments. The term "acquisition," as used in this item, includes among other things every ". . . purchase, acquisition by lease, exchange, merger, consolidation, succession or other acquisition. . . ." [29] The acquisition of securities is deemed to be an indirect acquisition of the assets represented by the securities if control of such assets results therefrom.

[26] *Ibid.*, Form 8–K, as amended to August 16, 1958.
[27] *Ibid.*
[28] *Ibid.*
[29] *Ibid.*

ITEM 7 OF FORM 8–K: INCREASE IN AMOUNT OF SECURITIES OUTSTANDING. Item 7 of the form requires that a report be filed if the aggregate amount of previously unreported increases in any class of securities of the issuer exceeds 5 per cent of the outstanding securities of the class. No report need be made, however, if the aggregate amount unreported does not exceed $50,000 face value or 1,000 shares or other units. The item has application to reissued treasury shares and indebtedness for which the maturity date has been extended.

A company that has been involved in a corporate acquisition or other business combination that does not meet the "significance test" set forth in item 2 of Form 8–K may still have to file the form if the number of shares or principal amount of the securities issued in this and other unreported transactions in the aggregate exceed 5 per cent of the outstanding securities of the class.

ITEM 11 OF FORM 8–K: SUBMISSION OF MATTERS TO A VOTE OF SECURITY HOLDERS. Item 11 of the form requires that a report be filed if any matter has been submitted to a vote of its shareholders.

A company that has submitted a proposal relating to a business combination to a vote of its shareholders, whether through solicitation of proxies or not, would be required to report on such an event in Form 8–K even though the transaction does not fall within the requirements of items 2 and 7 of the form.

PROPOSED AMENDMENTS TO FORM 8–K. The Securities and Exchange Commission recently circulated, for comment, a proposed amendment to Form 8–K that contained a variety of revisions, the majority requiring additional and more detailed reporting of certain specified events affecting the issuer or its affairs. Accordingly, inquiry should be made of the current status of the proposed amendment to determine the necessity of filing a report on this form.[30]

[30] *Ibid.* Release No. 6770, April 5, 1962.

Chapter 11

FINANCIAL DATA REQUIRED IN S.E.C. FILINGS

Financial statements, schedules, and statistical data submitted in a proxy or registration statement generally constitute the most significant sections of such statements. These are the data that have an important bearing on investment decisions to be made by offerees of securities.

FINANCIAL STATEMENTS—GENERAL

Instructions specifying the financial statements required in a particular situation and their timeliness will be found in the form on which the filing is to be made. The form will also specify any special requirements that may be appropriate and the need for certification of such statements. In most forms issued by the Commission, there is what is often referred to as a "Mother Hubbard" rule. This rule permits the Commission in its discretion to permit the omission of any financial statements otherwise required by the form, or to request the filing of additional financial statements not specifically called for by the form, if, in either case, the Commission considers it advisable to so rule for the protection of investors.

REGULATION S–X

The form and content of financial statements in all filings under the federal securities laws, including the 1933 and 1934 Acts, are governed by Regulation S–X [1] of the Securities and Exchange Commission and are not detailed in the various forms. This regulation sets forth in considerable detail the data that balance sheets, income statements, and notes to financial state-

[1] Originally adopted in *Accounting Series Release No. 12*, February 21, 1940, and amended a number of times since.

ments must show for proper disclosure of financial position and income.

Certain matters not generally shown in a company's report to stockholders are required to be detailed as a part of financial statements in a filing with the Commission. For example, the company's policy regarding depreciation, including the rates in effect; its accounting policy for sales and retirement of fixed assets; description of stock option and pension plans; and in certain instances, data on non-consolidated subsidiaries. Amounts for rent, royalties, maintenance and repairs, charges for depreciation and depletion of tangible assets, and amounts of amortization of intangibles must be indicated. Details of various types of taxes such as payroll taxes, franchise taxes, and property taxes are also required.

Regulation S–X Only Intended as a Guide. Regulation S–X is intended for use only as a *guide* to form and content. There has been a tendency on the part of some registrants to look upon its provisions as a tax return type of form in which amounts applicable to each item, regardless of size, are required to be set forth. Such an approach has resulted in statements that contain such a volume of information that material items are lost in a maze of insignificant detail. Thus, two rules contained in this regulation are important: (1) one that states that financial statements may be set forth in such form and employ such generally accepted terminology as will best indicate their significance and character in the light of applicable S–X provisions,[2] and (2) another that states the amounts that are not material need not be separately set forth in the manner prescribed.[3] The Commission's definition of "material" information relates to those matters that an average prudent investor ought reasonably to be informed of before purchasing the security registered.[4]

The various statutes administered by the Commission give it broad rule-making power regarding the preparation and presentation of financial statements contained in filings with it.[5] Among

[2] Regulation S-X, Rule 3.01(a), as amended to December 29, 1950.
[3] *Ibid.*, Rule 3.02.
[4] *Ibid.*, Rule 1.02.
[5] Securities Act of 1933, Sec. 19(a), May 27, 1933.

other things, the Commission may prescribe the methods to be followed in the preparation of accounts; appraisal or valuation of assets and liabilities; and the determination of recurring and non-recurring items, income, and expense.[6]

Accounting Series Releases. As the need arises, the Commission publishes new or amended rules and regulations as well as opinions of its Chief Accountant relating to major accounting questions or administrative policy regarding financial statements. These releases are called *Accounting Series Releases* and are of great significance in preparing financial statements for inclusion in a filing with the Commission. The first such release was issued in 1937, and since that time there have been ninety-six issued through January 10, 1963.

Probably the release of most lasting significance is Release No. 4, issued by the Commission in 1938. This release states the Commission's administrative policy with respect to financial statements filed with it and reads in part as follows:

In cases where financial statements filed with this Commission pursuant to its rules and regulations are prepared in accordance with accounting principles for which there is no substantial authoritative support, such financial statements will be presumed to be misleading or inaccurate despite disclosures contained in the certificate of the accountant or in footnotes to the statement provided the matters involved are material. In cases where there is a difference of opinion between the Commission and the Registrant as to the proper principles of accounting to be followed, disclosure will be accepted in lieu of correction of the financial statements themselves only if the points involved are such that there is substantial authoritative support for the practices followed by the Registrant and the position of the Commission has not previously been expressed in rules, regulations or other official releases of the Commission, including the published opinions of its chief accountants.[7]

SIGNIFICANCE OF RULE 4. The essence of this release is that if the statements filed with the Commission are based on unsupportable accounting principles, disclosure of this information in the accountant's opinion or the notes to financial statements will not correct them. Furthermore, if a company files financial statements that reflect an accounting principle that has been formally disapproved by the Commission, the financial statements will be presumed to be misleading. The importance of the release should

[6] *Ibid.*
[7] *Accounting Series Release No. 4,* April 25, 1938.

be apparent. It means that the company filing financial statements with the Commission is charged not only with the knowledge of the rules and regulations of the Commission, but also with its accounting opinions, whether in the form of releases in the Accounting Series or in official decisions and reports.

If the accounting treatment for a given transaction is not clearly indicated, either because principles have not been well established or there are differences of opinion regarding the weight to be given the known facts, it may be desirable to discuss such problems with the Commission staff informally in advance of filing.

FINANCIAL STATEMENT REQUIREMENTS—PROXIES

As indicated in item 15 of Schedule 14A,[8] the financial statements required in a proxy statement soliciting shareholder approval of a proposed business combination are the same for both parties to the transaction. These requirements are the same as those in an original application (generally Form 10) for the registration of securities under the 1934 Act. Although item 15(b) provides that the financial statements of the persons specified in item 14(b) "need not be certified," [9] in practice, one rarely sees a proxy statement containing uncertified financial statements for the following reasons:

1. *The officers and directors* of the issuer are subject to civil and criminal proceedings under the 1934 Act if false or misleading information is included in a proxy statement. To afford maximum protection against the liabilities imposed by the Act, it is to the advantage of the officers and directors to have as much of the material as possible in the proxy statement "expertized."
2. *The SEC has long held the view* that a proxy statement soliciting shareholder approval of a merger or acquisition should contain substantially the same information as that in a prospectus in a Form S-1 registration statement, which will be discussed later in this chapter. Since the financial statements included in a Form S-1 must be certified, any attempt to file financial statements that have not been certified would undoubtedly be questioned by the Commission.

[8] Securities Exchange Act of 1934, Regulation X-14, Schedule 14A, as amended to January 26, 1956.
[9] *Ibid.*

Item 15(c) of Schedule 14A provides that any or all of the financial statements "not material for the exercise of prudent judgment in regard to the matter to be acted upon may be omitted if the reasons for omission are stated" [10] in the proxy statement. However, the Commission has consistently taken the position that *all the required financial statements are material for the exercise of prudent judgment in cases involving the issuance of securities in a merger or acquisition.*

ANNUAL REPORT TO STOCKHOLDERS MAY BE INCORPORATED IN A PROXY STATEMENT. Item 15(d) of Schedule 14A permits incorporation by reference, in a proxy statement, of financial statements contained in an annual report to shareholders, provided such financial statements substantially meet the requirements of the form. Although this seems an expeditious means of meeting the financial statement requirements of the regulation, very few companies have availed themselves of this provision. The probable reason for this is that all required financial statements are seldom embodied in one document.

Proxy Financial Statements Governed by Requirements for Form 10 Under the Securities Exchange Act of 1934. Pursuant to item 15(a) of Schedule 14A of the Proxy Rules, companies filing proxy statements containing financial statements will be governed by the financial statement requirements for Form 10 under the Securities Exchange Act of 1934. These requirements include a certified balance sheet as of the close of the latest fiscal year and certified profit and loss (income) statements for each of the three fiscal years preceding the date of the balance sheet. In addition, there are specific requirements relating to separate financial statements for unconsolidated subsidiaries and 50 per cent owned persons.

For the most part, the financial statement requirements for a proxy statement are the same as those for a Form S–1 under the 1933 Act. The major differences between the two forms relate to the timeliness of the financial statements required and the omission in a proxy statement of most of the supporting schedules required in a Form S–1 filing. *Accordingly, the instructions*

[10] *Ibid.*

*for financial statements for a Form S–1 are reproduced as
Appendix G and should be referred to.*

DIFFERENCE IN TIMELINESS OF FINANCIAL STATEMENTS IN A
FORM S–1 AND IN A PROXY STATEMENT. The latest balance sheet
in a registration statement on Form S–1 must be as of a date
within ninety days of the filing date or within six months, if the
issuer files reports pursuant to Section 13 or 15(d) of the 1934
Act and meets other specified conditions. In a proxy filing, the
latest balance sheet may, in most cases, be as of the end of the
preceding fiscal year. While there are no specific requirements
to include a balance sheet as of a more current date and a comparative income statement for the interim period, such current
data are frequently included in proxy statements relating to
mergers or acquisitions, either at the request of legal counsel or
of the Securities and Exchange Commission. This is particularly
the case when a proposal is placed before the shareholders late
in the issuer's fiscal year.

Summary of Earnings. Although there is no requirement for a
summary of earnings in the proxy rules or in the instructions on
financial statements for Form 10, the Commission invariably requests that summaries for both parties to the proposal be included
in a solicitation for shareholder approval of a merger or acquisition. If a summary is included in a proxy statement, it should
meet the standards for a summary of earnings prescribed in item
6 of Form S–1, which is reproduced as Appendix H. The principal
features of a summary of earnings are described below.

DATA INCLUDED IN A SUMMARY OF EARNINGS. The summary of
earnings should cover the last five fiscal years, except where the
life of the company and its immediate predecessors is less. In
addition, it should cover any period between the end of the latest
fiscal year and the date of the latest balance sheet furnished and
the corresponding interim period of the preceding fiscal year. The
summary should show net sales, cost of goods sold, interest
charges, income taxes, net income, special items (if any), and net
income and special items as a final figure.

The summary of earnings is one of the most significant items
of information in a proxy statement relating to a proposed busi-

ness combination; and, accordingly, the utmost care must be taken in its preparation. The summary is prepared in the light of current circumstances and therefore may warrant hindsight adjustments of previously reported data. Some aspects of a summary of earnings that should be kept in mind are:

1. In lieu of a summary, the income statement of the company may be substituted in its entirety.
2. Although there is no requirement that the summary be certified by an independent accountant, as a matter of custom this is generally done. Whenever an independent accountant is named in a summary, the Commission requires that he express an opinion thereon. His opinion should, of course, be based on "an examination for such period in accordance with generally accepted auditing standards applicable in the circumstances." [11]
3. Retroactive adjustments of any material items affecting the comparability of results should be reflected in the summary. Although comparability as between years is of the utmost importance in constructing a summary of earnings, care should be taken to avoid "normalizing" income to the extent that the data thus reflected do not give a true picture of the historical operations of the company.
4. Explanation of items of material significance in appraising the results shown should be reflected in the summary; or reference should be made to such information set forth elsewhere, such as the notes to the financial statements. The footnote disclosure to the summary should be limited to information that is essential to understanding the summary.
5. Earnings and dividends per share should be included for each year in the summary. In view of the importance attached to per share computations in evaluating the fairness of exchange ratios, it is essential that they be made in accordance with generally accepted accounting practices. Accounting Research Bulletin No. 49 provides a working guide of the proper methods to be followed in such computations.[12]

PRO FORMA FINANCIAL STATEMENTS

Although the only specific requirement for pro forma financial statements in proxy statements soliciting shareholder approval

[11] Securities and Exchange Commission, *Accounting Series Release No. 62,* June 27, 1947.
[12] American Institute of Certified Public Accountants, *Accounting Research Bulletin No. 49,* April, 1958.

of a merger or acquisition is contained in instruction 11(b) to the financial statements in Form 10,[13] such statements, as a matter of practice, are generally included in proxy statements. The principal objective of such statements is to present the necessary financial data in the most useful and informative manner to enable the investor to arrive at an intelligent decision regarding the merits of the proposed exchange.

Pro forma financial statements in an exchange offer would ordinarily represent both companies' historical financial statements combined on a retroactive basis to give effect to the proposed terms of the offer. The circumstances governing adjustments made to properly present pro forma statements will vary, but there are guides that should be followed in their preparation.

Pro Forma Statements Should Be Clearly Distinguished from Historical Statements. Statement headings should describe the financial statements as "Pro Forma Balance Sheet" or "Pro Forma Income Statement (or summary of earnings)" and include references to footnotes or comments describing the basis on which such statements are prepared. If the pro forma statements are based principally on historical statements with only a few easily understandable assumptions, it may be sufficient to describe the assumptions in a footnote.

However, if the assumed transactions are numerous or complicated, it is advisable to show by columnar presentation (1) the historical figures for each company, (2) the adjustments arising from the assumed transactions, and (3) the pro forma amounts resulting from such adjustments. It is desirable to have a notation to the pro forma statements to the effect that, "These pro

---

[13] Securities Exchange Act of 1934, Form 10, "Instructions to Financial Statements," as amended to October 25, 1955:

(b) If the registrant by merger, consolidation or otherwise is about to succeed to one or more businesses, there shall be filed for the constituent businesses financial statements, combined if appropriate, which would be required if they were registering securities under the Act. In addition, there shall be filed a balance sheet of the registrant giving effect to the plan of succession. These balance sheets shall be set forth in such form, preferably columnar, as will show in related manner the balance sheets of the constituent businesses, the changes to be effected in the succession and the balance sheet of the registrant after giving effect to the plan of succession. By a footnote or otherwise, a brief explanation of the changes shall be given.

forma statements should be read in conjunction with the other financial statements appearing elsewhere in this Prospectus."

FINANCIAL STATEMENTS THAT GIVE EFFECT TO FORECASTS GENERALLY NOT ACCEPTABLE. Pro forma statements should be based on completed transactions or on proposed transactions expected to occur in the near future. Except for certain real estate companies, financial statements or earnings summaries that give effect to forecasts and projections are not permitted in filings with the Securities and Exchange Commission. Generally, it is also unacceptable to adjust historical statements for estimated reductions in expenses resulting from proposed mergers and acquisitions. This does not preclude giving pro forma effect to a reduction in expenses if the amount can be fairly determined, and *it is clearly evident that the expenses so eliminated will not be replaced by other expenses.*

It should be noted that the 1934 Act regulations specify certain types of information that, if included in a proxy statement, may be misleading, depending upon the particular facts and circumstances. Prominent among these are "predictions as to specific, future market values, earnings, or dividends." [14]

Proposed transactions in pro forma statements should reflect all changed conditions during the period that materially affects the pro forma presentation. It could be misleading to give effect to certain proposed transactions, while at the same time ignoring other conditions affecting the pro forma statements. When, for example, a company proposes to purchase another and intends to revise the operations of the acquired business to such an extent that they will no longer be comparable to those of prior years, the pro forma combination of both companies' past income statements to show the effect on earnings from the business combination may not be appropriate. If the effect of all changed conditions or significance cannot be properly reflected on a pro forma basis, the appropriate course may be to present the historical statements only, together with a footnote describing the changed conditions and explaining the impracticability of determining their effect on the historical statements.

[14] *Ibid.*, Rule X–14A–9, as amended to January 26, 1956.

There are few published rules and decisions of the Securities and Exchange Commission regarding pro forma statements. Rule X–15C1–9 under the 1934 Act states in part:

The term manipulative, deceptive, or other fraudulent device or contrivance . . . is defined to include the use of . . . "[pro forma]" . . . financial statements purporting to give effect to the receipt and application of any part of the proceeds from the sale or exchange of securities unless the assumptions upon which each . . . is based are clearly set forth as part of the caption to each such statement in type at least as large as that used generally in the body of the statement.[15]

The same requirement is contained in Rule 170 under the 1933 Act.[16] Although these rules require that the assumed conditions be set forth in the heading captions, in practice an acceptable alternative is to describe such assumptions in a footnote with reference thereto being made in the statement heading. The types of pro forma financial statements to be included in a proxy will depend largely on the accounting treatment of the transaction.

PRO FORMA STATEMENTS IN A POOLING

The "pooling of interests" concept implies a continuing entity and a continuation of the old basis of accounting. The pro forma financial statements included in a pooling would generally be an arithmetic combination of the income statements and balance sheets of the constituents, after giving effect to (1) any adjustment necessary to place both companies on a uniform accounting basis, and (2) the adjustments required to give effect to the terms of the proposed combination.

EXAMPLE OF PRO FORMA FINANCIAL STATEMENTS IN A POOLING OF INTERESTS. In Chapter 7, an analysis was made of the pro forma adjustments to the stockholders' equity section in a pooling of interests in 1960 of Federal Pacific Electric Co. and Cornell-Dubilier Electric Corp. In this transaction, Federal Pacific made an exchange offer of one share of 5½ per cent convertible preferred stock to stockholders of Cornell-Dubilier for each share of that company's common stock. On the assumption that enough Cornell-Dubilier stockholders would accept the exchange offer so

[15] *Ibid.*, Rule X–15C1–9, as amended to June 28, 1938.
[16] Securities Act of 1933, Rule 170, as amended to October 20, 1956.

that there would not be a significant minority interest remaining, the transaction was accounted for as a pooling of interests.

In addition to the historical financial statements of the respective companies, pro forma financial statements were in the proxy statement (which was required for the authorization of a new class of stock) and also in a prospectus included in a Form S-1 registration statement, which was required because the exchange offer was made directly to the stockholders of Cornell-Dubilier.

The following pro forma summary of combined earnings was included in the Federal Pacific prospectus: [17]

PRO FORMA SUMMARY OF COMBINED EARNINGS

The amounts in the following condensed summary have been obtained from the foregoing statements of earnings by combining for each of the years the amounts of Federal for the year ended June 30 with the respective amounts of Cornell for the year ended September 30. The summary should be read in conjunction with the foregoing statements and with the other financial statements and related notes appearing elsewhere herein.

	1955	1956	1957	1958	1959
Net sales	$68,794,334	$72,363,544	$82,052,609	$81,257,969	$87,454,464
Cost of products sold	52,428,152	55,224,964	62,843,742	61,433,434	67,902,567
Pro forma earnings (excluding special nonrecurring charges of Cornell-Dubilier Electric Corporation) before estimated taxes based on income	5,843,582	6,087,675	6,584,860	5,568,883	2,422,424
Estimated taxes based on income	3,119,000	3,199,000	3,365,000	2,654,000	607,600
Pro forma earnings (excluding special nonrecurring charges of Cornell-Dubilier Electric Corporation)	2,724,582	2,888,675	3,219,860	2,914,883	1,814,824
Less— Dividends on outstanding Preferred stocks	59,396	78,648	169,421	164,387	156,947
Pro forma earnings available for Common Stock before dividends on new 5½% Convertible Preferred Stock	$ 2,665,186	$ 2,810,027	$ 3,050,439	$ 2,750,496	$ 1,657,877
Pro forma earnings per share of Federal based on issuance of 484,590 shares of 5½% Convertible Preferred Stock for common stock of Cornell: Assuming that all of the outstanding Common Stock, Class B, (whether convertible at the time or not) had been converted: Assuming no conversion of Convertible Preferred Stock.	$1.17	$1.22	$1.33	$1.12	$.50
Assuming conversion of all shares of Convertible Preferred Stock into Common Stock of Federal at $28 per share of Common Stock (minimum conversion price)	$1.23	$1.28	$1.37	$1.20	$.67

NOTE:

Reference is made to Note 6 to financial statements of Federal Pacific Electric Company, and Note 5 to financial statements of Cornell-Dubilier Electric Corporation.

[17] Federal Pacific Electric Co., Prospectus, February 18, 1960.

The effect of the tax loss carry forward of Fifty Avenue L, Inc. a subsidiary of Federal, described in Note 6 was to decrease estimated taxes based on income and increase net earnings of that company by approximately $307,000 and $703,000 for the 1958 and 1959 fiscal years, respectively. The above pro forma earnings per common share (assuming conversion of all Common Stock, Class B) for 1958 and 1959, respectively, would have been reduced by the following amounts if the tax loss carry-forward had not been available:

Assuming no conversion of Convertible Preferred Stock......	$.16	$.34
Assuming conversion of all Convertible Preferred Stock......	.13	.28

As of June 30, 1959 Fifty Avenue L, Inc. had net operating loss carry-forward in the amount of approximately $980,000, and as of September 30, 1959 Cornell-Dubilier Electric Corporation had net operating loss carry-forward in the amount of approximately $1,200,000, available under present Federal tax laws for offsetting against future taxable income; the utilization of these amounts will depend on the availability of taxable income in such companies.

The pro forma balance sheet combining the balance sheets of Federal Pacific and Cornell-Dubilier are shown below. It is suggested that reference be made to pages 123 and 124 in Chapter 7 for an understanding of the adjustments made in this pro forma statement, which were somewhat complicated.

FEDERAL PACIFIC ELECTRIC COMPANY AND CONSOLIDATED SUBSIDIARIES
PRO FORMA COMBINED BALANCE SHEET COMBINING THE SEPTEMBER 30, 1959 BALANCE SHEETS OF FEDERAL PACIFIC ELECTRIC COMPANY AND SUBSIDIARIES AND CORNELL-DUBILIER ELECTRIC CORPORATION AND WHOLLY OWNED SUBSIDIARIES

(Not covered by opinion of independent public accountants)

	Federal Pacific Electric Company and subsidiaries	Cornell-Dubilier Electric Corporation and wholly owned subsidiaries	Pro forma adjustments Add (Deduct)	Pro forma combined
ASSETS				
Current Assets:				
Cash	$ 959,985	$ 1,624,535		$ 2,584,520
Receivables, less allowance for doubtful accounts	12,824,962	2,773,714		15,598,676
Inventories	25,265,600	6,420,607		31,686,207
Prepaid expenses	484,888	248,154		733,042
Other current assets		2,394,824(3)		2,394,824
Total Current Assets	39,535,435	13,461,834		52,997,269
Investments and Advances—foreign subsidiaries	699,574			699,574
Investment in Cornell-Dubilier Electric Corporation	637,568		($637,568)(2)	–
Property, Plant and Equipment	18,787,504	6,722,211		25,509,715
Accumulated depreciation	5,516,629	3,847,062		9,363,691
	13,270,875	2,875,149		16,146,024
Other Assets and Deferred Charges	668,269	324,330		992,599
	$54,811,721	$16,661,313		$70,835,466

LIABILITIES

Current Liabilities:

Notes payable to banks	$ 9,168,846	$ 1,800,000	$10,968,846
Accounts payable	6,108,584	867,805	6,976,389
Federal income taxes	1,050,535	66,642	1,117,177
Other current and accrued liabilities..	2,521,118	879,197	3,400,315
Current portion of long-term debt....	1,208,199	200,000	1,408,199
Total Current Liabilities....	20,057,282	3,813,644	23,870,926
Long-Term Debt	9,260,171	2,900,000	12,160,171
Deferred Federal Income Taxes........	347,800		347,800
	29,665,253	6,713,644	36,378,897

INVESTMENT OF SHAREHOLDERS

Capital Stock:

6% prior cumulative preferred stock..	1,805,000			1,805,000
$5.25 cumulative preferred stock, Series A		802,656		802,656
5½% convertible preferred stock......			11,145,570 (1)	11,145,570
Common stock	1,441,463	512,390	{ (484,590)(1) } { (27,800)(2) }	1,441,463
Common stock—Class B	581,040			581,040
Amount in excess of par value of capital stocks	15,854,508	3,499,199	{(10,660,980)(1)} { (189,874)(2) }	8,502,853
Retained earnings	5,486,535	5,257,331	(516,977)(2)	10,226,889
Treasury stock, at cost: Common stock—Class B	(22,078)			(22,078)
$5.25 cumulative preferred stock, Series A		(26,824)		(26,824)
Common stock		(97,083)	97,083 (2)	–
	25,146,468	9,947,669		34,456,569
	$54,811,721	$16,661,313		$70,835,466

FEDERAL PACIFIC ELECTRIC COMPANY AND SUBSIDIARIES
NOTES TO PRO FORMA COMBINED BALANCE SHEET

The foregoing pro forma combined balance sheet, which combines the September 30, 1959 consolidated balance sheets of Federal Pacific Electric Company and Subsidiaries and of Cornell-Dubilier Electric Corporation and Wholly-Owned Subsidiaries, each of which appears elsewhere herein, should be read in conjunction with such balance sheets and the related notes to financial statements. The pro forma combined balance sheet gives effect to the acquisition of all of the outstanding common stock of Cornell-Dubilier Electric Corporation in exchange for 5½% convertible preferred stock of Federal Pacific Electric Company and presents the combined financial position as if such acquisition had been consummated at September 30, 1959. For the purposes of this pro forma balance sheet the transaction has been accounted for as a "pooling of interests" on the assumption that the stockholders of Cornell-Dubilier Electric Corporation not accepting the exchange offer described under "Exchange Offer" will not constitute a significant minority interest. The transactions to which effect has been given are:

(1) The issuance on a share-for-share basis of 5½% convertible preferred stock of Federal for all of the issued shares of common stock, par value $1 each, of Cornell exclusive of 5,000 shares held in treasury and 22,800 shares previously acquired for cash. The 5½% convertible preferred

stock will have a par value of $23. In the pro forma combined balance sheet, the excess of the aggregate par value of $22 over the par value of Cornell common stock has been charged to "Amount in excess of par value of capital stocks." See "Terms of Convertible Preferred Stock" elsewhere herein for further information with respect to the 5½% convertible preferred stock.

(2) The elimination of Federal's investment in 22,800 shares and the cost of Cornell's acquisition of 5,000 shares of common stock of Cornell. The par value thereof has been charged to "Common stock," the portion of Cornell's "Amount in excess of par value of capital stocks" attributable to such shares has been charged to such account and the balance of cost has been charged to "Retained earnings."

(3) At September 30, 1959 Cornell was in process of negotiating the sale of its Norwood plant and a building in Worcester for which it expects to realize $1,541,500 after expenses of sale. These transactions have not been reflected in the accompanying financial statements and the cost of the two properties less depreciation and the mortgage payable on one of the properties has been included in other current assets in the net amount of $694,824. The net gain after applicable Federal income tax on these properties, which are under leaseback agreements, will be amortized against rental payments over the terms of the leases.

Reference is made to "Dividend and Other Restrictions" under "Capital Stock of Federal" for a description of the effects of the acquisition on restrictions on the combined retained earnings.

PRO FORMA FINANCIAL STATEMENTS IN A PURCHASE

The "purchase" concept gives rise to a new basis of accountability; and, accordingly, the pro forma financial statements included in a purchase would be (1) a combined balance sheet of the two entities and (2) a combined income statement of the two entities, generally for the latest full fiscal year only, each statement being adjusted to give effect to any changed conditions arising from the transaction.

A significant difference in the pro forma financial statements used in a purchase as opposed to those in a "pooling of interests" is that in a purchase situation the combined income statement ordinarily would be limited to the latest full year only, while a pooling would include a combined income statement for the full period reported on (generally five years in an S.E.C. filing).

The primary reasons for limiting the pro forma income statement to one year in purchases are:

1. It would be impossible to determine what the purchase or terms of the exchange offer would have been five years ago. This pre-

cludes a determination of the cost of the capital that would have been employed in the acquisition that, if disregarded, results in an overstatement of net income to the extent of the interest cost of the capital.

2. There could be many other areas where the results of operations of the business would be affected by reason of the acquisition, which could not be given retroactive effect to in a combined statement.

However, where a business combination involves only the exchange of equity securities but is accounted for as a "purchase," the Securities and Exchange Commission will generally request that a combined pro forma summary of earnings for the customary five-year period be provided in the proxy or registration statement.

EXAMPLE OF PRO FORMA FINANCIAL STATEMENTS IN A PURCHASE. In November, 1960, Kayser-Roth Corp., through one of its subsidiaries, offered to the shareholders of A. Stein & Co. $34.375 principal amount of Kayser's 5½ per cent convertible subordinated debentures in exchange for each share of common stock of Stein.

The transaction apparently was accounted for as a purchase because:

1. The shareholders of A. Stein & Co. were without voting rights in the combined entity.
2. In the event the debenture holders chose not to convert their bonds into common stock, a significant amount of cash would be withdrawn from the business upon payment.

The following pro forma financial statements of the combined companies, which were in addition to their respective historical statements, were included in the Kayser-Roth prospectus.[18]

PRO FORMA STATEMENT OF COMBINED EARNINGS
For The Year Ended June 30, 1960

The following statement has been prepared by combining the audited statement of consolidated earnings of Kayser-Roth Corporation and consolidated subsidiaries and the unaudited statement of consolidated earnings of A. Stein & Company and consolidated subsidiaries for the year ended June 30, 1960, and by giving effect to $425,964 of annual interest (net of income taxes) applicable

[18] Kayser-Roth Corp., Prospectus, October 13, 1960.

to the Debentures. The pro forma statement does not purport to indicate the results of the future integrated operations.

Revenues:

Net sales	$137,931,165
Royalties	1,569,666
Sundry	621,959
	$140,122,790

Costs and expenses:

Cost of products sold	$ 95,891,014
Selling, shipping, administrative and general expenses	32,254,629
Interest	1,867,823
Minority interest in net earnings of subsidiaries	40,300
Sundry	334,747
	$130,388,513
Earnings before taxes on income	$ 9,734,277

Provision for taxes on income—estimated:

United States	$ 4,178,470
Canada	223,241
	$ 4,401,711
Net earnings	$ 5,332,566
Gain on sales of property (less applicable taxes thereon)	932,907
Net earnings and gain on sales of property	$ 6,265,473
Preferred dividend requirement	375,000
Earnings and gain on sales of property applicable to Common Stock	$ 5,890,473

See Note (2) to "Pro Forma Combined Statement of Financial Position" regarding excess of cost of investment in Stein over its net asets.

PRO FORMA COMBINED STATEMENT OF FINANCIAL POSITION

June 30, 1960

	Kayser-Roth Corporation and Consolidated Subsidiaries	A. Stein & Company and Consolidated Subsidiaries	Pro Forma Adjustments	Pro Forma Combined Statement of Financial Position
ASSETS				
Current assets:				
Cash	$ 4,989,583	$ 936,154		$ 5,925,737
Marketable securities	–	1,282,128		1,282,128
Notes and accounts receivable—net..	15,676,557	2,509,874		18,186,431
Inventories	33,507,468	4,309,810		37,817,278
Prepaid expenses	1,436,380	–		1,436,380
Total current assets	$55,609,988	$ 9,037,966		$64,647,954
Investments	264,388	1,996,814		2,261,202
Property, plant, and equipment—net..	10,378,728	1,242,172		11,620,900
Other assets and deferred charges.....	2,993,743	706,608		3,700,351
Patents, trademarks and good will...	892,813	1		892,814
Excess of cost of investment in Stein over its net assets			$ 4,862,414	4,862,414
	$70,139,660	$12,983,561	$ 4,862,414	$87,985,635

LIABILITIES

Current liabilities:

Notes payable to banks	$ 5,000,000	$ -		$ 5,000,000
Accounts payable and accrued expenses	9,561,839	1,095,698		10,657,537
Taxes on income	2,541,502	506,352		3,047,854
Dividends payable	365,234	-		365,234
Long-term debt maturing within one year	2,687,134	-		2,687,134
Total current liabilities....	$20,155,709	$ 1,602,050		$21,757,759
Long-term debt	12,926,382	-	$16,135,000	29,061,382
Other liabilities	-	81,160		81,160
Reserve for unrealized gain on foreign exchange	-	27,765		27,765
Minority interest in subsidiaries......	627,668	-		627,668

Shareholders' equity:

Capital stock:

$1 Convertible Preferred Stock, without par value—authorized and issued 375,000 shares........	5,875,000	-		5,875,000
Common Stock, par value $1 per share—authorized 7,500,000 shares (2,289,430 shares reserved for issuance under terms of the debentures, convertible preferred stock and stock options); issued 2,-985,000 shares	2,985,000	-		2,985,000
Common stock, no par value......		1,800,000	(1,800,000)	-
Capital surplus	7,406,945	164,630	(164,630)	7,406,945
Retained earnings	21,580,326	9,384,107	(9,384,107)	21,580,326
	$37,847,271	$11,348,737	($11,348,737)	$37,847,271
Less Common Stock in treasury—at cost	1,417,370	76,151	(76,151)	1,417,370
Total shareholders' equity	$36,429,901	$11,272,586	($11,272,586)	$36,429,901
	$70,139,660	$12,983,561	$ 4,862,414	$87,985,635

(1) The pro forma combined statement of financial position has been prepared by combining the audited statement of consolidated financial position of Kayser-Roth Corporation and consolidated subsidiaries and the unaudited consolidated balance sheet of A. Stein & Company and consolidated subsidiaries at June 30, 1960, each of which appears elsewhere herein, and gives effect to the proposed issuance of the entire authorized principal amount of the 5½% Convertible Subordinated Debentures in exchange for all the outstanding shares of Stein.

(2) The Corporation does not have sufficient information at the present time to make an allocation to the accounts of Stein of the excess of the principal amount of Debentures (as stipulated in Agreement dated July 14, 1960, as amended) over Stein's net assets. To the extent that the excess is allocated (a) to property, plant, equipment and patents it will be written off over the remaining lives of such assets, and the effect upon net earnings per share of Common Stock will not be significant and (b) to good will it may not be amortized, since it is the Corporation's present policy not to amortize good will.

(3) This statement should be read in conjunction with the respective financial statements and related notes of Kayser-Roth and Stein.

The only adjustment given effect to in the pro forma statement of combined earnings was the additional interest expense that would be incurred, net of income taxes, on the assumption that all the debentures would be issued in the exchange offer. As indicated in Note 2 to the pro forma statement of financial position, Kayser did not have sufficient information at the time of filing to allocate the excess of the cost of the investment in Stein over the net assets acquired. If this information had been available, a pro forma adjustment would have been made for the amount of increased depreciation arising from a stepup in the carrying value of depreciable assets. There would be no pro forma adjustment of any amount allocated to goodwill since the company's stated policy is not to amortize goodwill.

COMPARATIVE PER SHARE DATA

Although not specifically required in the proxy rules, the Commission generally requires the inclusion, in a proxy statement soliciting approval of a business combination, of comparative per share data for earnings, net assets, and occasionally the dividends paid, for both parties to the proposed combination. These data, customarily presented in tabular form, would, depending upon circumstances, consist of all or part of the following:

A. *Earnings.*
  1. The historical earnings per share for each company for each of the five years included in the related summary of earnings and interim periods, if any, based on the number of shares outstanding during the respective periods.
  2. The pro forma earnings per share for the company to be acquired for each of the five years included in the related summary of earnings and interim periods, if any, based on the number of shares to be issued in the exchange offer.
  3. The pro forma combined earnings per share as follows:
     a) Pooling of interests—for each of the five years included in the pro forma summary of earnings, after giving retroactive effect to the number of shares to be issued upon consummation of the proposed exchange offer.
     b) Purchase—for the latest full fiscal year, based on the number of shares to be outstanding after consummation of the proposed exchange offer.

B. *Net Assets.*
  1. The historical net asset value per share for each company at the date of the latest balance sheet included in the proxy statement.
  2. The pro forma net asset value per share of the company to be acquired, based on the number of shares to be issued in the exchange offer.

3. The pro forma combined net asset value per share, based on the number of shares to be outstanding after the proposed exchange.

C. *Dividends.*

1. The dividends paid or accrued per share for each company for the latest full fiscal year, based on the number of shares outstanding during the respective periods.
2. The pro forma dividends paid or accrued per share for the company to be acquired, based on the number of shares to be issued in the exchange offer. If the stock to be issued in the exchange bears a fixed dividend rate, the per share amount thereof would ordinarily be included in lieu of pro forma per share figures.

Although the foregoing information in one form or another is frequently included in proxy statements relating to merger or acquisition proposals, the Commission's position in this regard is flexible; and if such information may be misleading or is not of material signficance for the exercise of prudent judgment by the investor, it will not be required.

Comparative Data in a Pooling of Interests. In 1961, the Burry Biscuit Corp. (whose capital stock was listed on the American Stock Exchange) solicited the approval of its shareholders for the acquisition of all the assets, subject to the liabilities, of Cal Ray Bakeries, Inc. As consideration for the net assets of Cal Ray, Burry proposed to issue not more than 187,497 shares of common stock to Cal Ray on the basis of one share of Burry for each two shares of Cal Ray. The following presentation of comparative data was included in the Burry proxy statement: [19]

COMPARATIVE DATA

Net Asset Values:

Based upon its Statement of Consolidated Financial Position at February 25, 1961, the net asset value per share of common stock of Cal Ray amounted to $3.19. If at that date Cal Ray's capitalization consisted of only 175,563 shares of common stock (the effect of the proposed transaction of exchanging one share of Burry for two shares of Cal Ray) the net asset value per share of common stock of Cal Ray would have been $6.38. Prior to the consummation of the proposed transaction, the net asset value of a share of Burry common stock, based upon its Consolidated Statement of Financial Position at March

---

[19] Burry Biscuit Corp., Proxy Statement, May 17, 1961.

18, 1961 was $5.18. Based on the Pro Forma Combined Statement of Financial Position (giving effect to the consummation of the acquisition of Cal Ray on the basis of one share of Burry for each two shares of Cal Ray) the net asset value per share would have been $5.44.

Net Income per Share:

	Years ended October 31,					Twenty-weeks ended	
						March 19, 1960	March 18, 1961
	1956	1957	1958	1959	1960		
Based on the Summary of Consolidated Earnings of Burry	$ .57	$ .41	$ .58	$ .66	$1.10	$ .35	$ .37

	Years ended					Forty-eight weeks ended	
	March 31, 1956	March 31, 1957	March 31, 1958	March 28, 1959	March 26, 1960	February 27, 1960	February 25, 1961
Based on the Summary of Consolidated Earnings of Cal Ray	$ .58	$ .78	$ .59	$ .49	$ .51	$ .49	$ .65
Based on the Summary of Consolidated Earnings of Cal Ray on the basis of 175,563 shares of Burry to be issued for 351,127 shares of Cal Ray	1.16	1.56	1.18	.98	1.02	.98	1.30

	Years ended October 31,					Interim Period	
	1956	1957	1958	1959	1960	1960	1961
Based on the Pro Forma Summary of Combined Earnings	$ .67	$ .54	$ .68	$ .73	$1.15	$ .36	$ .37

Comparative Data in a Purchase. In 1962, the Kimberly-Clark Corp. (whose capital stock was listed on the New York Stock Exchange) solicited the approval of its shareholders for the acquisition of the remaining 59.2 per cent of the common stock of the Coosa River Newsprint Co. Under the terms of the merger agreement, Kimberly proposed to issue 1.36 shares of its common stock in exchange for each share of common stock of Coosa, exclusive of those Coosa shares already owned by Kimberly. The following presentation of comparative data was included in the Kimberly-Clark proxy statement: [20]

COMPARATIVE FINANCIAL INFORMATION

Net Earnings Per Share of Common Stock
Kimberly-Clark Corporation for the twelve months ended January 31, 1962:
Earnings before inclusion of equity in undistributed net earnings of Coosa River Newsprint Company .... $ 3.14

[20] Kimberly-Clark Corp., Proxy Statement, April 16, 1962.

Earnings after inclusion of equity in undistributed net earnings of
  Coosa River Newsprint Company 3.17
Coosa River Newsprint Company net earnings for the year ended De-
  cember 31, 1961 .... 4.15
Net earnings per one share of the combined companies 3.16
Net earnings per 1.36 shares of the combined companies 4.30

Dividends Per Share of Common Stock
  Kimberly-Clark Corporation for the twelve months ended January 31,
    1962 .... 1.76
  Coosa River Newsprint Company for the year ended December 31, 1961:
    Actual 2.75
    Pro forma—equivalent to 1.36 times the K-C dividends 2.39

Book Value Per Share of Common Stock
  Kimberly-Clark Corporation:
    Actual at January 31, 1962 * 31.79
    Pro forma combined 34.01
  Coosa River Newsprint Company:
    Actual at December 31, 1962 .... 91.41
    Pro forma—equivalent to 1.36 times K-C pro forma combined 46.25

* Adjusted to include 193,273 shares for stock dividend payable to stockholders
of record March 2, 1962.

FINANCIAL STATEMENTS IN FORM S–1

The financial statements, summary of earnings, data relating
to per share earnings, dividends, and net assets previously described are requirements for a Form S–1 registration statement.
As mentioned, the instructions to the financial statements for a
Form S–1 registration statement have been reproduced as Appendix G.

In addition, there are various supporting schedules required
that are not included in the prospectus or in a proxy statement.
These are required to be certified whenever the balance sheet or
statements of income to which they relate are certified. The
schedules are described in Regulation S–X, numbered from I to
XVII, although it would be rare to find a case where all would
be applicable. A brief description of the schedules is included as
Appendix I. Some or all of these schedules may be omitted in
any case where the required information is furnished in the financial statements or the notes thereto.

**Form S–1 Financial Statement Requirements Relating to Business
Combinations.** The instructions to financial statements in the form
require comprehensive financial information for both corporate

entities in an exchange offer, as indicated in the following abstracts:

Succession to Other Business:

11.(b) If the registrant by merger, consolidation or otherwise is about to succeed to one or more businesses, there shall be filed for the constituent businesses financial statements, combined if appropriate, which would be required if they were registering securities under the Act. In addition, there shall be filed a balance sheet of the registrant giving effect to the plan of succession. These balance sheets shall be set forth in such form, preferably columnar, as will show in related manner the balance sheets of the constituent businesses, the changes to be effected in the succession and the balance sheet of the registrant after giving effect to the plan of succession. By a footnote or otherwise, a brief explanation of the changes shall be given.

11.(c) This instruction shall not apply with respect to . . . any acquisition of a business by purchase.

Acquisition of Other Businesses:

12.(a) There shall be filed for any business directly or indirectly acquired by the registrant after the date of the latest balance sheet filed pursuant to Part A or B above and for any business to be directly or indirectly acquired by the registrant, the financial statements which would be required if such business were a registrant.

12.(b) The acquisition of securities shall be deemed to be the acquisition of a business if such securities give control of the business or combined with securities already held give such control. In addition, the acquisition of securities which will extend the registrant's control of a business shall be deemed the acquisition of the business if any of the securities being registered hereunder are to be offered in exchange for the securities acquired.[21]

FINANCIAL STATEMENTS IN FORM 8–K

The only financial statements required in Form 8–K are those of businesses acquired by the issuer, as described in item 2 of the form and are briefly as follows: [22]

1. A balance sheet reasonably close to the date of acquisition. If not certified, a certified balance sheet is required at the close of the preceding fiscal year.
2. A statement of income for each of the last three full fiscal years and for the period, if any, between the close of the latest fiscal year and the date of the latest balance sheet filed. The statements for only the last three full fiscal years need be certified.

---

[21] Securities Act of 1933, Form S–1, "Instructions as to Financial Statements," 11(b), 11(c), 12(a), 12(b).

[22] Securities Exchange Act of 1934, Form 8–K, as amended to August 16, 1958.

3. Individual, consolidated, or group financial statements are required for the company and its subsidiaries on the same basis as in an original application (Form 10) or annual report (Form 10–K) filed under the 1934 Act.

Because of the nature of Form 8–K and the problems frequently encountered in obtaining accurate financial information on many acquired businesses, the Commission has frequently modified its requirements, pursuant to item 4 of the form, as to financial statements of the business acquired.

4. Filing of other statements in certain cases:

The Commission may, upon the informal written request of the registrant and where consistent with the protection of investors, permit the omission of one or more of the statements herein required or the filing in substitution therefor of appropriate statements of comparable character. The Commission may also by informal written notice require the filing of other statements in addition to, or in substitution for, the statements herein required in any case where such statements are necessary or appropriate for an adequate presentation of the financial condition of any person for which financial statements are required, or whose statements are otherwise necessary for the protection of investors.[23]

The provisions of this item, in effect, allow the Commission considerable discretion in determining what financial statements should be included in an 8–K filing. In the event an unreasonable amount of difficulty or expense would result from meeting the financial statement requirements of Form 8–K, a prefiling conference with the accounting staff of the Commission may result in a considerable reduction in the information requested.

[23] *Ibid.*

Chapter 12

STOCK EXCHANGE LISTING REQUIREMENTS

As mentioned in Chapter 10, companies whose securities are listed on a national securities exchange are subject not only to the filing and reporting requirements of the Securities and Exchange Commission, but also to those of the exchange upon which they are listed. Although some of the exchanges had requirements for financial reporting prior to the passage of the federal securities laws, these were not too comprehensive until after the enactment of the Securities Exchange Act of 1934, which brought the exchanges under the authority of the Commission. The major exchanges have continued to amend their requirements over the years with the view toward improving the standards of financial reporting and disclosure and the timeliness of the publication of data.

NATIONAL SECURITIES EXCHANGES

At the present time, the following exchanges are registered under the 1934 Act as national securities exchanges: [1]

American Stock Exchange	New York Stock Exchange
Boston Stock Exchange	Pacific Coast Stock Exchange
Chicago Board of Trade	Philadelphia-Baltimore Stock Exchange
Cincinnati Stock Exchange	Pittsburgh Stock Exchange
Detroit Stock Exchange	Salt Lake Stock Exchange
Midwest Stock Exchange	San Francisco Mining Exchange
National Stock Exchange	Spokane Stock Exchange

[1] A "national securities exchange" is defined in Sections 5 and 6 of the Securities Exchange Act of 1934 as an exchange registered with the Commission.

In addition, there are the following four exchanges exempted from registration, pursuant to Section 5 of the Act: [2]

Colorado Springs Stock Exchange   Richmond Stock Exchange
Honolulu Stock Exchange   Wheeling Stock Exchange

However, based on figures for 1960, the New York Stock Exchange accounted for 68.48 per cent and the American Stock Exchange 22.27 per cent of the total trading volume of all national exchanges.[3] Accordingly, the following discussion will be confined to the requirements of these two principal securities exchanges.

CORRELATION OF S.E.C. AND LISTING REQUIREMENTS

Before a security is traded on a national securities exchange, it must be registered for trading under the Securities Exchange Act of 1934.[4] The only exceptions to this are for "exempt" [5] securities (as defined in the Act), securities that have unlisted trading privileges, and certain securities traded temporarily on a "when-issued" basis.[6] Registration is accomplished by filing a listing application with the exchange and at the same time filing a registration statement on the prescribed form (generally Form 10 of the 1934 Act) with the Securities and Exchange Commission. The registration statement will become effective and the securities listed either thirty days after the exchange has notified the Commission that the listing application has been approved "or within such shorter period of time as the Commission may determine." [7] In practice, the Commission has granted acceleration in most cases, in accordance with their policy to "cooperate with registrants and with the exchanges by acting upon requests for acceleration as promptly as possible." [8]

---

[2] Section 5 of the Securities Exchange Act of 1934 provides that the Commission may exempt an exchange from registration if "by reason of the limited volume of transactions effected on such exchange, it is not practicable and not necessary or appropriate in the public interest or for the protection of investors to require such protection."

[3] Securities and Exchange Commission, 27th Annual Report, 1961.

[4] Securities Exchange Act of 1934, Sec. 12(a).

[5] *Ibid.*, Sec. 3 (a)(12).

[6] *Ibid.*, Rule X–12A–5.

[7] *Ibid.*, Sec. 12(d).

[8] *Ibid.*, Release No. 3085.

Incorporation by Reference. As permitted by Rule X–12B–35 of the Securities Exchange Act of 1934, an issuer may use a registration statement that has been effective for not more than one year under the 1933 Act and incorporated as part of the application. Any data required in the application that is not contained in the prospectus would then be attached to the prospectus as cover pages.

Effective in 1954, the Commission adopted rules that permitted all applications for registration under the 1934 Act to ". . . apply for registration of the entire class of such security." [9] Prior to that date, an issuer could only register the number of shares actually issued at the date of the application. This meant filing a registration statement under the 1934 Act each time additional securities were listed.

The 1954 change, however, applied only to the registration requirements under the 1934 Act. Listing applications with the exchanges still apply only to the number of shares of an issuer that are presently outstanding, or reserved for a specific corporate purpose. The policy of the New York Stock Exchange in this regard is set forth in their company manual as follows:

The Exchange will authorize listing of unissued securities only if such securities have been duly authorized to be issued for a specific purpose which can be adequately described, with its related terms and conditions, in the listing application.

Such listing authorization is effective only if the securities are issued for the purpose, and under the terms and conditions, specified in the listing application. If, after authorization of listing by the Exchange, the company desires to make a change in the specified purpose of issuance, or in the specified terms and conditions of issuance, there may be required (depending upon the circumstances), a further listing application, or a supplement to the prior application.[10]

As explained, the initial registration of securities with the Securities and Exchange Commission under the 1934 Act effectively registers the entire class of securities, including any shares unissued at that time. However, when listing any new class of securities, it is necessary to register them with the Commission. To facilitate this procedure, the Commission has adopted Form 8–A, a simplified registration form for use by issuers wishing to

[9] *Ibid.*, Rule X–12D1–1.
[10] *New York Stock Exchange Company Manual*, June 26, 1958, p. B–59.

register an additional class or series of securities on a national exchange. Most of the required information may be incorporated by reference to a prospectus, proxy statement, or current report previously filed with the Commission.

LISTING APPLICATION

The New York Stock Exchange has two kinds of listing applications (as does the American Stock Exchange): one for original listing and another for listing additional securities. These are designed to meet the following basic disclosure objectives.

1. Original listing application
   a) To provide the stock exchange with the necessary information for determining the suitability of the securities for trading on the exchange
   b) To provide the investing public with the necessary information for making an intelligent decision on the investment merits of the security
2. Subsequent listing application
   a) To provide the stock exchange with full information regarding the purpose for which the securities are to be issued and the consideration to be received therefor
   b) To bring up-to-date certain significant information to the extent this has not been done in preceding applications [11]

Companies entering into business combinations will occasionally have an original listing of the securities of the combined enterprise on a securities exchange shortly after a merger or consolidation, particularly where neither company prior to the combination was of sufficient size by itself to meet the necessary listing qualifications. However, since the vast majority of acquisitions and mergers involving stock exchange listings are by companies who already have their shares listed, the requirements discussed in this chapter will be those relating to applications for listing additional amounts of securities. The original listing qualifications of the New York and American Stock Exchanges are set forth as Appendixes K and L.

Listing Agreements. Companies making application for the listing of their securities on either the New York or American Ex-

[11] *Ibid.*, April 3, 1959, p. B–5.

change, as a regular part of the listing procedure, enter into a listing agreement with the exchange through which they commit themselves to a code of performance, regarding the matters dealt with by the agreement. As the public interest in corporate affairs has become more clearly defined, the listing agreement has expanded in scope.

Basic Objectives of Current Form of Agreement. The *New York Stock Exchange Company Manual* defines the basic objectives that the listing agreement attempts to achieve, as follows:

1. Timely disclosure, to the public and to the exchange, of information which may affect security values or influence investment decisions, and in which stockholders, the public and the exchange have a warrantable interest;
2. Frequent, regular and timely publication of financial reports prepared in accordance with accepted accounting practice, and in adequate detail;
3. Providing the exchange with timely information to enable it to perform, efficiently and expeditiously, its function of maintaining an orderly market for the company's securities and to enable it to maintain its necessary records;
4. Preclusion of certain practices not generally considered sound;
5. Allowing the exchange opportunity to make representations as to certain matters before they become accomplished facts.[12]

Thus, it is clear that the overriding objective of the listing agreement is the timely disclosure of information. The American Stock Exchange also has similar basic objectives.

UNLISTED TRADING ON AMERICAN EXCHANGE

In addition to the trading in listed securities on the American Stock Exchange, at June 30, 1961, there were 179 stock issues with unlisted trading privileges. By comparison, prior to the passage of the Securities Acts, there were over 1,800 such issues trading on that exchange. Although given serious consideration in 1934, the S.E.C. did not terminate unlisted trading entirely for fear that it would drive most of the issues into the over-the-counter market and thereby damage the securities markets and investors without providing any protection to the latter. Instead,

[12] *Ibid.*, December 1, 1959, pp. A–19 to A–20.

the Commission was empowered to continue unlisted trading in the following circumstances:

1. Securities that were admitted to unlisted trading before March 1, 1934
2. Securities listed and registered on another national securities exchange
3. Securities for which the provisions of Sections 13, 14, and 16 of the Exchange Act already have application

PREDISCLOSURE

The *New York Stock Exchange Company Manual* contains the following statement regarding predisclosure handling of corporate matters:

Unusual market activity in a security accompanied by a substantial price change has on occasion occurred shortly before the announcement of an important corporate action or development. Such incidents are extremely embarrassing and damaging to both the company and the Exchange since the public may quickly conclude that someone acted on the basis of "inside" information.

Acquisitions, mergers, stock splits, changes in dividend rates or earnings, new contracts, products or discoveries are the type of development most likely to be involved. Frequently these matters require discussion and study by corporate officials before final decisions can be made. The extreme care which must be used in keeping such studies and discussions on a confidential basis is evident. The market action of a company's securities should be closely watched at a time when consideration is being given to such matters, so that if the occasion should arise the company would be prepared to make a public announcement of the matter under consideration.

There have been instances in the past where it became necessary for a company to make such a public announcement of a matter it was preparing for presentation to its Board of Directors. Obviously, such an action places the Board, which must exercise judgment on the proposal, in an embarrassing and undesirable position.[13]

NOTICES TO EXCHANGES

Certain of the events that, under listing agreements, require notice to the exchanges also require the filing of a Form 8–K report with the Securities and Exchange Commission, a copy of which is filed with the stock exchange. Since the 8–K is not filed until the month after the event and the exchange requires prompt notice, the filing of an 8–K does not constitute suitable notice to the exchange. The New York Stock Exchange has com-

[13] *Ibid.,* February 18, 1962, p. A-21.

piled a list of corporate events not dealt with in the listing agreement that require direct notice to the exchange.[14]

NEW YORK STOCK EXCHANGE

Applications for Listing of Additional Securities. The New York Stock Exchange requires a company, already having securities listed on the exchange, to file a listing application subsequent to original listing in the event:

1. The company proposes to issue an additional amount of a listed class, issue, or series.
2. The company desires listing of a class, issue, or series different from the securities already listed.
3. The company proposes to make a change in a listed class, issue, or series, which in effect creates a new security, or which alters any of its rights, preferences, privileges, or terms.
4. The company desires to have a previously granted listing authorization changed.[15]

Companies creating a new class of security, such as preferred stock, for issuance in a business combination could list the new class merely by filing a subsequent listing application with the exchange. As indicated, a simplified registration, Form 8–A, would also have to be filed with the Securities and Exchange Commission in such cases.

MINIMUM VOTING RIGHTS REQUIRED FOR LISTING. If a company is considering the creation of a new class of securities for issuance in a business combination, the requirements of the New York and American Stock Exchanges regarding stockholder voting rights should be considered carefully. Generally, neither exchange will extend listing privileges to a non-voting stock that is, in effect, a common stock, or to a preferred stock that does not have certain minimum voting rights.[16]

The exchange recommends that where there is any doubt as to the eligibility of a security for listing, the necessary data be presented informally for confidential study by the exchange, prior to the preparation of a complete formal application.

[14] *Ibid.,* "Summary List of Events Requiring Notice to Exchange," February 18, 1962, pp. A–91 to A–104.
[15] *Ibid.,* February 1, 1954, p. B–58.
[16] *Ibid.,* October 19, 1961, pp. A–280 to A–282.

In certain instances involving the issuance of additional securities, the exchange feels that stockholder approval is essential and requires it to be secured through the solicitation of proxies pursuant to Regulation X–14 of the Securities Exchange Act of 1934 as a condition of the listing.[17]

Situations Requiring Solicitation of Proxies. The situations requiring solicitation of proxies are as follows:

1. Granting of options to or providing special remuneration plans for directors, officers, or key employees
2. The acquisition of a company or property in which directors, officers, or substantial security holders have an interest
3. Acquisition of a company or property where:
   a) The amount of stock to be so issued represents an increase in outstanding shares at 20 per cent or more, or
   b) The combined value of stock (including securities convertible into common stock) and all other consideration approximates 20 per cent or more of the market value of the outstanding common stock
4. Actions resulting in a change in the control of the company

In any proposed listing involving a business combination, the exchange does not approve of a transaction that would have the effect of circumventing its standards for original listing and result in a so-called "backdoor listing." By this is meant that an unlisted company that proposes to combine with, and into, a listed company under circumstances that, in the opinion of the exchange, constitute an acquisition of a listed company by an unlisted company, the resulting company must meet the standards for original listing. If the resulting company would not qualify for original listing, the exchange will ordinarily refuse to list the additional shares for that purpose.[18]

In deciding whether or not a proposed transaction constitutes a "backdoor listing," the exchange gives consideration to all relevant factors, including changes in ownership of the listed company, changes in management, whether the size of the company being acquired is larger than the listed company, and if the two businesses are related on a horizontal or a vertical basis. All

---

[17] *Ibid.*, p. A–284.
[18] *Ibid.*, p. B–11.

circumstances will be considered collectively and weight given to compensating factors.[19] As a precautionary measure, it is recommended that any plan of this nature be submitted for an informal opinion prior to filing an application, particularly where the shareholders of the listed company emerge with less than 50 per cent of the voting power of the combined enterprise.

Subsequent Listing Applications. Basically, subsequent (additional) listing applications are designed to provide the exchange and the investor with pertinent information regarding the proposed use of the securities and to update information previously filed.

To allow time for preliminary examination and revision, four draft copies of the application should be submitted to the Department of Stock List at least two weeks in advance of the date on which it is desired to have the application acted upon.

Final approval of the listing application rests with the Board of Governors of the exchange, and action is usually taken as soon as practicable after all the information and other requirements are complied with. As soon as the listing has been authorized, the exchange distributes copies of the final listing application to all member firms and to all others requesting a copy.

Accordingly, if a company has followed the practice of disclosing to the public through its annual reports to stockholders, or otherwise, the data required in the application, a simplified form [20] may generally be used with only the following information:

1. Heading
2. Description of transaction
3. Recent developments
4. Authority for issuance
5. Opinion of counsel

If a company has not met the disclosure requirements of the listing application on a continuing basis, the type of information needed in a subsequent listing application would be generally the same as in the company's original listing application.

[19] *Ibid.*
[20] *Ibid.*, p. B–61.

Outline of Information To Be Included in a Subsequent Stock Listing Application. An indication of the scope of the information required in the application may be derived from the following items included in the directions:

1. Heading
2. Description of transaction
3. Recent developments
4. Authority for issuance
5. Business
6. Property description
7. Affiliated companies
8. Management
9. Employees—labor relations
10. Stockholder relations
11. Dividend record
12. Changes in capitalization
13. Options, warrants, conversion rights, etc.
14. Funded debt
15. Stock provisions
16. Litigation
17. Business, financial, and accounting policies
18. Financial statements
19. Opinion of counsel
20. General information

Although the scope of the indicated information required is considerable, because this information is required only for the period since the company's last listing application, and in view of the high standards of corporate disclosure currently being practiced, relatively little of this information is needed in the subsequent listing application.

USE OF PROSPECTUSES AND PROXY STATEMENTS IN SUBSEQUENT LISTING APPLICATIONS. If the securities being listed are to be issued in connection with a transaction that was fully described in a prospectus under the Securities Act of 1933 or a proxy statement under Regulation X–14 of the Securities Exchange Act of 1934, either of such documents may be used as a part of the listing application. Any additional data required by the application would be furnished with either document.

Description of Transaction. Since the subsequent listing application is designed to provide the exchange and the investor with information regarding the proposed use of the securities, in a business combination, certain of the instructions included under "Description of Transaction" are of particular interest:

> If the securities are to be issued in connection with the acquisition of a controlling interest in, or a major part of the business and assets of, another company, describe briefly the history and business of such other company. Appropriate financial statements, usually the most recent annual financial statements, supplemented by the latest available interim earnings statement, should be included. A recent balance sheet and/or pro forma or combined statements may be considered appropriate in some circumstances. Independently audited annual statements are preferred but where these are not available company statements may be accepted. Interim statements would usually be unaudited company statements. The foregoing data should be appended as an exhibit and reference made to it under the caption "Description of Transaction."
>
> If the securities are to be issued for property, securities, or for any form of consideration other than cash, describe such properties, securities or consideration in detail sufficient to indicate the relative values of the securities to be issued and the consideration to be received. A statement should be made as to why the company regards the acquisition as a favorable one from the standpoint of the company. Indicate whether or not any officer, director or principal stockholder of the company (or any of its affiliates) has any direct or indirect beneficial interest in the property, securities, or other consideration to be received and, if such interest does exist, describe it.
>
> Describe the accounting treatment to be accorded the transaction on the books of the company. State the policy to be followed with respect to amortization whenever intangible assets are acquired or created. State the treatment to be given in consolidation where it differs from the method followed in recording the transactions on the books. Where other than routine transactions such as issue of securities for cash, stock dividends, stock splits, etc., are involved, the accounting treatment should be reviewed with the company's independent accountants and mention of their review and approval included under this heading. This section does not apply, however, if the securities to be listed are already issued and outstanding.[21]

EXAMPLE OF "DESCRIPTION OF TRANSACTION" IN A LISTING APPLICATION INCORPORATING A PROSPECTUS FILED UNDER THE SECURITIES ACT OF 1933. In August, 1962, the Sharon Steel Co. applied for listing of 165,781 additional shares of common stock that was to be issued in exchange for all the stock of Macomber, Inc. and described the transaction as follows:

> One hundred sixty-five thousand, seven hundred eighty-one additional shares of common stock, without par value, of Sharon Steel Corporation are issuable in exchange for shares of common stock, par value $1.00 per share, of Macomber, Incorporated pursuant to an exchange offer described in the

[21] *Ibid.*, April 3, 1959, p. B-62.

attached prospectus relating to such offer, which prospectus is incorporated herein by reference and constitutes a part of this listing application. The exchange offer will expire at the close of business on August 29, 1962.

If the proposed exchange is made, the transaction will be treated for accounting purposes as a pooling of interests, and the difference between the aggregate stated value ($10 per share) of the Corporation's common stock issued for Macomber common stock and the aggregate par value ($1.00 per share) of the Macomber common stock exchanged will be transferred to the Corporation's common stock account from its capital contributed and earnings capitalized in excess of stated value of common stock account. The Corporation's independent accountants have reviewed and approved such accounting treatment as being in conformity with generally accepted accounting principles.

The Corporation believes that consummation of the exchange offer will benefit the Corporation and its shareholders by enabling it to enter a desirable new field (steel for light construction) and to have an assured outlet for a substantial tonnage, thereby providing the Corporation's operations with better diversity and stability. Reference is made to "Sharon's Reasons for the Macomber Acquisition" in the prospectus.

The Corporation, through certain of its officers, employees and agents, has investigated the management, financial condition and physical properties of Macomber and is satisfied that full and fair consideration will be received for the additional shares of the Corporation's common stock to be issued.

No officer, director or principal stockholder of the Corporation has any direct or indirect beneficial interest in the common stock of Macomber being acquired by the Corporation.[22]

EXAMPLE OF "DESCRIPTION OF TRANSACTION" IN A LISTING APPLICATION INCORPORATING A PROXY STATEMENT FILED UNDER THE SECURITIES EXCHANGE ACT OF 1934. In January, 1962, Mohasco Industries, Inc. applied for listing of 407,716 additional shares of common stock that was to be issued in exchange for all the stock of Firth Carpet Co. and described the transaction as follows:

The Firth Carpet Company, a New York corporation ("Firth") will be merged into Mohasco Industries, Inc. ("Mohasco"). The name of the surviving corporation will remain Mohasco Industries, Inc. Upon consummation of the merger, each issued and outstanding share of common stock of Firth will be converted into two thirds of one share of Mohasco common stock, par value $5 per share. Based on the 563,574 shares of Firth common stock outstanding on December 1, 1961, up to 375,716 shares of Mohasco common stock will be issued upon the above conversion.

In addition, 32,000 shares of Mohasco common stock will be reserved for issuance upon the exercise of options for 48,000 Firth shares outstanding under Firth's restricted stock option plan, for which Mohasco options will be substituted.

[22] Sharon Steel Co., Listing Application to the New York Stock Exchange, August, 1962.

It is presently contemplated that the merger will become effective on January 31, 1962. Reference is made to the Mohasco proxy statement, which is incorporated herein and made a part hereof, for a statement concerning the reasons for the merger, a description of the history and business of both companies and certain financial information concerning both companies. The merger will be treated for accounting purposes as a "purchase" by Mohasco, which treatment has been approved by Mohasco's independent accountants as being in accordance with generally accepted accounting principles. Reference is made to the pro forma balance sheet appearing on page F–18 of the proxy statement for details concerning the accounting treatment.[23]

Financial Statements in a Subsequent Listing Application—General Requirements. The financial statement requirements for a subsequent listing application are less extensive than for an original application and may be summarized briefly as follows:

1. The latest available consolidated balance sheet and statements of income and surplus of the company and its subsidiaries that have been certified by an independent accountant, together with the accountant's certificate.
2. If the statements of income and surplus referred to in item 1 relate to a period that is less than a full fiscal year, then such statements for the previous full fiscal year must be included, together with the accountant's certificate thereon.
3. If the company has released for publication earnings data relating to a period subsequent to the statements referred to in item 1, such data must be included in the application, and it must be certified to by the company's principal accounting officer.
4. If a major financing, acquisition, reorganization, or recapitalization is planned, a "pro forma" balance sheet giving effect to the proposed changes may be required.

The financial statements of the issuer are seldom included in a subsequent listing application for acquisition of another company, even though the Company Manual indicates that such statements are required. It is understood that the exchange waives this requirement because it feels its regular reporting requirements for listed companies are adequate for the investor and the inclusion of the issuer's financial statements in a listing application for the acquisition of another company would involve unnecessary expense.

[23] Mohasco Industries, Inc., Listing Application to the New York Stock Exchange, January, 1962.

INCORPORATION OF FINANCIAL INFORMATION BY REFERENCE. As noted, the exchange permits the incorporation by reference in a listing application of material contained in a proxy statement or prospectus. In addition, any required financial statements, which were included in a previous listing application, may be incorporated by reference in the current application.

Where a subsequent listing application incorporates a proxy or prospectus, the New York Stock Exchange ordinarily will not require an amendment to the application if the financial statements in the incorporated material do not comply to its requirements. However, the exchange will require the company to make the necessary changes to conform to its requirements in the next annual report to stockholders.

Special Financial Statement Requirements. In addition to the general requirements that apply to most applicants, there are other financial statement requirements that have application only in special cases, as follows:

Subsidiaries Not Included in the Consolidated Financial Statements: If there are any subsidiary or controlled companies not included in the consolidated financial statements, the consolidated income account shall include a footnote reflecting the parent company's proportion of the undistributed profits or of the losses of such companies. There shall also be a footnote to the consolidated balance sheet showing the amount by which the parent company's equity in the unconsolidated subsidiary or controlled companies has increased or decreased, since the date of acquisition, as a result of profits, losses and distributions.

Separate financial statements of any such unconsolidated subsidiary or controlled company may be required in the application if the investment in such company represents a substantial part of the assets of the parent company, or if the parent company's proportion of the profits or losses of such company is substantial in relation to the consolidated net income.[24]

Parent Company Statements: There may also be required statements of the company as a separate corporate entity, if, in the Exchange's opinion, such statements appear to be essential. In general, parent company statements are not required in cases where the subsidiaries are wholly owned and do not have any substantial amount of funded debt outstanding.[25]

FINANCIAL STATEMENTS OF ACQUIRED COMPANY. If the securities being listed are to be issued in connection with the acquisition of a controlling interest in or the net assets of another

[24] *New York Stock Exchange Company Manual,* June 26, 1958, p. B–69.
[25] *Ibid.*

company, the latest available balance sheet and statements of income and surplus of such company must be included in the application. The statements must be certified to either by an independent accountant or by the chief accounting officer of the company.[26]

Although the exchange does not attempt to prescribe the form or content of financial statements included in listing applications, it is expected the statements will meet two general criteria, viz.:

1. They will be reasonably informative without being overburdened with detail.
2. The accounting principles employed in their preparation will conform to generally accepted practice.[27]

It is the practice of the exchange to request that an applicant for original listing submit its financial statements, initially, in the form in which they have been published in previous annual reports to stockholders. These statements are then examined by the Department of Stock List of the exchange, and any recommended changes are discussed with the company's representatives.[28]

One of the listing agreements the company must enter into as a condition of its original listing is an agreement that all financial statements contained in the company's future annual reports to stockholders be in the same form as the statements contained in the original listing application.[29] This has been interpreted as meaning that the financial statements in future annual reports of the applicant should contain substantially the same information as included in the original listing application. This is done to establish a standard of disclosure rather than an inflexible form for reporting.

AMERICAN STOCK EXCHANGE

Applications for Listing of Additional Securities. The American Stock Exchange requires the filing of a subsequent listing appli-

[26] *Ibid.*
[27] *Ibid.,* September 1, 1953, p. B–44.
[28] *Ibid.*
[29] New York Stock Exchange Current Listing Agreement II(2), November 15, 1956.

cation by a company already having securities listed on the exchange in the event of:

1. The issuance of an additional amount of a listed security
2. A change in a listed security that creates a new security or that alters any of the listed securities rights, preferences, or terms
3. The assumption of a listed security by another company
4. Reincorporation under the laws of another state
5. Merger or consolidation into or with one or more corporations [30]

The requirements and procedures for listing and registering a new class of securities in addition to those previously listed on the American Exchange are basically the same as for the New York Exchange in that they require the filing of a subsequent listing application with the exchange and a simplified registration statement with the Securities and Exchange Commission. See page 222 for further comments with regard to this and the minimum voting rights required for listing any class of securities.[31]

Solicitation of Stockholders by Proxy Under Regulation X–14 Required Under Certain Conditions. The Exchange has adopted a policy of requiring the solicitation of shareholder approval pursuant to Regulation X–14 of the Securities Exchange Act of 1934 as a prerequisite to approval of applications to list additional shares to be issued as sole or partial consideration for an acquisition of the stock or assets of another company in the following circumstances:

1. If any director, officer, or substantial stockholder of the listed company has an interest, directly or indirectly, in the company or assets to be acquired or in the consideration to be paid in the transaction

[30] American Stock Exchange, Division of Securities, *Applications Subsequent to Original Listing,* April 5, 1962.

[31] The American Stock Exchange's policy with regard to minimum voting rights as stated on page 2 of *Requirements for Original Listing Applications* is as follows:

"The American Stock Exchange will not view favorably applications for the listing of (a) Common Stocks which are non-voting or which have unduly restricted voting rights, and (b) non-voting Preferred Stocks which do not acquire voting rights upon specified defaults (maximum two years) in the payment of fixed dividend requirements. However, in applying the above policy the Exchange will consider each case individually and on its own merits, and may make certain exceptions thereto depending upon the circumstances in each case."

2. If the acquisition will result directly or indirectly in an increase of 20 per cent or more in the number of outstanding shares of the listed class of stock (including for the purpose of this calculation any shares issuable in conversion of convertible securities issued in the transactions)

3. If the market value of the additional shares to be issued plus the fair value of any other consideration to be paid in the transaction equals 20 per cent or more of the aggregate market value of the outstanding shares of the listed class of stock [32]

"BACKDOOR LISTINGS." The American Stock Exchange follows the same general policy regarding "backdoor listings" as does the New York Stock Exchange.

Subsequent Listing Applications. The requirements for subsequent (additional) listing applications generally are the same as for an original listing. The company may use either the regular long-form application containing all the required information or the short-form application in which a prospectus or proxy statement is incorporated to provide certain of the information. The requirements as to form and content in an application are set forth in the exchange's publications: *Requirements for Original Listing Applications* and *Applications Subsequent to Original Listing.*

The requirements for a subsequent listing application are designed to bring information up-to-date that was provided in previous listing applications concerning the applicant and its securities. When the short-form is not used, the information requirements are basically the same as for an original application.

SCOPE OF INFORMATION IN SUBSEQUENT LISTING APPLICATION. An indication of the scope of the information in the application may be derived from the following items included in the directions:

1. Data concerning securities to be listed
2. Capitalization
3. Funded debt
4. Authority for and purpose of issuance
5. Opinion of counsel
6. Registration under Securities Act of 1933
7. Business and operations

[32] American Stock Exchange, Listing Form L, April 5, 1962, p. 6.

8. Properties
9. Subsidiary and affiliated companies
10. Dividend record
11. Changes in capitalization
12. Stock provisions and description of bonds
13. General corporate information
14. Business, financial, and accounting policies
15. Financial statements
16. Certificate [33]

The subsequent listing requirements indicate the need for a considerable amount of information to be filed. However, most listed companies maintain a high level of disclosure in their corporate reporting practices so that much of the data above will have been furnished in periodic reports.

SPECIAL REQUIREMENTS FOR BUSINESS COMBINATIONS. When securities to be used in a business combination are being listed, the information of most significance in a short-form application is that relating to the purpose of the proposed issuance. These requirements follow:

State the purpose of issuance and the consideration to be received:

(a) If to be issued for cash, state net amount to be received by the applicant and the purpose to which the proceeds will be applied. If any underwriting, option or similar agreement has been entered into, include summary of all important provisions thereof.

(b) If the securities applied for are to be issued in exchange for, or will result from modification of, previously listed securities, state the basis of exchange or the nature and effect of the proposed modification.

(c) If the securities applied for are to be issued to acquire securities or business of another company, the history and business of the acquired company should be described. Financial statements of the business to be acquired should also be furnished.

(d) If the securities applied for are to be issued to acquire properties, describe such properties.

In the case of either (c) or (d) above, furnish (1) the names of the persons from whom the securities or properties are to be acquired, and their relationship to the applicant, if any; (2) state the principle followed in determining the amount at which the securities or properties are to be acquired; and (3) identify the persons making the determination, and their relationship to the applicant. If any engineering, geological or appraisal reports, etc., were obtained in connection with the proposed acquisition refer to such reports and include appropriate excerpts therefrom in the listing application.

[33] American Stock Exchange, Division of Securities, *Applications Subsequent to Original Listing*, April 5, 1962, pp. 2–5.

If the security applied for is stock, state the amounts to be credited to capital and capital surplus accounts respectively, and state what disposition, if any, is to be made of any capital surplus resulting from its issuance.[34]

EXAMPLE OF "PURPOSE OF ISSUE" IN A BUSINESS COMBINATION. In 1962, Argus, Inc. (formerly Mansfield Industries, Inc.) entered into an agreement with Sylvania Electric Products, Inc. whereby Argus would purchase all the assets subject to the liabilities of the "Argus Business" of Sylvania. To provide funds for the proposed transaction, Argus proposed to sell a maximum of $4,000,000 of convertible debentures. The sale of debentures involved a public offering of securities, so it was necessary to register them with the Securities and Exchange Commission. Since the company already had its common stock listed on the American Stock Exchange, it was also necessary to list the additional shares of common stock reserved for issuance upon conversion with the exchange and to solicit proxies under Regulation X–14 for stockholder approval of the proposed transaction. The purpose of issue of the transaction was described in the stock listing application, as follows:

The company has authorized the issuance of (i) a maximum of $8,200,000 aggregate principal amount of its 6% convertible subordinated debentures due July 15, 1972, a maximum of $4,000,000 principal amount of which are to be publicly offered, $3,200,000 principal amount of which are to be offered in exchange for a short-term promissory note of a similar amount of the company held by Sylvania Electric Products, Inc. and $1,000,000 of which are to be offered in exchange for a similar principal amount of existing debentures (the latter exchange being described on page 6 of the attached prospectus) and (ii) the granting of common stock purchase warrants to purchase 24,000 shares of its common stock, all in connection with the purchase by the company of the assets and properties of the Argus Business (as defined) of Sylvania Electric Products, Inc. in accordance with the agreement relating to such purchase dated March 1, 1962 (the "Agreement"), as described on pages 8–10 of the attached prospectus, the related financing thereof and the discharge of a note of the company in the principal amount of $1,000,000 payable to Kirkeby-Natus Corporation.

For more complete details of the transaction, including a description of the properties and assets of the company and of the Argus Business and the financial statements of each, reference is made to the proxy statement and prospectus of the company, dated April 26, and July 18, 1962, respectively, which are attached to this application, included herein, and a part hereof.

The Board of Directors of the company, at meetings thereof held February 26, May 7 and July 16, 1962, approved the agreement and the related financing.

[34] *Ibid.*, p. 3.

It is in connection therewith that certain of the shares of common stock covered by this application are being reserved for issuance. The agreement (and therefore the related financing), as well as the amendments to the certificate of incorporation to increase the authorized number of shares of common stock and change the name of the company, and the amendment to the existing restricted stock option plan to increase the number of shares of common stock authorized for issuance thereunder, were approved in each instance by the affirmative vote of the holders of a majority of the outstanding common stock of the company at a special meeting thereof authorized by the Board of Directors of the Company and held on May 7, 1962.[35]

The Short-Form Listing Application. The exchange permits the simplified procedure of incorporating by reference in the listing application any material included in a recent prospectus or proxy statement relating to the proposed transaction. An application making use of the incorporation technique is called a "short-form" in that the information required is substantially shortened. If this approach is used, the prospectus or proxy statement must be attached to and made part of the listing application. Any data required by the application that is not in the prospectus or proxy statement should be included separately in the application.

INFORMATION IN THE SHORT-FORM LISTING APPLICATION. When a "short-form" application is used, the required information will generally be limited to the following:

1. Data regarding stock to be listed
2. Capitalization
3. Funded debt
4. Authority for and purpose of issuance
5. Opinion of counsel
6. Registration under Securities Act of 1933
7. General corporate information
8. Financial statements
9. Corporate certificate

Financial Statements in a Subsequent Listing Application. GENERAL REQUIREMENTS. The financial statement requirements for a subsequent listing application are as follows:

1. A balance sheet and statements of income and surplus of the company "in reasonable detail" as of the close of the latest fiscal

---

[35] Argus, Inc., American Stock Exchange, Stock Listing Application, dated May 11, 1962, amended July 18, 1962.

year that have been certified by an independent accountant, together with the accountant's certificate. If the applicant so desires, it may satisfy this requirement by submitting its annual report to stockholders with the certificate of the independent accountant manually signed.

2. If the statements submitted pursuant to the above requirements are as of a date more than six months prior to the date of the listing application, supplemental statements must be submitted, similar in form and content, as of a date not more than six months prior to the date of the listing application.

INCORPORATION BY REFERENCE PERMITTED. Applicants may incorporate by reference a proxy statement or prospectus in which the accountants have manually signed their certificate relating to the financial statements contained therein. If such financial statements are as of a date more than six months prior to the date of the listing application, the supplemental statements referred to above shall be submitted and included at the end of the listing application.

FINANCIAL STATEMENTS OF ACQUIRED COMPANY. If an application is submitted for securities to be issued to acquire a stock interest in another corporation, a balance sheet at a recent date and a statement of income and profit and loss and surplus to the date of the balance sheet of such other company is required to be furnished.

The exchange requires that the basic financial statements be certified by a properly qualified practicing public accountant or certified public accountant who is not an officer, director, or employee of the applicant corporation, who shall, if requested, submit to the exchange a statement setting forth his or their qualifications.

In ordinary cases, the supplemental financial statements may be certified either by a properly qualified practicing public accountant or certified public accountant, or by the chief accounting officer of the applicant corporation.

Chapter 13

OTHER ASPECTS OF BUSINESS COMBINATIONS

Other factors pertinent to business combinations include general or business corporation laws, state blue sky laws, and those pertaining to taxation and the transfer of assets, and federal antitrust laws. These and matters such as finders' fees, "corporate raiders," and the timing and type of public announcements of impending business combinations will be discussed in this chapter.

GENERAL OR BUSINESS CORPORATION LAWS

The general or business corporation laws, which vary from state to state, govern the formation of corporations, their powers, the maintenance of corporate records, the election of officers and directors, the issuance of capital stock and debt securities, mergers and consolidations, dissolutions, solvency, and reorganizations. The discussion of these laws will be limited to their relation to acquisitions, mergers, and consolidations.

Business combinations, whether taxable or tax free, often involve legal requirements in such matters as board of director and stockholder action, rights of dissenting shareholders, and the filing with state authorities of various papers, pursuant to their corporation laws. The problems in this area require management officials entering into a business combination to seek expert legal advice. The discussion below will accordingly be limited to outlining some of the considerations involved.

Stockholder Approval Requirements for Business Combinations. In general, the extent to which stockholder approval is required under state laws depends upon the form that a business combination may take. A statutory merger or consolidation (an "A"-

type tax-free reorganization [1]) ordinarily requires approval by the stockholders of all corporations that are parties to the merger or consolidation. A taxable purchase or a tax-free acquisition of net assets for capital stock (a "C"-type reorganization [2]) ordinarily requires approval by the stockholders of the selling or transferor corporation in most states, but not by those of the acquiring corporation. A state customarily does not require approval of stockholders of either the acquired or acquiring corporation in a taxable or a tax-free acquisition of capital stock (a "B"-type reorganization).[3]

STATUTORY MERGER OR CONSOLIDATION. State laws ordinarily require prior approval by the stockholders of each corporation entering into a statutory merger or consolidation. The percentage of stock required to be voted in favor of the merger varies from a simple majority in many states to as much as 80 per cent in Texas. Several states, including Ohio and Minnesota, permit the percentage to be established by the corporate articles, provided that it be not less than 50 per cent. Requirements for the use of preferred stock, non-voting stock, debt securities, and other special circumstances vary from state to state.

ACQUISITION OF ASSETS. At the present time, the various states, except Arizona, Mississippi, and Wyoming, have adopted statutes that require a corporation to seek the approval of its stockholders before disposing of substantially all its assets and business, whether in a tax-free or taxable transaction. Here, too, the percentage of assenting votes required varies from state to state, typically from one-half to two-thirds of the total outstanding shares.

Acquiring Corporation Not Presently Required To Seek Approval of Stockholders in the Acquisition of Net Assets and Business of Another Corporation. On the other hand, state statutes do not presently require the acquiring corporation, in such a transaction to seek the approval of its stockholders. However, in the case of a tax-free acquisition of the assets of one corporation in exchange for

---

[1] Int. Rev. Code of 1954, § 368(a).
[2] *Ibid.*
[3] *Ibid.*

the stock of another corporation, some courts have held that statutory merger requirements must be complied with where the practical effect of the transaction is the same as would result from a formal merger of the two companies. Thus, in the leading case of *Farris v. Glen Alden Corp.*,[4] the Pennsylvania Supreme Court prevented Glen Alden from consummating the acquisition of the assets of another company in a "C"-type reorganization, holding that it should have complied with statutory merger requirements with respect to action by its stockholders. The rationale in decisions holding that such combinations are *de facto* mergers is to the effect that the stockholder should not be compelled to accept an investment in an entirely different corporation.

ACQUISITION OF STOCK. As in the case of an asset acquisition, states do not presently require a corporation to seek the approval of its stockholders to acquire the stock of another company. With regard to the acquired corporation, each stockholder acts as an individual in determining whether or not to transfer his shares to the acquiring corporation. Hence, in this type of business combination, no formal action is taken by the acquired corporation as such, which under state law would require approval by any designated percentage of its stockholders acting as a body. Of course, in a "B"-type exchange of stock, the Internal Revenue Code requires that at least 80 per cent of the stock of the acquired corporation must be obtained in order to qualify the transaction as a tax-free reorganization.

As in the case of asset acquisitions, some courts have held that acquisitions of stock having the same practical effect as a merger must satisfy statutory merger requirements. Thus, in the recent case of *Applestein v. United Board & Carton Co.*[5] a New Jersey court held that a "B"-type reorganization was in substance a statutory merger where it was to be followed by immediate dissolution of the acquired corporation.

Furthermore, although an acquirer may not be required by corporate law or its stock listing agreement to submit an acquisi-

---

[4] Farris v. Glen Alden Corp., 393 Pa. 427, 143 A.2d, 25 (1958).

[5] Applestein v. United Board & Carton Co., Super. Ct. N.J. Ch. Div., 159 A.2d 146 (1960).

tion transaction for approval to its stockholders, it may still require such approval because of related matters resulting from the combination, such as an increase in capital stock or in the number of shares available for employee stock options, or because of a requirement to amend its charter to add additional corporate purposes and powers.

Rights of Dissenting Stockholders. In the case of a statutory merger or consolidation, all states except Utah and West Virginia grant stockholders who dissent from a business combination the right to demand appraisal of their shares and payment of the value in cash. In the case of an acquisition of assets, whether in a taxable transaction or a "C"-type reorganization, general rights to demand an appraisal are given dissenting shareholders of the acquired corporation in more than thirty states. Generally, appraisal rights are not granted to dissenting stockholders of the acquiring corporation in this type of combination, nor are any appraisal rights given to stockholders of either the acquiring or acquired corporation in the case of an acquisition of stock, whether a taxable purchase or a "B"-type reorganization.

If, however, either a "B"- or "C"-type tax-free reorganization [6] has the practical effect of a merger, precedent established by court decisions such as the *Glen Alden* and *United Board & Carton* cases may give dissenting shareholders of both the acquiring and acquired corporations in such situations the appraisal rights granted under the merger statutes of the states concerned.

The question of the rights of dissenting stockholders who oppose a business combination is a complex one. As indicated, not all states provide for appraisal rights in all cases; nor is the appraisal right where it exists necessarily the exclusive remedy. Moreover, those state statutes that do provide for appraisal differ widely in the phraseology, scope, and requirements for exercising the right. For example, some states have varying concepts of valuing shares. Suffice it to say that dissenting sharesolders can cause difficult problems in a business combination, resulting at times in costly and prolonged litigation.

[6] Int. Rev. Code of 1954, § 368(a).

Moreover, in any stock acquisition in which less than 100 per cent of the outstanding shares of the acquired corporation is secured by the acquiring corporation, so that a minority interest in the acquired corporation remains, that interest may have to be reckoned with, if, at some future date, the liquidation of the acquired company into its parent is desired.

EFFECT OF PRE-EMPTIVE RIGHTS. The concept of stockholders' pre-emptive rights refers to the right of a present stockholder in a corporation to subscribe to new stock that that corporation may issue in order to maintain his proportionate share of ownership in the company. Many states have qualified this common law concept by statute, so that it is often possible for a corporation to limit or entirely eliminate this right by so providing in its articles of incorporation. In fact, in a few states, including Pennsylvania and California, pre-emptive rights are denied unless the articles specifically provide for them.

To the extent that pre-emptive rights do apply to a corporation, they are not generally considered to extend to the issuance of shares in exchange for specific property or in a merger. In the case of a "C"-type reorganization,[7] however, where one company acquires the assets of another in exchange for its stock, pre-emptive rights could have some application if the acquiring corporation acquires the cash, along with the other assets, of the acquired corporation. In some states, the existence of such rights might give the stockholders of the acquired corporation a cause for action against that company. Hence, the question of possible application of pre-emptive rights is another matter to be considered in determining the form that a proposed business combination should take.

General Comments on Corporation Laws. Even though stockholder approval may not be required in some business combinations, particularly on behalf of an acquiring company, it may be prudent to obtain such approval. This is most important where a deal is large relative to the resources of the acquiring company.

[7] *Ibid.*

COMPETENT AND TIMELY LEGAL ADVICE IMPORTANT. In reading the foregoing discussion on aspects of corporation laws, as they affect business combinations, it should be borne in mind that state statutes are amended and judicial interpretations of them change as a result of court decisions. Accordingly, there is no substitute for competent and timely legal advice as to the form a business combination should take to avoid some of the potential problems discussed above.

BLUE SKY LAWS

State statutes governing the regulation of the offering for sale or the sale of securities are generally referred to as "blue sky laws." This term of reference was suggested by a United States Supreme Court opinion, in which it was stated: "The name that is given to the law indicates the evil at which it is aimed, that is, to use the language of a cited case 'speculative schemes which have no more basis than so many feet of *blue sky.'* " [8]

Laws Vary Among States. Blue sky laws vary among the states from those designed primarily to provide penalties for the fraudulent sale of securities to those that are quite comprehensive in regulating the sale of securities. Some states exempt, from provisions of their blue sky laws, transactions in securities resulting from mergers and reorganizations. Others require the filing of an application for permission to issue securities in a merger, consolidation, or reorganization, including the furnishing of financial data on the constituent companies and copies of all documents used in soliciting security holders.

The states that have comprehensive laws governing the issuance of securities are in the majority. The administrators of the securities laws in many such states have adopted a uniform application form for qualification of securities and certain other uniform policies.

In the case of acquisitions, mergers, or consolidations, the requirements for obtaining negotiating permits or permits for the issuance of securities should be ascertained by legal counsel for

---

[8] Hall v. Geiger-Jones Co., 242 U.S. 539 (1916).

the states of domicile of the several constituent companies involved and for other states in which they have property.

STATE TAX CONSIDERATIONS

Taxable Consequences of a Business Combination for State Tax Purposes Not Always Apparent. At the state tax level, characterization of a combination as either taxable or tax free is not always so evident as it is for federal income tax purposes (see Chapter 9). For one thing, there are various types of state taxes whose effect must be considered in connection with any business combination: income taxes (both corporate and personal), franchise taxes (taxes based on capital values, such as net worth or total assets or on income), sales taxes, and stock transfer or original issue corporation taxes and fees. Moreover, a corporation engaged in other than a strictly local business is probably subject to one or more of these taxes in several states.

STATE TAXES GENERALLY NOT TOO MATERIAL. State taxes generally are a minor matter relative to potential federal income tax effects. Nevertheless, state tax consequences must be considered in a business combination; and under certain circumstances, they may be significant.

Because tax statutes vary considerably from state to state, there is no substitute for carefully checking the applicable tax rules of each state to which the constituents to a business combination pay a significant tax, in order to gauge the effect of state taxes on the combination. The discussion that follows presents a broad outline of the points that should be considered in this review.

Corporate Income Taxes. In the numerous states that impose an income tax on corporations, the question of possible tax liability to the transferor corporation must be considered in any transaction involving the transfer of assets by one corporation to another. For federal tax purposes, gain on transfers of assets is not recognized if the transfer is made in exchange for stock and the transaction qualifies as a reorganization under Section 368 of the Internal Revenue Code. If the transfer is made for cash or other consideration that does not meet the requirements of a reorganization, gain still will not be recognized to the transferor corporation if the transfer is made pursuant to a plan of complete liquidation, which is completed within a twelve-month period, and the other requirements of Section 337 of the Code are met, as explained in Chapter 9.

In those states such as New York, Pennsylvania, and New Jersey where taxable income for state purposes is based principally on taxable income reported for federal purposes, an asset transfer on which taxable gain is not recognized for federal purposes should be similarly exempt for state income tax purposes. A number of states have adopted their own detailed income tax statutes, following the general lines of the Federal Internal Revenue Code. In many of these states, including California, Minnesota, and Louisiana, the state statutory provisions on reorganizations and twelve-month liquidations closely parallel the Internal Revenue Code. Accordingly, in such states, asset transfers, on which gain is not recognized for federal purposes, should also be exempt for state purposes, provided the transaction qualifies under the related statutory provisions of the state.

On the other hand, it may be assumed, generally, that if gain on the sale of the assets of a business is recognized for federal income tax purposes, it will similarly be subject to state taxation in such states. Exceptions arise in states such as Maryland, where all gains from the sale of capital assets, as defined by the state, are exempt from income tax.

INCOME TAX LAWS OF SOME STATES BEAR NO RESEMBLANCE TO FEDERAL LAWS. Greater problems are presented in those states whose income tax laws bear little resemblance to the Internal Revenue Code. State tax laws of this type are often written in broad general terms, and no specific provisions are made for reorganizations or sales of assets by liquidating corporations. Great discretionary power in prescribing regulations and administering the income tax law is often given the tax commissioner or other officials in such states.

In those states, of which Tennessee and Mississippi are examples, in which income tax statutes do not generally parallel the Internal Revenue Code, care must be exercised in checking the state rules to ascertain whether, for example, gain on sale of assets not recognized for federal purposes will be similarly exempted by the state. It may be prudent to request a specific ruling from the state tax authorities in appropriate cases.

Personal Income Taxes. A general personal income tax is imposed in many states and by the District of Columbia. Since most business combinations involve directly or indirectly the exchange of the stocks held by the shareholders of the acquired corporation for stock of the acquiring corporation or for cash or other consideration, the question of possible state income tax liability to the stockholders on such exchanges must be considered. While this is not of direct concern at the corporate level, it could be important if a closely held corporation is involved in a business combination.

Franchise Taxes. Many states and the District of Columbia impose a franchise or capital value tax. These may be divided into two general groups: (1) those that base the tax on stated or nominal capital values, such as par value or number of shares of stock; and (2) those that base the tax on real capital values, such as the market value of outstanding stock or net worth, as shown on the books. Illinois, Delaware, and New Hampshire are examples of the first group; and Pennsylvania, New Jersey, and Texas of the second.

FRANCHISE TAX LIABILITY MAY BE AFFECTED BY BUSINESS COMBINATION. Franchise tax liability in those states basing the tax on nominal or stated capital can be affected by any recapitalization or increase in capitalization incident to a merger, or an acquisition involving issuance of additional shares by the acquiring corporation. It is necessary to check the particular law of each state to which the acquiring corporation pays or will pay a franchise tax in order to evaluate the potential franchise tax effect of the merger. In some cases, credit may be available ˙ for taxes previously paid to the state by an acquired corporation absorbed in a merger.

More serious problems can be presented to the acquired corporation in certain of the states that base the franchise tax on actual capital values. For example, in New Jersey the annual franchise tax is ordinarily based, in part, on book net worth.

However, in the case of a corporation that sells or transfers its assets and business to an acquiring corporation and then liquidates, the state requires that net worth as reflected on the final return of the liquidating corporation be based on the actual value of the consideration received for its assets.[9] Thus, a corporation having book net worth of $1,000,000 prior to a sale of all its net assets and business, and which receives $3,000,000 as the selling price, will find its franchise tax base tripled on its final New Jersey return. Moreover, the state has been known to then assert a franchise tax deficiency for the year prior to the year of the sale, on the grounds that book net worth was substantially less than the actual market value of the company's net assets at that point as well.

Sales Taxes. Most states impose some form of sales or gross receipts tax or license tax measured by gross income. Such taxes are also imposed by the District of Columbia and by many municipalities in certain states. In these jurisdictions, a business combination involving a sale of assets must be checked for possible sales tax liability that might attach with respect to the tangible personal property—machinery, equipment, and inventories—included among the assets transferred.

In many states, a transaction involving the sale of all the assets of a business would be exempt from sales tax, either because of the specific exemption of casual sales or by reason of the classifications of taxable transactions prescribed by the state. However, this rule would not hold true in all states. In Colorado, for example, the regulations specifically provide that in the case of the sale of a business ". . . the sales tax must be paid on the purchase price paid for the equipment, furniture, fixtures, supplies and all tangible personal property included in the sale except a stock or inventory of goods acquired for resale in the trade or business."[10]

California is another state in which possible sales tax liability on the sale of a business often proves troublesome, despite an exemption in the law for occasional sales.

[9] New Jersey Regulations 16:10–10.120.
[10] Colorado Sales and Use Tax Rule No. 18.

Moreover, the fact that assets are transferred to an acquiring corporation for stock in a tax-free reorganization for federal purposes rather than for cash would not necessarily remove the transaction from the definition of a sale in some states.

Stock Transfer and Sundry Taxes. A few states impose stock transfer taxes, and most states impose various qualification and filing fees or fees based on increases in authorized capital stock. Hence, any business combination that requires recapitalization or formation of a new corporation or the qualification of the acquiring corporation in other states will be subject to fees or taxes of this type. In most cases, these may be expected to form a relatively minor part of the cost of effecting a business combination. In a few states, however, certain specialized types of "initial tax" might give rise to an unexpected tax liability.

Pennsylvania imposes an excise tax, which is in addition to the franchise tax, on foreign corporations for the privilege of employing capital in the state. The tax, a so-called "plateau" tax, is assessed only on increases in the amount of capital employed. If a New York corporation having a plant in Pennsylvania sells its assets and business to a Delaware corporation, the tangible property at that plant will be viewed as an increase in the amount of capital employed by the Delaware corporation in Pennsylvania, and accordingly will be subject to excise tax.[11] If the value of the tangible property (land, building, equipment, and inventories) at the plant is $3,000,000, for example, the excise tax would amount to $10,000, at present tax rates.

STATE BULK SALES LAWS

In any corporate acquisition involving the purchase of assets, whether for stock or cash, the requirements of the bulk sales laws of the various states should be considered. Bulk sales laws are designed to protect the creditors against the fraudulent sale of business assets, particularly inventories and fixtures. While the laws differ from state to state, the typical requirement is for notice to the creditors in the case of a sale or other disposition

[11] Pennsylvania, Act of July 25, 1953, P.L.560, Section 2. See also Commonwealth v. Merchants Shipbuilding Corp., 26 Dauph. 89, 3 D & C. 670 (1923).

in bulk of all or a part of the inventories and fixtures in a transaction not in the ordinary course of business.

Notice to Creditors Required. Usually, the law requires the purchaser to secure from the seller an itemized listing of the names and addresses of all the creditors of the business, together with the amounts owed to each. Within a stipulated period prior to the completion of the sale, the purchaser must give each of the listed creditors personal notice of the proposed transaction, together with the price, terms, and conditions of the sale. In some states, the seller is also required to furnish to the purchaser an itemized inventory of all the articles included in the sale, including cost prices, which the purchaser must retain for a period and exhibit to the creditors of the seller upon request.

COUNSEL SHOULD BE CONSULTED ON THE APPLICATION OF BULK SALES LAWS. Counsel should be consulted on the possible application of the bulk sales laws to any purchase of the assets of a business. Failure to comply may expose the purchaser to possible claims by the creditors of the seller. In appropriate circumstances, it may be possible to secure waivers of the requirements of the law.

FEDERAL STAMP TAXES

Real Property Conveyances—Deeds. A federal stamp (excise) tax is imposed on all deeds or other instruments whereby real property sold is conveyed or transferred to the purchaser. The basis for the tax is the value of or consideration for the property conveyed, less any mortgages or other encumbrances on the propery existing before the sale and not removed thereby. The rate of tax is $0.55 for each $500 or fractional part thereof of value conveyed, except that conveyances of $100 or less are exempted.

Since the tax attaches only to deeds relating to *sales* of property, it does not apply to transfers of realty pursuant to a statutory merger or consolidation. It does apply in the case of corporate acquisitions taking the form of a purchase of assets, including the stock-for-assets type of acquisition.

Original Issuance of Stock. A federal stamp (excise) tax is imposed on the original issuance of a stock by a domestic corporation. The rate of tax is $0.10 for each $100 (or major fraction thereof) of *actual value* of the stock certificates issued. Thus, if a corporate acquisition involves the issuance by the acquiring corporation of new shares of its stock having an aggregate market value of $5,000,000, the tax imposed on the issuance would be $5,000.

Stock Transfer. Many corporate acquisitions involve the imposition of the federal stamp (excise) tax on stock transfers. This tax is levied at the rate of $0.04 for each $100 (or major fraction thereof) of the *actual value* (market value) of the certificates transferred, subject to a maximum tax of $0.08 on *each share* of stock.

In the case of a corporate acquisition effected by an exchange of stock between the acquiring corporation and the stockholders of the acquired corporation:

1. The transfer tax applies to the transfer to the stock of the acquired corporation to the acquiring corporation.
2. The original issuance tax applies to the issuance of the new stock of the acquiring corporation to the shareholders of the acquired corporation.

Similarly, in the case of a statutory merger or consolidation, both the original issuance and stock transfer taxes will usually apply. In the case of the acquisition of the net assets of one corporation by another corporation, however, the surrender of the stock of the acquired (selling) corporation for extinguishment in connection with the dissolution of that company is not subject to the transfer tax.

FEDERAL ANTITRUST LAWS

Although there are other federal laws that could be pertinent, the basic antitrust laws invoked in business combinations are the Sherman Act and the Clayton Act. Most of the actions in antitrust cases arising out of business combinations during recent years have been instituted under the Clayton Act, either by the Federal Trade Commission or the Department of Justice.

For background purposes, developments under these laws are set forth below, in the order of their enactment. So that this antitrust problem in acquisitions and mergers may be viewed in perspective, it should be mentioned that there have been relatively few actions initiated by law enforcement agencies under these Acts because of alleged violations resulting from acquisitions and mergers. Most of the cases tried, until recent years, involved trade associations or non-affiliated companies and individuals allegedly conspiring to restrain trade, monopolize the market, fix prices, and interfere with the business rights of competitors.

Sherman Act. The Sherman Act was enacted July 2, 1890, for the purpose of controlling interstate trade and foreign commerce to prevent monopolistic practices or conspiracies in restraint of trade. Sections 1 and 2 of the Act, as amended, which are pertinent to business combinations, read as follows:

SECTION 1. *Every contract, combination in the form of trust or otherwise, or conspiracy, in restraint of trade or commerce among the several States, or with foreign nations, is hereby declared to be illegal:* Provided, That nothing herein contained shall render illegal, contracts or agreements prescribing minimum prices for the resale of a commodity which bears, or the label or container of which bears, the trade mark, brand, or name of the producer or distributor of such commodity and which is in free and open competition with commodities of the same general class produced or distributed by others, when contracts or agreements of that description are lawful as applied to intrastate transactions, under any statute, law, or public policy now or hereafter in effect in any State, Territory, or the District of Columbia in which such resale is to be made, or to which the commodity is to be transported for such resale, and the making of such contracts or agreements shall not be an unfair method of competition under section 5, as amended and supplemented, of the act entitled "An Act to create a Federal Trade Commission, to define its powers and duties, and for other purposes," approved September 26, 1914: *Provided further,* That the preceding proviso shall not make lawful any contract or agreement, providing for the establishment or maintenance of minimum resale prices on any commodity herein involved, between manufacturers, or between producers, or between wholesalers, or between brokers, or between factors, or between retailers, or between persons, firms, or corporations in competition with each other. Every person who shall make any contract or engage in any combination or conspiracy hereby declared to be illegal shall be deemed guilty of a misdemeanor, and, on conviction thereof, shall be punished by fine not exceeding fifty thousand dollars, or by imprisonment not exceeding one year, or by both said punishments, in the discretion of the court.

SEC. 2. *Every person who shall monopolize, or attempt to monopolize, or combine or conspire with any other person or persons, to monopolize any part of the trade or commerce among the several States, or with foreign nations, shall be deemed guilty of a misdemeanor, and, on conviction thereof, shall be punished by fine not exceeding fifty thousand dollars, or by imprisonment not exceeding one year, or by both said punishments, in the discretion of the court.*[12]

The first case under the Sherman Act, which involved a business combination, resulted from a petition filed in 1892 in the Circuit Court against the E. C. Knight Co. and others.[13] In this case, American Sugar Refining Co. acquired the capital stocks of four independent sugar refineries, including Knight, and thus gained control of over 90 per cent of the productive facilities of that industry in the United States. The Circuit Court in 1894 held for the defendants and ordered the petition dismissed. This decision was affirmed later that year by the Circuit Court of Appeals and in 1895 by the Supreme Court. Although this decision may have rested on some fine technicalities, the popular judicial interpretation of it, at that time, was to the effect that corporations could combine *by agreement* and not be in restraint of trade.

DECISION IN *Northern Securities* CASE RAISED SERIOUS QUESTIONS ABOUT BUSINESS COMBINATIONS. At any rate, there were no other petitions filed under the Sherman Act, involving business combinations, until that of the *United States v. Northern Securities Co.* in 1902. This action, filed in the Circuit Court, alleged that Northern Securities Co. (a holding company) and certain named individuals, pursuant to a combination or conspiracy in restraint of trade, had acquired and were voting a large majority of the capital stock of Great Northern Railway Co. and Northern Pacific Railway Co. In 1903, a decree was entered, which was affirmed by the Supreme Court in 1904,[14] declaring the combination illegal and enjoining the Northern Securities Co. from acquiring additional stock, from voting the stock it then held, and from exercising any control over the railroads. Some of the language used by the Court was broad enough

[12] Act of July 2, 1890, c. 647, 26 Stat. 209, 51st Cong., 1st Sess. (S. 1, Public 190), as amended by Act of March 3, 1911, c. 231, 36 Stat. 1167, and Act of August 17, 1937 ("Miller-Tydings Act"), c. 690, 50 Stat. 693, 75th Cong., 1st Sess. (H. R. 7472, Public 314).
[13] United States v. E. C. Knight Co., 156 U.S. 1 (1895).
[14] Northern Securities Co. v. United States, 193 U.S. 197 (1904).

to raise serious questions about business combinations of competing companies.

AFTERMATH OF *Northern Securities* DECISION. During the next several years, suits were filed under the Act against Standard Oil Co. of N. J., American Tobacco Co., and Du Pont de Nemours Co., the adjudication of which resulted in the dissolution of their existing combinations and divestment of many interests.

Clayton Act. The Clayton Act, enacted October 15, 1914, was considered by Congress to be in the nature of an amendment to the Sherman Act. One of the purposes of the Clayton Act was to exempt labor unions and agricultural cooperative organizations from being construed as illegal combinations or conspiracies in restraint of trade, when lawfully carrying out their legitimate objectives. The Act also contained a specific provision relating to acquisitions and mergers, which enabled the enforcing agencies to act to prevent such business combinations as well as to petition for their dissolution. In addition, the Clayton Act empowered either the Federal Trade Commission (which was created under a separate act in 1914) or the Attorney General to "prevent and restrain" violations under the Act.

Section 7 of the Clayton Act, as amended through July 7, 1955, is pertinent to business combinations and reads as follows:

SEC. 7. That no corporation engaged in commerce shall acquire, directly or indirectly, the whole or any part of the stock or other share capital and no corporation subject to the jurisdiction of the Federal Trade Commission shall acquire the whole or any part of the assets of another corporation engaged also in commerce, where in any line of commerce in any section of the country, the effect of such acquisition may be substantially to lessen competition, or to tend to create a monopoly.

No corporation shall acquire, directly or indirectly, the whole or any part of the stock or other share capital and no corporation subject to the jurisdiction of the Federal Trade Commission shall acquire the whole or any part of the assets of one or more corporations engaged in commerce, where in any line of commerce in any section of the country, the effect of such acquisition, of such stocks or assets, or of the use of such stock by the voting or granting of proxies or otherwise, may be substantially to lessen competition, or to tend to create a monopoly.

This section shall not apply to corporations purchasing such stock solely for investment and not using the same by voting or otherwise to bring about, or in attempting to bring about, the substantial lessening of competition. Nor shall anything contained in this section prevent a corporation engaged in commerce from causing the formation of subsidiary corporations for the actual carrying on of their immediate lawful business, or the natural and legitimate branches or extensions thereof, or from owning and holding all or a part of the stock of such subsidiary corporations, when the effect of such formation is not to substantially lessen competition.

Nor shall anything herein contained be construed to prohibit any common carrier subject to the laws to regulate commerce from aiding in the construction of branches or short lines so located as to become feeders to the main line of the company so aiding in such construction or from acquiring or owning all or any part of the stock of such branch lines, nor to prevent any such common carrier from acquiring and owning all or any part of the stock of a branch or short line constructed by an independent company where there is no substantial competition between the company owning the branch line so constructed and the company owning the main line acquiring the property or an interest therein, nor to prevent such common carrier from extending any of its lines through the medium of the acquisition of stock or otherwise of any other common carrier where there is no substantial competition between the company extending its lines and the company whose stock, property, or an interest therein is so acquired.

Nothing contained in this section shall be held to affect or impair any right heretofore legally acquired: *Provided,* That nothing in this section shall be held or construed to authorize or make lawful anything heretofore prohibited or made illegal by the antitrust laws, nor to exempt any person from the penal provisions thereof or the civil remedies therein provided.

Nothing contained in this section shall apply to transactions duly consummated pursuant to authority given by the Civil Aeronautics Board, Federal Communications Commission, Federal Power Commission, Interstate Commerce Commission, the Securities and Exchange Commission in the exercise of its jurisdiction under section 10 of the Public Utility Holding Company Act of 1935, the United States Maritime Commission, or the Secretary of Agriculture under any statutory provision vesting such power in such Commission, Secretary, or Board.[15]

As originally enacted, the Clayton Act prohibited acquisitions of stock but not of assets, where the effect of the business combination would be to lessen competition or create a monopoly, and applied specifically to the acquisition of competitors and not to acquisitions of suppliers, customers, or others. Subsequent amendments broadened the language to make vertical and conglomerate acquisitions, as well as those of assets, subject to

---

[15] Act of October 15, 1914, c. 323, 38 Stat. 730, 63d Cong., 2d Sess. (H. R. 15657, Public 212), as amended by Act of May 15, 1916, c. 120, 39 Stat. 121, 64th Cong., 1st Sess. (S. 4432, Public 75); Act of August 31, 1916, c. 427, 39 Stat. 674, 64th Cong., 1st Sess. (S. J. Res. 129, Public Res. 33); Act of September 7, 1916, c. 461, 39 Stat. 752, 64th Cong., 1st Sess. (H. R. 13391, Public 270); Act of March 4, 1917, c. 190, 39 Stat. 1201, 64th Cong., 2d Sess. (S. J. Res. 206, Public Res. 55); Act of January 12, 1918, c. 8, 40 Stat. 431, 65th Cong., 2d Sess. (S. J. Res. 106, Public Res. 20); Act of December 24, 1919, c. 18, 41 Stat. 378, 66th Cong., 2d Sess. (S. 2472, Public 106); Act of February 28, 1920, c. 91, 41 Stat. 456, 66th Cong., 2d.

provisions of the Act. In fact, lawyers claim the following language of the Clayton Act is manifestly unfair in that it enables the enforcing agencies to act not only before there is proof of a violation but before there is even evidence of potential wrongdoing:

> . . . no corporation . . . shall acquire the whole or any part of the assets of another corporation . . . where in any line of commerce in any section of the country, the effect of such acquisition *may be* substantially to lessen competition, or to tend to create a monopoly.[16]

ANTITRUST CASES INVOLVING BUSINESS COMBINATIONS. As a matter of interest, although there have been 1,652 suits filed in court by government enforcing agencies from 1890 through 1961, only 208 have been in connection with "business combinations." This does not include numerous complaints filed by the Federal Trade Commission that have been settled at the administrative level. These business combination suits include not only those dealing with prospective and recently completed acquisitions and mergers, but also cases in which the government has endeavored to break up companies that built up to their dominant positions over a long period. Examples of these are the early *Standard Oil* and *American Tobacco* cases, the more recent *Du Pont-General Motors* case, and those resulting in the separation of exhibiting from the production business in the motion picture industry.

This cumulative record of relatively few cases involving business combinations is not necessarily indicative of current or future activity of the law enforcement agencies in endeavoring to prevent business combinations in their incipient state, or to force their dissolution, if effected. As mentioned, some of the amendments to the Clayton Act extended its provisions, so that actions initiated by law enforcement agencies in recent years would not have been undertaken in earlier years. For example, the Federal Trade Commission filed a complaint against American Marietta Co. (now Martin-Marietta Co.) of Chicago, accusing it of violating the antitrust laws in conglomerate acquisitions of forty-nine companies throughout the country during the years 1953 to 1960.[17]

[16] *Ibid.*
[17] F.T.C. Docket of Complaints 8280 (1961).

The Brown Shoe Co. CASE. A United States Supreme Court decision in June, 1962, involving Brown Shoe Co. was of considerable interest in interpreting the 1950 amendment of Section 7 of the Clayton Antitrust Act. In this decision, the Supreme Court affirmed the Federal District Court order requiring Brown to divest itself of G. R. Kinney Co., which it had acquired in 1955.[18] Brown was then the fourth largest shoe manufacturer in the country but also had retail outlets, and Kinney was the largest retail shoe outlet and the twelfth largest manufacturer. The two companies together accounted for only 4½ per cent of national shoe production.

The Court's opinion pointed out that "in this industry no merger between a manufacturer and an independent retailer could involve a larger potential market foreclosure," and further that:

The trend toward vertical integration in the shoe industry, when combined with Brown's avowed policy of forcing its own shoes upon its retail subsidiaries, seems likely to foreclose competition from a substantial share of the market for men's, women's, and children's shoes, without producing any countervailing competition, economic, or social advantages.

The Court noted, with relation to the amended statute language, which reads *"may be* substantially to lessen competition," that it "requires a prognosis of the probably future effect of the merger." In summing up, it was the Court's position that:

We cannot avoid the mandate of Congress that tendencies toward concentration in industry are to be curbed in their incipiency, particularly when those tendencies are being accelerated through giant steps striding across a hundred cities at a time. In the light of the trends in this industry we agree with the Government and the court below that this is an appropriate place at which to call a halt.

Recent Antitrust Activity. There has been a noticeable stepup in total activity in recent years by the enlarged Anti-Trust Division of the Department of Justice. Also, the Federal Trade Commission is substantially increasing its staff. This acceleration in total activity will no doubt result in an increase in cases involving business combinations.

The primary purpose of the foregoing discussion of federal antitrust laws, as they affect acquisitions and mergers, is to alert

[18] Brown Shoe Co., Inc. v. United States, 370 U.S. 294 (1962).

the prospective acquirer to this aspect of a business combination. In some cases, there may be no problem involved; in others, there may. If there appears to be a problem, it is sometimes desirable to seek prior government clearance before effecting a deal, and at times it is not. It is therefore prudent to seek the advice of legal counsel regarding the antitrust aspects of any business combination undertaken.

FINDERS' FEES AND BROKERS' COMMISSIONS

Investment bankers, business brokers, and management consultants often act as "finders" in endeavoring to locate a company either for purposes of acquisition on behalf of their principal or to purchase or merge "upstream" the company represented by their principal. In addition to such organizations that make a business of bringing together principals wishing to negotiate mergers, acquisitions, and sales of companies, almost anyone can qualify as a finder and claim a fee for his services.

Some Organizations Perform Services in Addition to the Mere Act of "Finding." While the type of organizations mentioned act as finders, they also perform other services, such as assisting in negotiations and endeavoring to work out the terms of a deal. Therefore, their compensation for services may include a finder's fee, if the deal is consummated, in addition to other charges. If no deal is consummated, they may not render any charges; or else their fees may be based on time expended, provided an agreement is made with them to this effect prior to the undertaking.

When a Finder's Services Are Limited Merely to That Activity. A finder's services may be limited merely to the bringing together of a possible buyer and seller. Even if there is no written contract covering such services, he could be entitled to a fee if he can demonstrate that there was an implied contract or obligation to pay him a fee. Often, a finder will approach an investment banking or management consulting firm with the view to arranging a deal with some company for which he is acting and one of the clients of such firms.

A finder's fee or originating commission, as it is sometimes called, may be asserted against the acquirer or seller, whichever the finder is acting for. There have been many litigated cases involving claims for finders' fees, including some multiple claims for the same deal. It is therefore prudent, when a principal discusses with any person the possibility of locating an acquirer or seller who might be interested in a merger, purchase, or sale of a business, that there be a clear understanding of the services to be performed by the finder, investment banker, business broker, or management consultant. This understanding and the basis of compensation should be set forth in writing.

Range of Finders' Fees or Commissions. The fees or commissions paid to finders or brokers range generally from 1 to 5 per cent of the amount involved in the business transaction. The larger the transaction, the lower the percentage of fee relative to the amount of the deal. As mentioned, investment bankers or business brokers or consultants will often perform services in addition to the finding of a candidate for a business combination, on various prearranged fee bases.

Independent certified public accountants and commercial banks sometimes are of service in locating candidates for business combinations for their clients. The former are prohibited by their code of ethics from asserting finders' fees, and the latter generally do not claim such fees either through ethical or other considerations.

CORPORATE RAIDERS

All acquisitions and mergers are not the result of amicable planning by both parties involved in the combination. The managements of some companies are on the lookout for corporate bargains, with the view to buying an interest in them and ultimately effecting a business combination through an exchange of capital stocks.

Typical Company Vulnerable to a Raid. The typical company vulnerable to such a raid is one whose operating results have been poor for a period of several years, whose market price per share is considerably below its net book equity, and whose management is allegedly weak. If management is holding a very small percentage of outstanding shares of the company's capital stock, this is an added incentive to the would-be acquirer.

Procedure Followed by Would-Be Acquirers. The customary initial step in acquisitions involving companies taken over with some reluctance or downright dissent on the part of the management is the purchase of substantial amounts of capital stock by the would-be acquirer, usually in nominee names. Once the purchaser has become the beneficial owner (not necessarily the holder of record) of 10 per cent or more of the capital stock of a company that is listed on a national securities exchange, he must file a statement indicating such ownership with the exchange and with the Securities and Exchange Commission within ten days after the close of the calendar month.[19] Thereafter, if there is any change in his holdings, he must file continuing statements after the close of each calendar month in which there is a change.

Sometimes, a tender offer to buy a company's stock at a price above market may be made to stockholders by the would-be acquirer, initially or after he has accumulated some of the stock.

The disclosure of a company's holdings in another may not be wholly indicative of the voting strength it can muster. Very often, particularly if it appears that the company in which the stock is being purchased would show improvement in operating results under the management of the aspiring purchaser, a number of large investors, and investment bankers, may purchase stock in the company, primarily in nominee names. These investors probably would support the prospective acquirer in a show of voting strength.

Interesting Cases Involving Fights for Control in Recent Years. During recent years, there have been some interesting cases of

---

[19] Securities Exchange Act of 1934, Sec. 16(a):

"Every person who is directly or indirectly the beneficial owner of more than 10 per centum of any class of any equity security (other than an exempted security) which is registered on a national securities exchange, or who is a director or an officer of the issuer of such security, shall file, at the time of the registration of such security or within ten days after he becomes such beneficial owner, director, or officer, a statement with the exchange (and a duplicate original thereof with the Commission) of the amount of all equity securities of such issuer of which he is the beneficial owner, and within ten days after the close of each calendar month thereafter, if there has been any change in such ownership during such month, shall file with the exchange a statement (and a duplicate original thereof with the Commission) indicating his ownership at the close of the calendar month and such changes in his ownership as have occurred during such calendar month."

companies allegedly or actively endeavoring to force business combinations with others. Some were successful in effecting the combinations, though not necessarily successful in operating the combined enterprises. In other cases, the would-be acquirers were thwarted in their efforts.

THE *Fairbanks, Morse & Co.* CASE. The Fairbanks, Whitney Corp. (then Penn-Texas Corp.) acquisition of approximately 85 per cent of the capital stock of Fairbanks, Morse & Co., through a series of purchases and a proxy contest with the incumbent management of the latter, was so costly from the standpoint of the prices paid for the stock, and for interest on money borrowed to finance the purchases, that it substantially diluted the value of the parent company's stock. Furthermore, Fairbanks, Morse has had poor operating results since its acquisition by Fairbanks, Whitney.[20]

THE *E. L. Bruce Co.* CASE. Empire National Corp., which had acquired 81 per cent of the stock of E. L. Bruce Co. following a proxy fight in 1958, acquired the remaining outstanding shares via the merger route in 1961, despite the efforts of C. Arthur Bruce to block the combination through a suit filed in Chancery Court.[21] Later, E. M. Gilbert, who was credited with effecting the takeover of E. L. Bruce through Empire, a family corporation, endeavored to pyramid his corporate empire through the acquisition of shares of Celotex Corp., with a view to eventual merger of that company into E. L. Bruce Co. (name changed from Empire National Corp.).

This proved to be Mr. Gilbert's undoing when stock market prices plunged; and early in June, 1962, he admitted unauthorized withdrawals from E. L. Bruce approximating $2,000,000, reportedly to support his market operations in acquiring Celotex stock.[22]

These instances point up an important factor in considering the desirability of acquiring control of a company, other than by consent of both managements. The stock of a company selling

[20] See Chapter 3, page 38.
[21] Bruce v. E. L. Bruce Co., 174 A.2d 29 (1961).
[22] *Business Week,* June 16, 1962, p. 38.

at an apparently depressed price may be a bargain when you start to acquire its shares but may increase in price substantially through the buying support generated by the would-be acquirer. Furthermore, at some point in the acquisition plan, it may be necessary to offer tenders to stockholders at prices ranging up to 20 per cent or more above market in order to obtain sufficient control to force a business combination. During the course of such successive purchases of the stock at increasing prices, it may lose its bargain aspect.

PUBLIC ANNOUNCEMENTS OF BUSINESS COMBINATIONS

The timing and type of public announcements of business combinations is a matter of considerable importance. Various practices have been followed in the timing of announcements, ranging from those indicating that a preliminary offer has been made or preliminary negotiations are being conducted to announcements made after a formal agreement has been signed.

Usually, secrecy must be maintained in premerger discussions. However, when negotiations reach an appropriate stage, a company should inform its employees and stockholders of such actions as early as possible. This is particularly important where there are a number of individuals involved in the negotiations and the possibility exists of a news leak. Generally, the announcement should be made to employees the day that the published release is made. The published releases, by the two or more companies involved, should be identical.

Announcement to Employees. The method of informing executives and employees of an impending business combination may vary depending upon the size of the company and whether it is the prospective seller or acquirer. The seller's executives and employees will be most anxious about the future in such deals; and when negotiations have reached a stage of substantial agreement between the parties, it is generally wise, from a morale standpoint, to advise at least the other members of the executive group not participating in the negotiations and key personnel whose continuing services are important to the business combination.

An employee's interest in a business combination differs from that of a stockholder, although he may also have an interest in the latter capacity. Whether the proposed business combination will be carried out under the tax-free reorganization provisions, and treated as a pooling of interests for accounting purposes, will be of minor concern to him. What he will be interested in is whether he will lose his job or be downgraded or upgraded, or have his salary and fringe benefits maintained, increased, or cut. The answers to these questions will not be found in the press release. Accordingly, it is desirable to prepare an announcement particularly for employee purposes.

The major factors in such an employee communication may be summarized as follows:

1. Tell the employee as soon as you tell the world. Since he is involved directly, he should not have to read about the deal in the newspapers.
2. Explain generally why the business combination is desirable or necessary.
3. Indicate confidence in the desirability of the deal. You cannot expect employees to have confidence if your release implies a lack of it.
4. Outline the proposed organization after the business combination. Be careful not to make promises that you know cannot be fulfilled. It is better to face adverse issues immediately, if they are readily apparent.

An example of a type of release to employees of Food Packing Co., which was proposed to be merged into Ajax Products, Inc., follows:

To All Employees:

The attached press release of a proposed merger with Ajax Products, Inc., tells of another important step forward for our company. After stockholders approve this combination, your management believes the resulting company will be one of the best equipped to serve the public and industry with products they desire.

The new company's sales will be over $800 million. More important will be the combined resources and talents, including the extensive research departments, which are so vital today in the progress of any business. Our products will be put in an advantageous position for world-wide distribution because of the well-established trained sales organizations of Ajax Products and the favorable locations of its plants throughout the world.

Every day people are in a position to demand better products—new products that will help them in every way. With the resources of the combined companies, we will be able to go forward with the times. To do this will take personnel, probably more than we now have; and it should result in greater opportunities for everyone.

Both companies have excellent retirement plans, and nothing will be done to impair their good features or to deprive anyone of benefits under the plans.

You know how careful and, we think, successful your management has been in the past in acquiring new businesses. We feel sure that we are using the same good judgment in this merger. Ajax is the leader in its field, and merging two such companies of the same top caliber must produce a more successful one—to the best interests of all. To make it so, we have only to believe in it thoroughly.

Charles L. Peterson
President

An example follows of a letter circulated to key executives of Ajax Products, Inc., the surviving company in the merger:

Our negotiations for a merger with Food Packing have culminated in a preliminary agreement, the basis of which is outlined in the attached press release.

We will want to acquaint ourselves with pertinent facts about the company that will join us later this year. The attached Annual Report of Food Packing provides general background.

The news story, when it breaks today, will cause quite a stir. We can expect to be asked many questions. May I remind you that all questions coming from the press should be routed through the office of Edward Jones, our public relations director.

Our people will be asking questions, too. Probably they will be wondering whether jobs will be affected. The answer is that Food Packing will operate as an independent division. The merger of these two leading enterprises should result in greater opportunity for everyone.

We shall keep you advised of important developments.

John W. Williams
President

Releases to the Outside Public. Aside from the desirable public relations aspects of announcements of impending business combinations, regulatory bodies have requirements that affect the timely release of such information. For example, the New York

Stock Exchange, in its company manual, states as one of the objectives of its current form of listing agreement that it seeks to achieve, for companies whose stocks are listed on the exchange, "timely disclosure to the public and to the Exchange, of information which may affect security values or influence investment decisions, and in which stockholders, the public and the Exchange have a warrantable interest." [23]

Also, in some states, in the case of a statutory merger, a negotiating permit is required to be obtained under the provisions of their corporate security laws (blue sky laws) before an agreement of merger is completed and filed under the general corporation laws. The intention of the parties to the proposed merger accordingly becomes a matter of public record.

The following random selection of public releases on business combinations, in recent years, indicates the difference in "timing" followed by the various companies involved.

Stage of Negotiations at Time of Announcement	Announcement Date
Preliminary offer or preliminary negotiations:	
American Cyanimid Co.—Formica Co.	Dec. 13, 1955
Progress Mfg. Co.—Reading Tube Co.	May 21, 1960
Diamond Alkali—Bessemer Limestone Co.	Apr. 18, 1961
Quaker Oats Co.—Burry Biscuit Co.	July 11, 1961
U. S. Industries—National Associated Mills	Aug. 29, 1962
Approval (or approval "in principle") of terms of business combination by Board of Directors:	
Union Bag Paper Co.—Camp Mfg. Co.	May 30, 1956
Beech-Nut Packaging Co.—Life Saver Corp.	June 7, 1956
Lone Star Cement Co.—Superior Portland Cement Co.	Dec. 29, 1956
Kennecott Copper Co.—The Okonite Co.	Oct. 15, 1958
The Ruberoid Co.—Mastic Tile Corp. of America	July 1, 1959
Bell & Howell—Consolidated Electrodynamics Corp.	Oct. 28, 1959
Dow Chemical Co.—Allied Laboratories	Sept. 1, 1960
Midland Ross Corp.—Industrial Rayon Corp.	Feb. 22, 1961
National Biscuit Co.—Cream of Wheat	Apr. 12, 1961
Ford Motor Co.—Philco Corp.	Sept. 14, 1961
Lock Joint Pipe Co.—Gladding, McBean & Co.	May 22, 1962
Formal agreement signed and approved by Board of Directors:	
Monsanto Chemical Co.—Lion Oil Co.	July 22, 1955
Eaton Mfg. Co.—Fuller Mfg. Co.	June 21, 1958
Aluminum Company of America—Rome Cable Co.	Jan. 23, 1959
Warner-Lambert Pharmaceutical Co.—American Chicle Co.	Aug. 14, 1962

SOURCE: *The New York Times,* issues of dates of announcements.

[23] *New York Stock Exchange Company Manual,* Sec. A-2, December 1, 1959, p. 19.

In some instances, where the announcement was made after Board of Directors approval, or approval "in principle," letters of intent had already been signed by the respective managements.

Although early public releases on impending business combinations are recommended, it would appear desirable to withhold announcement until (1) substantial agreement has been reached on "price," or on the ratio of the exchange of shares of capital stock; and (2) the deal has been approved, at least "in principle," by the respective Boards of Directors. At times it may be necessary to announce negotiations in progress before this stage has been reached; but an announcement, which of necessity says nothing, does not create a good public image of the companies negotiating.

New York Stock Exchange Statements on Predisclosure Handling of Such Matters. Chapter 12 page 221 contains extracts from the exchange company manual regarding the care that must be exercised to keep matters such as business combination negotiations confidential prior to public disclosure.[24]

GOOD EXAMPLE OF PUBLIC ANNOUNCEMENT OF IMPENDING MERGER. The following public announcement of an impending merger between Lock Joint Pipe Co. and Gladding, McBean & Co. is a good example of a timely and informative release:

NEW YORK—Directors of Lock Joint Pipe Co., of East Orange, N.J., and Gladding, McBean & Co., Los Angeles, approved a merger of the companies, the companies announced. The merger is subject to approval of stockholders of each company at special meetings this summer.

A spokesman for Lock Joint said a name for the new corporation hasn't been determined, and no date had been set for the merger to go into effect.

Under the proposed merger, Gladding, McBean stockholders will exchange five shares of common stock for one share of 5% cumulative convertible preferred stock, $100 par value of the new corporation.

The preferred stock will be convertible into $2\frac{5}{8}$ shares of common stock. It will be noncallable for ten years, and thereafter callable at $110 a share.

Lock Joint stockholders will exchange common shares for common shares of the new corporation on a share-for-share basis.

Lock Joint manufactures pre-stressed concrete pipe and sewer and culvert pipes. The company recently entered the plastic pipe, fittings and corrosion resistant materials field.

[24] *Ibid.*, February 18, 1962, p. A–21.

Lock Joint operates 38 plants in the eastern U.S. and overseas. Its earnings in 1961 were $4,113,490 on sales of $59,660,000. The company has 1,829,938 common shares outstanding.

Gladding-McBean manufactures a diversified line of ceramic products. It operates 14 plants in the western U.S., and has working arrangements in a number of foreign countries. Last year Gladding-McBean had earnings of $1,949,000 on revenues of $33,768,000. The company has 1,724,937 common shares outstanding.

Gladding-McBean closed at $18.375 yesterday on the New York Stock Exchange, up 62½ cents from Friday's closing. Lock Joint, traded over-the-counter, was quoted at $39 bid and $43 asked late yesterday. The previous closing was $36 bid.[25]

[25] *The Wall Street Journal*, May 22, 1962.

APPENDIXES

Appendix A

CHECKLIST FOR PROPOSED ACQUISITIONS AND MERGERS

I. SUMMARY OF INFORMATION CONCERNING PROPOSED ACQUISITION OR MERGER

This general section has been designed for use as a summary, where a comprehensive review of the financial statements has been carried out. However, it also may be used as a modified checklist in a "quickie review" when supplemented by reference to pertinent questions in Section II.

A considerable amount of information may be obtained on a company from outside sources such as *Moody's Industrial Manual* or similar publications, annual reports to stockholders, Form 10–K or other reports and proxy statements filed with the S.E.C., and Dun & Bradstreet reports on unlisted companies. Marketing and sales information may be obtained from brochures distributed by the company, as well as from trade, industry, and United States government publications.

The Proposed Transaction

1. Summarize the known facts about the proposed transaction to outline the objectives of the acquisition. This should include any unusual reasons given as an advantage or disadvantage for the acquisition.
2. Prepare or obtain a summary of the business being acquired, including history, ownership, products, competition, geographical scope of operations, and trend in recent years.
3. Describe the objectives in obtaining either a company in this industry or this particular company. Indicate whether a competing business could be established without the acquisition of a going concern.
4. Describe the seller's objectives in disposing of the company or the need for additional financing. Any indication of possible weaknesses should be included in this summary.
5. Analyze the price that the seller has placed on the business and compare it with the acceptable rate of return or an acceptable price, if one has been established. Comment on possible profit improvements that seem attainable in the near future including the amount of any additional capital outlays that appear necessary to obtain such improvements.
6. Indicate if it appears that contributions in the form of management talent; cash investment; or a solution of difficult operating, labor, or other problems will be required in order to make the acquisition a success.

Tax Aspects

The tax aspects of a business combination are most important; therefore, an individual with considerable experience should be involved in the preliminary review or consulted at the outset of negotiations.

1. The taxable status of a proposed transaction should be set forth; i.e., will it result in a tax to the seller, or will it be tax free under the reorganization provisions of the Internal Revenue Code.
2. If it is a taxable transaction, can the major portion of the purchase price over the seller's tax basis be allocated to assets, other than goodwill, so that tax benefit will be obtained upon their disposition or through depreciation and amortization charges? Consider the possible effect of the 1962 Code changes with respect to depreciation "recapture" provisions.
3. If the contemplated transaction would be non-taxable, consider the best way to accomplish the objectives of the purchaser and seller under the various alternatives afforded in tax-free exchanges.

4. Obtain information as to operating losses, amortization of emergency facilities, the use of sum of the years-digits or declining balance methods of depreciation, and LIFO inventory valuations, if any. In the event of a "bargain purchase" of inventories, the advisability of preserving the low basis for inventories by adopting "LIFO" should be considered.

Securities and Exchange Commission Aspects

If the acquiring company is subject to the reporting requirements of the S.E.C. or will become so as a result of the transaction, consideration should be given to this factor. These requirements may include any or all of the following: (1) a registration statement under the Securities Act of 1933, (2) a proxy statement under Regulation X–14 of the Securities Exchange Act of 1934, (3) a Form 8–K under the Securities Exchange Act of 1934. The applicability of these various requirements should be discussed with legal counsel.

Also, consideration should be given to the desirability of conferring with members of the Securities and Exchange Commisison staff if any unusual accounting or related problems appear likely in the event the transaction is consummated.

Possible Pitfalls to Acquiring Company

1. Describe the conditions of the industry that gave rise to the company proposed to be acquired, and those that govern its rate of growth or decline. Indicate whether:
   a) These conditions can be duplicated or exceeded by competitors or others; or
   b) Present advantages may be eliminated by loss of government contracts, changes in laws, expiration of patents, etc.
2. Consider whether the transaction results in any shareholder of the acquired company becoming a controlling stockholder of the surviving company.

Status and Development of the Company

1. Show the company's development to date by comparing financial results for at least the last five years for each major division. Indicate for this period the amount of assets employed, the rate of return on investment, and the number of employees.
2. Describe the company's present and probable future competitive position, to the extent practicable, considering such factors as product development, market analysis, and geographical conditions.

3. Ascertain, if possible, whether or not the company carries a "full" product line, or in what respects it is deficient. Also, indicate which products are carried with low sales volumes or low gross profit margins.
4. Indicate whether products are manufactured for stock or against specific orders and if they are accompanied by guarantees or warranties. If so, describe the terms.
5. Indicate if the company purchases and sells on the basis of fixed long-term contracts and, if so, their impact on future earnings.
6. If products are based primarily on patents, indicate who owns them, expiration dates, and the possible impact of loss of patent protection.

Accounting Principles and Practices

The primary purpose of obtaining information regarding accounting principles and practices and certain other accounting information is to make comparisons of the net assets and net income of the company proposed to be acquired on a basis comparable to that of the acquiring company, to develop data pertinent to evaluation of the respective companies, and to project future operations of the combined enterprise.

1. Indicate whether the financial statements have presented the position of the company and its operating results on a consistent basis.
2. State the bases for valuing inventories, receivables, properties, investments, etc.
3. Indicate whether:
   a) Liabilities for taxes, renegotiation, warranties, etc., where definite amounts may not be known are either reserved for or indicated in footnotes to the financial statements.
   b) Liabilities or reserves for future items such as pensions, dismissal indemnities, vacations, etc., are either recorded or indicated in footnotes to the financial statements.
   c) Items of income applicable to future periods or provisions of reserves for future expenses are taken into the current period.
   d) Losses on unfavorable contracts are recorded.
4. Indicate major differences between book and tax basis of net assets and evaluate any net of tax reserves against probability of future taxable position to use such deductions.

The following sections of the checklist are intended for more comprehensive reviews, where the "quickie" type of review will not suffice. Of course, reference may be made to pertinent questions in any of these sections, particularly Section II, to supplement the more general questions in Section I, when the latter is used for a "quickie review."

II. CORPORATE, ACCOUNTING, AND FINANCIAL

Corporate, accounting, and financial information should be accumulated in a manner that highlights accounting considerations that affect the proposed transaction. Such information also should be in sufficient detail to permit restatement of the net assets of the companies involved on a comparable basis and to facilitate the estimate of future earnings.

Corporate

1. Schedule the present legal form of the organization and the legal forms through which it has passed.
2. List the principal provisions of the articles of incorporation, charter, by-laws, etc.
3. Describe the major rights and restrictions imposed on management by the outstanding common stock, preferred stock, long- or short-term debt.
4. Indicate the possibility of change in ownership through conversion of preferred stock or bonds to common stock, exercise of unexpired stock rights or options, pre-emptive privileges, or sale of treasury stock.

Accounting and Financial

A. *Cash.*

1. Schedule the maximum and minimum bank balances during the year.
2. Describe any restrictions in effect on cash as a result of debt or other agreements.
3. Schedule the current and cash position over the past five years with a rough statement of the cash flow for this period.
4. Indicate whether a line of credit has been available to the company and if a lack of credit has hampered growth.

B. *Marketable securities.*

List the marketable securities and the basis of recording them on the books together with present market values.

C. *Notes and accounts receivable.*

1. Indicate the number of open accounts.
2. Attach a schedule of all accounts with a balance exceeding 10 per cent of total receivables.
3. Review aging and schedule aged accounts receivable in total for the current and the balance sheet date of the previous year.

4. Attach a schedule of receivables from other than normal trade accounts, such as United States government, officers, employees, etc.

5. List notes and accounts discounted or hypothecated.

6. Attach a recap of accounts written off as uncollectible during the last year or two.

7. Indicate if the reserve for uncollectible accounts appears adequate.

D. *Inventories.*

1. Indicate the basis of recording inventories and describe the cost system in use.

2. Schedule inventories by type including items on consignment in or out.

3. Recap the latest physical inventory by major categories and show comparison with book amounts and perpetual records, if any.

4. Indicate date and results of latest review for obsolete, unusable, or unsalable stock on hand.

5. Indicate the months' or years' supply of the largest or typical large items of inventory on hand.

6. Ascertain if work in process will be completed at a normal profit. This applies particularly in the case of long-term contracts and where the production cycle requires a long period of time to complete.

E. *Fixed assets.*

1. Schedule fixed assets by type, indicating original cost or other basis and amount and rates of accumulated depreciation. Indicate whether there are idle or excess assets held and in what amounts.

2. Attach details of any current appraisals or estimates of value of fixed assets and indicate whether the appraisal was for insurance or other purposes.

3. Indicate whether tax basis and book basis are identical. If not, schedule major differences.

4. Indicate mortgages and other liens.

5. Indicate whether guideline lives are used for tax purposes but not for books and if so whether deferred tax has been provided for in the accounts.

F. *Prepaid expenses and deferred charges.*

1. Attach schedule of major items deferred to subsequent periods and the method of write-off or amortization.

2. Comment on any change in company policy over last few years in order to ascertain consistency of application.

3. Evaluate whether deferred charges are of value to purchaser.

G. *Investments.*

1. Schedule the investments showing the basis for book amounts and the current market values or underlying equities.

2. Describe ownership in unconsolidated subsidiary companies and method of recording income of such companies.

3. Prepare schedules showing for each unconsolidated subsidiary the excess of underlying assets and the unrecorded income for the last five years. Indicate clearly the source from which such data are compiled.

4. Record all advances and payables to affiliated companies or unconsolidated subsidiaries.

H. *Goodwill, trade-marks, patents, etc.*

1. Schedule all intangible assets recorded in the accounts showing the book basis and amortization policy.

2. Indicate whether company has any intangible or other assets that may not be shown in the accounts.

I. *Current liabilities.*

1. Schedule major current liabilities being sure to indicate whether company accrues for profit-sharing bonuses, vacations, dismissal indemnities, and pension costs.

2. Indicate the basis for recording the above liabilities—whether deferred or current and if net of tax or gross.

J. *Income taxes.*

1. Indicate which years are still open for federal and major state taxes.

2. Schedule items of significance that have been disallowed in revenue agents' reviews of prior years' tax returns.

3. Schedule major differences between tax and book income for last five to ten years to determine if book income is reasonable and if any unrecorded future tax liabilities exist. Schedule any available operating loss carry-forwards by years.

4. Evaluate the effect of prior adjustments on the unexamined years and indicate any major items that are apt to be disputed.

K. *Short- and long-term debt from banks, insurance companies, bonds payable, etc.*

1. Show the following information by type of loan: amount, interest rates, due date, liens on assets, advance-payment privileges and penalties, and renewal privileges.

2. Read indentures for restrictions on working capital, dividends, mergers, etc.

L. *Contingent liabilities.*

1. Determine if there are any contingent liabilities outstanding—other than those covered elsewhere—being particularly careful about lawsuits, and third party endorsements on behalf of customers, officers and employees, affiliates, etc.
2. Show whether company protects itself by insurance or is a self-insurer and whether self-insurance coverage has been adequate in the past.

M. *Commitments.*

List the major outstanding commitments, being particularly careful in relation to fixed asset purchases; inventory purchases; hedging transactions; advertising campaigns; long-term sales agreements to sell civilian products, military products, or to carry out construction projects; guarantees of work or products; and renegotiation and price redetermination.

N. *Leases, franchise and royalty agreements.*

Schedule the following information on leases, franchise and royalty agreements that involve (1) substantial sums of money or (2) the company's right to use an important piece of property or manufacturing process or to make or sell a major product, etc.: (*a*) basis and amount of payment; (*b*) expiration date and renewal privileges; (*c*) cancellation notice and penalties by (i) company, (ii) other party; and (*d*) transferability by sales or sublease, subcontract, sublicense, etc.

O. *Capital stock, surplus, and retained earnings.*

1. Describe the classes of stock outstanding.
2. Prepare a schedule of capital surplus accounts indicating the history of current balances.
3. Ascertain whether company has adjusted surplus or retained earnings accounts for items that should have been reflected in the income account.
4. Schedule recent transactions in treasury stock.
5. Show redemption price of preferred stock outstanding, if any.
6. Describe any restrictions on retained earnings.

P. *Statement of income.*

1. Prepare a brief summary of earnings for five latest years on a consistent basis.
2. Explain any significant variations in income or expense.
3. Schedule amounts and percentages of gross profit by major product lines or by products during recent years.

4. Indicate anticipated changes in product line or costs and list expected gross profit margin for ensuing two years.

5. Schedule amount of estimated increases or decreases in major expense categories for ensuing two years. These might include, for example:

   a) Effect of including acquired company employees under the acquiring company's profit-sharing and pension plans, etc.

   b) Changes in management personnel or broad changes in personnel policies.

   c) Increase in depreciation if transaction results in higher fixed asset book values or new equipment is to be acquired.

   d) Changes in volume of production.

   e) Changes in promotion or distribution policies.

   f) Amortization of goodwill arising from this acquisition.

Q. *Financial ratios.*

Schedule the following ratios based on summarized financial statements: (1) ratio of sales to accounts receivable, (2) ratio of sales to inventory, (3) ratio of inventory turnover, (4) working capital ratio, (5) net book value of capital stock outstanding, (6) earnings per share, and (7) comparison of company ratios with industry ratios, where possible.

III. TAX CONSIDERATIONS

The intricacies of the Internal Revenue Code are extremely important in the area of mergers and acquisitions. Consequently, the income tax aspects of a proposed transaction should be carefully considered during the course of the negotiations. The following is a very general summary of some of the principles.

Corporate acquisitions are considered to be either taxable or tax free for income tax purposes. The tax status has reference generally to the position of the seller, as ordinarily no tax arises on the acquisition of property. The distinction is significant from the point of view of the buyer, however, since the taxability of the transaction is a major factor in determining the tax basis of the assets or stock acquired.

A tax-free transaction is generally of the merger type in which the seller accepts stock in the acquiring company in exchange for the assets or the stock of the company being sold. This type of transaction is treated for tax purposes essentially as a pooling of interests; and the earnings and profits (i.e., earned surplus) of the two companies are considered to be, in effect, aggregated.

The seller ordinarily does not recognize a gain or loss on this type of transaction. His tax basis or tax cost for the stock received is the same as that for the stock given up. His tax on the transaction is deferred until he disposes of the stock received from the purchasing company.

Tax Aspects

1. Outline the proposed transaction as to consideration given and assets transferred.
2. Indicate whether the transaction is considered taxable or tax free and the applicable Code section governing its status.
3. For tax-free transactions, indicate the following:
    a) Method of deducting bad debts—reserve or direct charge-off.
    b) Inventory valuation method.
    c) Depreciation practices and estimated lives for major asset classifications.
    d) Amount and nature of any reserves per books not allowable as tax deductions.
    e) Amount of any operating loss carry-overs.
4. For taxable transactions, indicate the following:
    a) Whether buyer purchased stock or assets.
    b) Whether company is to be retained as a wholly owned subsidiary or is to be liquidated.
    c) Amount to be paid in excess of the present tax basis of the assets to be acquired.
    d) Method of allocation of excess in *c*) above.
5. In a purchase of assets (including a purchase of stock followed by a liquidation), the purchase price must be allocated among all the assets acquired.
    a) Schedule all limited-term intangible assets (i.e., patents, copyrights, contracts, leases, and franchise for a fixed term) and tangible assets previously charged off (i.e., supplies, jigs, dies, small tools, etc.).
    b) Obtain details of any appraisal of fixed assets and indicate whether such values may reasonably be relied upon for purchase price allocation purposes.
    c) Indicate sales value of inventory, less normal distribution cost, for possible allocation of purchase price at such values rather than at seller's basis.
    d) Indicate any assets not listed above that may be of value to the buyer and therefore assigned some portion of the purchase price.

IV. SECURITIES AND EXCHANGE COMMISSION CONSIDERATIONS

The primary responsibility for determining the S.E.C. reporting requirements necessitated by the proposed transaction rests with legal counsel. The appropriate accounting treatment of the transaction and the determination of the financial statements required are the responsibility of the reporting company. The following information should assist in determining the method of reporting the proposed transaction.

Acquiring Company

1. Consider whether a report on Form 8–K will be required by the company by reference to items 2, 7, 11, and 13 of Form 8–K and instructions therein as to "Financial Statements of Businesses Acquired."

2. Consider whether the Proxy Rules are applicable and whether it is intended to solicit proxies from shareholders with respect to the plan for acquisition or merger. See items 12, 14, and 15 of Schedule 14A to Regulation X–14 under the Securities Exchange Act of 1934. Note particularly the requirements of paragraph (b) of item 15 with reference to financial statements of the acquired company.

3. If the plan of acquisition or merger involves the issuance of securities, consider whether the issuance of such securities constitutes:

   a) A public offering requiring registration under the Securities Act of 1933. If so, a Registration Statement may be required.

   b) A private offering exempt from registration under the second clause of Section 4(1) of the 1933 Act.

   c) A transaction meeting the terms of Rule 133 of the Securities Act of 1933. If so, the registration and prospectus requirements of the Act may be inapplicable.

4. The attitude of the S.E.C. staff as to appropriate methods of accounting for the proposed transaction by the acquiring or surviving corporation should be considered:

   a) If the proposed transaction is deemed to be a "pooling of interests," this position should be taken only if it can be effectively sustained with the staff of the S.E.C. A preliminary discussion with the S.E.C. accounting staff may be desirable if some doubt exists in this area.

   b) If "goodwill" arises in accounting for the transaction, the acquiring company should consider a policy of amortization of such goodwill over a reasonable period of time, either to commence immediately or at some future date.

Company Whose Assets or Outstanding Securities Are Being Acquired

1. Consider whether a report on Form 8–K will be required. See items 1, 2, 8, and 11 to Form 8–K.

2. Consider whether the company is subject to the Proxy Rules and whether the company intends to solicit proxies from its share-

holders with respect to the plan of merger or sale or other transfer of all or any substantial part of its assets. See items 14, 15, and 16 of Schedule 14A to Regulation X–14 under the Securities Exchange Act of 1934. Note particularly the requirements of paragraph (b) of item 15 with reference to financial statements of the *acquiring* company when the transaction involves the issuance or exchange of securities.

3. If the plan of acquisition or merger involves the issuance of securities by the acquiring company, consider whether the issuance of such securities constitutes:

   a) A public offering requiring registration under the Securities Act of 1933. If so, a Registration Statement containing certified financial statements of the *acquired* company will probably be required.

   b) A transaction meeting the terms of Rule 133 of the Securities Act of 1933. If so, the *acquired* company must submit the transaction to a vote of its stockholders and must obtain approval of the required majority in order to qualify the transaction under this Rule.

4. Consider whether the transaction results in any shareholder of the acquired company becoming a controlling stockholder of the surviving company. Such stockholder might be considered an "issuer" under the terms of the 1933 Act and accordingly might be required to meet the registration and prospectus requirements of the Act at the time a portion of the acquired shares is in turn sold to the public.

5. Inquire whether any of the major shareholders of the acquired company intend to dispose of their holdings in securities of the acquiring company shortly after the proposed transaction. If so, the S.E.C. may require that the registration and prospectus requirements of the Act be met.

6. Consider whether the transaction results in any shareholder, director, or officer of the acquired company becoming a director, officer, or principal holder of equity securities (10 per cent or more) in the surviving company. If so, and if the surviving company has securities listed on a national securities exchange, such persons must comply with the "insider trading" and reporting requirements of Section 16 of the 1934 Act.

V. MANAGEMENT AND ADMINISTRATION

A summary of the general policy of the acquired company should be helpful in evaluating the following matters. If no general policy exists, a statement as to the general goals established by officials of the company should suffice.

Administrative Departments

1. List the principal administrative departments and the number employed by each. Indicate whether any department seems excessively large or has an unusual concept as to its functions.
2. Characterize the financial departments in such matters as:
   a) Number and experience of personnel.
   b) Contribution to planning of company operations.
   c) Contribution to control of operations.
   d) Extent of dominance by top management or a particular department.
   e) Efficiency of methods, extent of mechanization, etc.

Management

1. Obtain the following information about executives and other key men: names and ages, family relationships, positions, investment in the company, portion of time devoted to business, areas of responsibility, experience and background, intention to continue after merger (or at least intention *not* to continue after merger), and apparent skill in discharging duties.
2. List each of the following for the executives and key men for the preceding five years: salary, bonus/profit-sharing, pension fund contribution, insurance paid, stock option plans, other present compensation, and other deferred compensation.
3. Obtain details and, if practical, copies of compensation plans, management contracts, etc.
4. Indicate the extent it seems likely that additional management talent will have to be provided.
5. Characterize the management and control as:
   a) "A one-man show," highly centralized, highly decentralized, or a combination.
   b) Formalized through budgets, reports, etc., or informal and personal.
6. Briefly, summarize management's reputation in business circles.
7. Detail the organizational relationship of the officers and key employees. Obtain or prepare a rough organizational chart.
8. List any other companies doing business with the subject company in which the management and/or owners have a financial interest but which are not being acquired.

Research and Development

1. Schedule the amounts that have been spent by the company in each of the past five years on research and development of a military nature, of a civilian nature, and of mixed value.

2. Describe principal projects briefly.
3. Indicate amounts spent for research billed to the government and others.
4. Describe the types of physical facilities and equipment provided for research.
5. Indicate type and cost of research purchased from outside consultants, laboratories, etc.
6. Indicate whether the research effort seems well organized in the sense that there are well-defined projects; means of measuring progress; and proper considerations of how much effort to put into an individual project and when to increase, decrease, or discontinue this effort.
7. Indicate the rate of turnover of the research staff. List the new commercially salable products that have resulted from this research and the portion of sales derived from these products.

VI. MANUFACTURING

General

Summarize the basic manufacturing function of the company. For example, indicate if the company manufactures most products from basic materials or whether numerous subassemblies are necessary. List areas where subcontracting plays an important part in the manufacturing process.

Facilities

1. Obtain the following data for major facilities:
   a) Locations.
   b) Products manufactured.
   c) Capacity.
   d) Production in recent years.
   e) Anticipated production in future years.
   f) Dates of construction or purchase of major items of plant and equipment.
   g) Evidences of obsolescence such as partial replacemant of a group of machines, few purchases of equipment in recent years, emergence of products with more difficult specifications, machines with substantially idle time, proposed (perhaps budgeted) purchases, etc.
   h) Any estimate of cost of putting plant equipment in modern condition.
   i) Depreciation rates and accumulated reserves.
2. If facilities (land, buildings, equipment) are leased, detail terms of applicable leases.

3. Indicate any problems likely to occur in expansion of facilities: availability or condition of land, zoning, adequate streets, sidings, etc.; location in relation to markets; location in relation to transportation, employee parking facilities, etc.
4. Obtain a recent appraisal of company facilities, if one exists.
5. Indicate any known plans for governmental or private projects that would enhance or reduce the value of the company's land or buildings—roads, parks, clearance projects, etc.

Materials

1. List the principal materials and purchased parts used in products, their availability, and their prices.
2. Indicate the type of arrangements for material purchases, including lead time, probable outstanding commitments, and number of vendors.
3. Review materials and parts to ascertain extent of their being out of balance and/or obsolete.
4. List any significant specification changes for materials and parts as the result of changes in the end use of the products and the effect of such changes on current business.
5. Describe the purchasing function and establish whether it is so organized as to result in effective purchasing considering such matters as: price, service, quality, and alertness for better materials.

Work Force

1. Give principal characteristics of work force: number, sex, skilled/unskilled, seasonal/non-seasonal, and union/non-union.
2. List the principal provisions of union contracts and obtain copies of contracts.
3. Indicate the principal features of pay plan: (a) hourly, weekly, or incentive; (b) holiday and overtime provisions; (c) profit-sharing; (d) guarantees and indemnities.
4. Briefly describe how employee compensation compares with other companies with which this company is or wishes to be competitive.
5. List the indirect ("fringe") benefits and whether they are fully paid.
6. Detail the past history and present status of union-management relations.
7. Show whether or not the work force can be varied in accordance with changes in volume.
8. List the rate of turnover and, if exceptionally high or low, to what this can be attributed.

Methods

1. Describe your impressions of the efficiency of plant operations with the following guides:
    a) Is there adequate space to provide for:
       (1) A smooth manufacturing operation?
       (2) Storage of materials, finished products, etc.?
    b) Are the facilities so arranged that the work flows logically from one process to the other with minimum of movement?
    c) In moving materials, are modern materials handling devices extensively employed (i.e., conveyors, lift trucks, pallets, etc.) or are hand-powered trucks, etc., used?
    d) Have machines been acquired, where feasible, that combine machine processes to eliminate the need for separate machines and operators, for handling materials between machines, etc.?
    e) Is the plant an attractive place to work?
    f) Do union agreements, trade practices, or company practices act to limit labor efficiency to any appreciable extent through such means as "feather-bedding," output limitations, and jurisdictional inefficiencies? To what extent and by what methods have these been overcome in the past?
2. For the company's production control department and the industrial engineering department, if one exists, indicate number of employees, type of work, and major changes initiated by the department in recent years.
3. If a consulting firm has made a recent survey, list its recommendations.

VII. SELLING AND DISTRIBUTION

Characteristics of Market

1. Prepare a general description of company's sales and distribution methods. Indicate whether sales are made by salesmen or brokers. If by salesmen, outline the general sales organization; if by broker, indicate the usual arrangement. Indicate whether distribution is from public warehouses, centralized warehouses, or other method of accumulating products for sale to customer.
2. For each of the principal products or product lines manufactured or purchased for resale by the company, indicate for the last five to ten years (a) the company's principal competitors and (b) the company's share of the total market and (better) also the respective shares of the market held by the principal competitors.

3. Schedule the company and industry's expected sales performance in the next five to ten years.
4. Indicate how expected total demand compares with expected industry capacity.
5. List the most important factors of the company's sales policy, evaluating this with factors concerned with who makes a sale and how the company compares with others in this respect: price, service, transportation costs, advertising and other promotional support, attractiveness of packaging, rental versus sale, credit terms, sales return policy and experience, other.
6. List the company's principal customers: largest by name and volume, by type of industry, by military and non-military, and by domestic and export (export by major countries).
7. Show possible effect of price change on volume and effect of volume changes on cost (and indirectly on selling price).
8. Describe whether the product brings about repeat customers and whether the company retains its customers.
9. If the products carry maintenance agreements as a separate contract or as part of original sales agreement, indicate if these are profitable or unprofitable and to what extent.
10. If company rents as well as sells its products, indicate under what terms. If not, indicate if it should consider this method of marketing.
11. Describe the importance of competition from foreign sources and whether tariff restrictions, quota limitations, etc., are significant.
12. If company sells under a franchise granted by another, indicate the basis for termination and to what extent the franchise limits sales territory, volume, type of customers, etc.

Marketing Methods

1. Schedule the percentages of the company's products that are marketed through (a) its own sales organization, (b) franchised dealers or agents (how many), (c) general distributors or brokers (how many), (d) direct mail, and (e) other (if this varies significantly by product lines, report data separately).
2. List the basis of compensation of distributors.
3. List the most important terms of selling agency (i.e., franchise and other) agreements.
4. Describe how the non-company sales organization is either tightly or loosely controlled and directed.
5. Detail the extent that sales are supported by advertising by amount and type of media.
6. If sales effort is supported by service engineering, describe important factors of servicing.

Marketing Organization

1. Describe the sales organization and indicate if it appears to be effective in (a) management abilities, (b) degree of aggressiveness, and (c) cost per sales dollar.
2. Obtain details of the company sales divisions, their numerical and geographical (territorial) strengths.

Sales Pricing Policies

1. Describe the type of price structure(s) used by the industry.
2. List allowances made to certain (classes of) customers because of volume and/or cooperative and other promotional efforts.
3. Describe how and when these allowances are paid.

Transportation and Distribution

1. Indicate how company's products are normally moved to its customers: (a) direct from factory, (b) from company warehouses, (c) from jobber's warehouses, (d) from public warehouses, (e) through company-owned retail outlets, and (f) other.
2. List the means of transportation used (train, truck, boat, plane, etc.).

   (In answering questions 1 and 2, it may be helpful to make a map.)
3. Indicate if the transportation and distribution system provides the desirable elements of (a) low cost, (b) adequate customer service, and (c) low inventories. If not, show how it can be improved.

REQUEST FOR TAX RULING FROM THE COMMISSIONER OF INTERNAL REVENUE

March 22, 1962

Commissioner of Internal Revenue
Washington 25, D. C.

Dear Sir:

RE: PLAN AND AGREEMENT OF REORGANIZATION
BETWEEN THE A COMPANY AND B CORPORATION
AND PLAN OF REORGANIZATION INCLUDED
THEREIN

A ruling as hereinafter set forth is respectfully requested concerning the federal income tax effects of the various steps to be taken under the Plan and Agreement of Reorganization (hereinafter referred to as "Agreement") between A Company and B Corporation dated March 15, 1962, and the plan of reorganization to be effected pursuant to such Agreement. A copy of the Agreement is included in the preliminary copy of the proxy statement to be submitted to B stockholders in connection with a shareholders' meeting to be held June 1, 1962 (hereinafter referred to as the "Proxy Statement"), a copy of which is attached hereto as Exhibit A.

1. Parties to the Reorganization:

The A Company (hereinafter referred to as "A"), a corporation organized and existing under the laws of the State of New Jersey, has its principal office located at Newark, N. J. A was incorporated in 1930. A is engaged directly and through its wholly owned subsidiaries in the business of manufacturing, distributing, and selling widgets on an international basis. A maintains its records on the basis of a fiscal year ending September 30 and uses the accrual method of accounting. A has a number of active wholly owned subsidiaries, the assets and operations of which are reflected in the financial statements included in the Proxy Statement attached hereto and marked Exhibit A.

As of March 15, 1962, there were authorized 25,000 shares of A 6 per cent Cumulative Preferred Stock of the par value of $100 per share, of which 18,000 (including treasury shares) were issued. A's remaining authorized capitalization consists of 1,600,000 shares of Common Stock having a par value of $1 per share, of which 789,107 were issued and outstanding on March 15, 1962. Of the unissued shares of Common Stock, 5,000 shares were reserved for issuance to employees under A's restricted stock option plan, under which options covering 2,922 shares were outstanding and unexercised.

A's consolidated statement of financial position as of September 30, 1961, and a summary of its consolidated earnings for the fiscal year ended with that date are included in the Proxy Statement.

B Corporation, a corporation organized and existing under the laws of the State of Delaware, has its principal office at New York City. B was incorporated in 1950. B is engaged directly and through its wholly owned subsidiaries in the business of manufacturing, distributing, and selling nuggets throughout the United States. B keeps its records on the basis of a fiscal year ending November 30 and uses the accrual method of accounting. B has a number of active wholly owned subsidiaries, the assets and operations of which are reflected in the B financial statements included in the Proxy Statement.

B's authorized capitalization consists of 1,000,000 shares of Common Stock having a par value of 10¢ per share, of which 861,308 were issued and outstanding on February 15, 1962.

It is anticipated that prior to the closing date under the Agreement, the outstanding capitalization of B will be affected by the issuance of not more than 700 shares of Common Stock to employees of B pursuant to the exercise of restricted stock options previously granted to said employees. As a result of the foregoing transactions, it is anticipated that no more than 862,008 shares of B's stock will be outstanding as of the exchange date.

B's consolidated statement of financial position as of August 31 and a summary of its consolidated earnings for November 30, 1961, the period ending with that date, are included in the Proxy Statement.

There is no known substantial common ownership of A and B. A owns no stock in B.

2. Proposed Plan of Reorganization:

The terms of the plan of reorganization contemplated by the Agreement are in substance as follows:

(a) Prior to closing, B shall liquidate all of its government securities and apply to the reduction of B's liabilities all cash on hand and on deposit, except as set forth in subparagraph (b) below.

(b) On the closing date provided by the Agreement, B will transfer to A all of B's property, assets, and business of all types whatsoever except an amount of cash on deposit with a commercial bank that B shall deem suffiicent to enable it to pay all expenses in connection with carrying out the Agreement and the plan of reorganization provided for therein, including all liquidation and dissolution expenses and taxes; provided, however, that any balance remaining after the expiration of 120 days from the closing or exchange date under the Agreement shall be used to pay liabilities shown on the B statement of financial position as of date of closing. It is contemplated that the amount retained for this purpose will not exceed $10,000.

(c) Concurrently with the transfer of assets by B described in subparagraph (b) above, A will issue and transfer to B that number of shares of A presently authorized Common Stock that is equal to one-third of the number of shares of B Common Stock issued and outstanding on the closing date. Under the Agreement, the number of shares transferred by A will in no event exceed 287,336.

(d) A will assume all liabilities of B other than (i) any federal tax imposed upon B by reason of B's liquidation pursuant to the terms of the Agreement; and (ii) the expenses of B incurred in carrying out its obligations under, or its dissolution and liquidation contemplated by, the Agreement. A shall not be liable for federal capital gains or other taxes imposed upon the B shareholders as a result of the exchange.

(e) On or as soon as practicable after the closing date, B shall completely dissolve and distribute the A stock described in subparagraph (c) above to its shareholders in return for their B stock, at the ratio referred to above. The distribution and exchange of the A stock for the B stock will be administered as follows:

B will deposit with a New York bank, as depository for its shareholders, all A certificates received by it. The bank, upon receipt from the B shareholders of their B certificates, will make delivery of the A share certificates to the shareholders entitled to such certificates. No fractional shares will be issued in this connection.

The bank, as agent for the shareholders of B, two-thirds of whom must approve the Agreement and plan of reorganization, shall sell a sufficient number of A shares to pay said fractions in cash. On or after June 1, 1963, A may require the bank to transfer all unclaimed shares and accumulated dividends thereon then held by the bank to A; and thereafter, A shall hold such shares and such dividends for the shareholders entitled thereto.

3. Nature of B Assets To Be Transferred Pursuant to Agreement:

The assets of B as of November 30, 1961, are summarized in the statement of financial position included in the Proxy Statement attached hereto and marked Exhibit A. Under the terms of the Agreement, B warrants that it will, until the transfer of assets contemplated by the Agreement, conduct its business diligently and only in the ordinary course of business without making any distributions to its shareholders other than its usual cash quarterly dividends on its common stock.

Accordingly, the assets of B at the time of the contemplated exchange are expected to be substantially as shown by the November 30, 1961, statement of financial position, subject only to changes occurring in the ordinary course of business and as stated in paragraph 2(a) of the Agreement. From such assets, B, as noted in paragraph 2(b) above, will retain cash on deposit with a commercial bank in an estimated amount not exceeding $10,000.

4. Business Purpose of the Reorganization:

As indicated above, A is engaged primarily in the business of manufacturing, distributing, and selling widgets. B, on the other hand, is engaged in the business of manufacturing, distributing, and selling nuggets. Accordingly, the acquisition will permit A to distribute and sell a more diversified line of products; and the combined base of the two corporations will permit capital expenditures, not now feasible for B, to acquire the latest and most efficient machinery developed in the nugget field. In addition, the management of both companies believes that the acquisition will result in economies in production and distribution, and in other significant business advantages. The advantages of the acquisition are outlined in detail in the Proxy Statement.

5. Requested Ruling:

Accordingly, a ruling is respectfully requested as follows:

(a) The acquisition of B's assets by A pursuant to the terms of the Agreement will consitute the acquisition by one corporation, in exchange solely for part of its voting stock, of substantially all of the properties of another corporation and will therefore constitute a reorganization within the meaning of Section 368(a)-(1)(C) of the Internal Revenue Code of 1954.

(b) Pursuant to the provisions of Section 357 and 361(a) of the Internal Revenue Code of 1954, no gain or loss will be recognized to B with respect to the transfer of assets, assumption of liabilities, and issuance of stock involved in the reorganization, all pursuant to the Agreement.

(c) Under the provisions of Sections 118 and 1032 of the Internal Revenue Code of 1954, no gain or loss will be recognized to A in connection with the acquisition of the B's assets.

(d) Under the provisions of Section 362 of the 1954 Code, the basis of the assets of B in the hands of A after consummation of the reorganization exchange will be the same as the basis of such assets in the hands of B immediately prior thereto.

(e) Under Section 354(a)(1) of the Internal Revenue Code of 1954, no gain or loss (except gain or loss relating to fractional shares of A stock that are sold) will be recognized to the former shareholders of B upon the receipt by them of A's stock in complete cancellation of the B stock held by them.

(f) Gain that is derived from the sale of fractional shares by the bank on behalf of the former shareholders of B will be taxable to said shareholders as capital gain, the amount of said gain being equal to the excess of the amount received by each shareholder over his basis for said fractional share as determined under Section 358(a)(1) of the Code.

(g) Under the provisions of Sections 358(a)(1) and 1223 of the Code, the basis and holding period of A stock in the hands of the former B shareholders will be the same as the basis and holding period of the B stock that was exchanged for said stock, the basis, however, being adjusted by that portion of said basis that is allocable to fractional shares that are sold.

Pursuant to the Agreement, B's obligations are specifically conditioned upon the successful obtaining of the ruling requested herein. The Agreement will therefore not be consummated until said ruling has been obtained.

We believe that the requested ruling is adequately supported by the statutes set forth above. We will, however, be pleased to submit such additional information as may be required. Further, in the event an adverse ruling is contemplated, we respectfully request the privilege of a conference prior to the issuance of such a ruling.

Copies of all requests for additional information and other materials, and of all correspondence in connection with this request for ruling, should be addressed to _____. Duplicate executed copies of the power of attorney authorizing such representation are enclosed herewith.

Respectfully submitted,

_____

(Signature)

Appendix C

FAVORABLE TAX RULING FROM
THE INTERNAL REVENUE SERVICE

B Corporation
New York, New York

Dear Sirs:

This is in reply to the letter dated March 22, 1962, requesting a ruling as to the federal income tax consequences of the proposed transaction described below. Additional information was furnished by letters dated April 12, and 26, 1962. From the information furnished, the relevant facts appear to be as set forth below.

The A Company is a New Jersey corporation that was incorporated in 1930. It is engaged directly and through its wholly owned subsidiaries in the business of manufacturing, distributing, and selling widgets on an international basis. As of September 15, 1961, A had 18,000 shares of 6 per cent cumulative preferred stock with a par value of $100 per share issued (including treasury shares). As of this date, it also had 789,107 shares of common stock with a par value of $1 per share issued and outstanding. The common and preferred stock of A is listed on the New York Stock Exchange.

B is a Delaware corporation that was incorporated in 1950. B is engaged directly and through its wholly owned subsidiaries in the business of manufacturing, distributing, and selling nuggets throughout the United States. On March 15, 1962, the outstanding capital stock of B consisted of 861,308 shares of common stock with a par value of 10¢ per share. It is anticipated that prior to the closing date of the proposed transaction, the outstanding common stock of B will be affected by the issuance of not more than 700 shares of common stock to the employees of B pursuant to the exercise of restricted stock options previously granted to such employees.

It is stated that there is no known substantial common ownership of A and B stock, and that A owns no stock of B.

In order to diversify the line of products of A and to allow B to make greater capital expenditure and effect economies in production, the following plan is proposed.

(1) Prior to closing, B will liquidate all of its government securities and apply to the reduction of B's liabilities all cash on hand and on deposit, except as set forth in (2) below.

(2) On the closing date, B will transfer to A all of B's property, assets, and business of all types whatsoever except an amount of cash on deposit with a commercial bank that B will deem sufficient to pay all expenses in connection with carrying out the agreement and plan of reorganization, including all liquidation and dissolution expenses and taxes; provided, however, that any balance remaining after the expiration of 120 days from the closing or exchange date under the agreement will be used to pay liabilities shown on the B statement of financial position as of the date of closing. It is contemplated that the amount retained for this purpose will not exceed $10,000.

(3) Concurrently with the transfer of assets by B, A will transfer to B that number of A shares of common stock that is equal to one-third of the number of shares of B common stock that is issued and outstanding on the closing date. Under the agreement, the number of A shares transferred will in no event exceed 287,336 shares.

(4) A will assume all liabilities of B other than (a) any federal tax imposed upon B by reason of B's liquidation; and (b) the expenses of B incurred in carrying out its obligations under, or its dissolution and liquidation contemplated by, the agreement. A will not be liable for federal capital gains or other taxes imposed upon the B shareholders as a result of the exchange.

(5) On or as soon as practicable after the closing date, B will completely dissolve and distribute to its shareholders the A stock received in exchange for their stock of B, at the ratio referred to above. The distribution of A stock by B will be effected by depositing such shares with a New York bank. Bank will deliver to the shareholders of B all full shares to which they are entitled, together with any dividends that the bank, as depository, will have received subsequent to the closing date. No fractional shares will be delivered. Bank as agent for the shareholders of B will, at the written direction of each of B's shareholders entitled to a fractional share, either (a) purchase at the expense of such shareholder an additional fractional share interest to round his holding to a full share, or (b) sell his fractional interest and remit the proceeds to him. After a

date that is at least sixty days subsequent to the giving of notice to the B shareholders, bank will sell for cash a number of shares of A stock equivalent to all remaining fractional interests and thereafter pay over the proceeds to the shareholders entitled thereto upon receipt of their certificates of B stock. At such time, on or after June 1, 1963, as A will request, bank will deliver and pay to A any and all certificates representing shares of common stock of A and moneys then held by it with respect to shares of B stock not yet surrendered to bank. Thereafter, the holders of such shares of B common stock will look only to A for delivery of such shares and payment of such moneys upon surrender of their shares for exchange.

B warrants that it will, until the transfer of assets, conduct its business diligently and only in the ordinary course of business without making any distributions to its shareholders other than its usual cash dividends.

Solely on the basis of the information submitted, it is held as follows:

(1) The proposed acquisition of substantially all the assets of B by A solely in exchange for a portion of the voting stock of A will constitute a reorganization within the meaning of Section 368(a)(1)(C) of the Internal Revenue Code of 1954 provided that A acquires at least 90 per cent of the fair market value of the net assets of B. No gain or loss will be recognized to B or A as a result of the proposed transfers of property in exchange for stock (Sections 361 and 1032, respectively, of the Code).

(2) Under Section 362 of the Code, the basis of the property acquired by A solely in exchange for its stock will be the same as the adjusted basis of such property in the hands of B.

(3) Under the provisions of Section 354(a)(1) of the Code, no gain or loss will be recognized to the shareholders of B upon the receipt of common stock (including fractional shares to which they would be entitled) of A exchanged for their stock of B.

(4) The basis and holding period of the stock of A received by the shareholders of B (including fractional shares to which they would be entitled) will be the same as the adjusted basis and holding period, respectively, of the stock surrendered therefor (Sections 353(a)(1) and 1223 of the Code). The basis should be allocated proportionately to the whole and fractional shares received.

(5) It will be considered that the B shareholders actually received the fractional interests to which they are entitled. Accordingly,

upon the sale by the bank of such fractional interests for the accounts of the shareholders, each shareholder entitled thereto will realize gain or loss measured by the difference between the amount of cash received and the basis of his stock properly allocable to the fractional share sold. To those shareholders in whose hands the stock of B constituted a capital asset, such gain or loss will constitute capital gain or loss subject to the provisions and limitations of Subchapter F of Chapter 1 of the Code.

It is important that a copy of this communication be attached to the federal income tax returns of the parties involved for the taxable year in which the proposed transaction is consummated.

In accordance with the instructions contained in the power of attorney on file with this office, a copy of this communication has been sent to Mr. _____.

Yours very truly,

Chief, Reorganization Branch

Appendix D

RULE 133 OF THE SECURITIES ACT OF 1933

(as revised July 16, 1959)

(a) For purposes only of Section 5 of the Act, no "sale," "offer," "offer to sell," or "offer for sale" shall be deemed to be involved so far as the stockholders of a corportion are concerned where, pursuant to statutory provisions in the state of incorporation or provisions contained in the certificate of incorporation, there is submitted to the vote of such stockholders a plan or agreement for a statutory merger or consolidation or reclassification of securities, or a proposal for the transfer of assets of such corporation to another person in consideration of the issuance of securities of such other person or voting stock of a corporation which is in control, as defined in Section 368(c) of the Internal Revenue Code of 1954, of such other person, under such circumstances that the vote of a required favorable majority (1) will operate to authorize the proposed transaction so far as concerns the corporation whose stockholders are voting (except for the taking of action by the directors of the corporation involved and for compliance with such statutory provisions as the filing of the plan or agreement with the appropriate state authority), and (2) will bind all stockholders of such corporation except to the extent that dissenting stockholders may be entitled, under statutory provisions or provisions contained in the certificate of incorporation, to receive the appraised or fair value of their holdings.

(b) Any person who purchases securities of the issuer from security holders of a constituent corporation with a view to, or offers or sells such securities for such security holders in connection with, a distribution thereof pursuant to any contract or arrangement, made in connection with any transaction specified in paragraph (a), with the issuer or with any affiliate of the issuer, or with any person who in connection with such transaction is acting as an underwriter of such securities, shall be deemed to be an underwriter of such securities within the meaning of section 2(11) of the Act. This paragraph does not refer to arrangements limited to provision for the matching and combination of fractional interests in securities into whole interests, or the purchase and sale of such fractional interests, among security holders of the constituent corporation and to the sale on behalf of, and as agent for, such security holders of such number of fractional or whole interests as may be necessary to adjust for any remaining fractional interests after such matching.

(c) Any constituent corporation, or any person who is an affiliate of a constituent corporation at the time any transaction specified in paragraph (a) is submitted to a vote of the stockholders of such corporation, who acquires securities of the issuer in connection with such transaction with a view to the distribution thereof shall be deemed to be an underwriter of such securities within the meaning of section 2(11) of the Act. A transfer by a constituent corporation to its security holders of securities of the issuer upon a complete or partial liquidation shall not be deemed a distribution for the purpose of this paragraph.

(d) Notwithstanding the provisions of paragraph (c) a person specified therein shall not be deemed to be an underwriter nor to be engaged in a distribution with respect to securities acquired in any transaction specified in paragraph (a) which are sold by him in brokers' transactions within the meaning of section 4(2) of the Act, in accordance with the conditions and subject to the limitations specified in paragraph (e) hereof, if such person—

(1) does not directly or indirectly solicit or arrange for the solicitation of orders to buy in anticipation of or in connection with such brokers' transactions;

(2) makes no payments in connection with the execution of such brokers' transactions to any person other than the broker; and

(3) limits such brokers' transactions to a sale or series of sales which together with all other sales of securities of the same class by such person or on his behalf within the preceding six months will not exceed the following:

(A) if the security is traded only otherwise than on a securities exchange, approximately one per cent of the shares or units of such security outstanding at the time of receipt by the broker of the order to execute such transactions, or

(B) if the security is admitted to trading on a securities exchange, the lesser of approximately (i) one per cent of the shares or units of such security outstanding at the time of receipt by the broker of the order to execute such transactions or (ii) the largest aggregate reported volume of trading on securities exchanges during any one week within the four calendar weeks preceding the receipt of such order.

(e) For the purposes of paragraph (d) of this rule

(1) The term "brokers' transactions" in section 4(2) of the Act shall be deemed to include transactions by a broker acting as agent for the account of the seller where (a) the broker performs no more than the usual and customary broker's functions, (b) the broker does no more than execute an order or orders to sell as a broker and receives no more than the usual or customary broker's commissions, (c) the broker does not solicit or arrange for the solicitation of orders to buy in anticipation of or in connection with such transactions and (d) the broker is not aware of any circumstances indicating that his principal is failing to comply with the provisions of paragraph (d) hereof;

(2) The term "solicitation of such order" in section 4(2) of the Act shall be deemed to include the solicitation of an order to buy a security, but shall not be deemed to include the solicitation of an order to sell a security;

(3) Where within the previous 60 days a dealer has made a written bid for a security or a written solicitation of an offer to sell such security, the term "solicitation" in section 4(2) shall not be deemed to include an inquiry regarding the dealer's bid or solicitation.

(f) For the purposes of this rule, the term "constituent corporation" means any corporation, other than the issuer, which is a party to any transaction specified in paragraph (a). The term "affiliate" means a person controlling, controlled by or under common control with a specified person.

Appendix E

REGULATION X-14 OF THE SECURITIES EXCHANGE ACT OF 1934, SCHEDULE 14A, ITEMS 14 AND 15

Item 14. *Mergers, Consolidations, Acquisitions and Similar Matters.*

Furnish the following information if action is to be taken with respect to any plan for (i) the merger or consolidation of the issuer into or with any other person or of any other person into or with the issuer, (ii) the acquisition by the issuer or any of its security holders of securities of another issuer, (iii) the acquisition by the issuer of any other going business or of the assets thereof, (iv) the sale or other transfer of all or any substantial part of the assets of the issuer, or (v) the liquidation or dissolution of the issuer:

(a) Outline briefly the material features of the plan. State the reasons therefor, the general effect thereof upon the rights of existing security holders, and the vote needed for its approval. If the plan is set forth in a written document, file three copies thereof with the Commission at the time preliminary copies of the proxy statement and form of proxy are filed pursuant to Rule X-14A-6(a).

(b) Furnish the following information as to each person (other than totally-held subsidiaries of the issuer) which is to be merged into the issuer or into or with which the issuer is to be merged or consolidated or the business or assets of which are to be acquired or which is the issuer of securities to be acquired by the issuer in exchange for all or a substantial part of its assets or to be acquired by security holders of the issuer.

(1) Describe briefly the business of such person. Information is to be given regarding pertinent matters such as the nature of the products or services, methods of production, markets, methods of distribution and the sources and supply of raw materials.

(2) State the location and describe the general character of the plants and other important physical properties of such person. The description is to be given from an economic and business standpoint, as distinguished from a legal standpoint.

(3) Furnish a brief statement as to dividends in arrears or defaults in principal or interest in respect to any securities of the issuer or of such person, and as to the effect of the plan thereon and such other information as may be appropriate in the particular case to disclose adequately the nature and effect of the proposed action.

(c) As to each class of securities of the issuer, or of any person specified in paragraph (b), which is admitted to dealing on a national securities exchange or with respect to which a market otherwise exists, and which will be materially affected by the plan, state the high and low sale prices (or, in the absence of trading in a particular period, the range of the bid and asked prices) for each quarterly period within two years. This information may be omitted if the plan involves merely the liquidation or dissolution of the issuer.

Item 15. *Financial Statements.*

(a) If action is to be taken with respect to any matter specified in Item 12, 13, or 14 above, furnish certified financial statements of the issuer and its subsidiaries such as would currently be required in an original application for the registration of securities of the issuer under the Act. All schedules other than the schedules of supplementary profit and loss information may be omitted.

Instruction. Such statements shall be prepared and certified in accordance with Regulation S–X.

(b) If action is to be taken with respect to any matter specified in Item 14(b), furnish financial statements such as would currently be required in an original application by any person specified therein for registration of securities under the Act. Such statements need not be certified and all schedules other than the schedules of supplementary profit and loss information may be omitted. However, such statements may be omitted for (i) a totally-held subsidiary of the issuer which is included in the consolidated statement of the issuer and its subsidiaries, or (ii) a person which is to succeed to the issuer or to the issuer and one or more of its totally-held subsidiaries under such circumstances that Form 8–B would be appropriate for registration of securities of such person issued in exchange for listed securities of the issuer.

(c) Notwithstanding paragraphs (a) and (b) above, any or all of such financial statements which are not material for the exercise of prudent judgment in regard to the matter to be acted upon may be omitted if the reasons for such omission are stated. Such financial statements are deemed material to the exercise of prudent judgment in the usual case involving the authorization or issuance of any material amount of senior securities, but are not deemed material in cases involving the authorization or issuance of common stock, otherwise than in exchange.

(d) The proxy statement may incorporate by reference any financial statements contained in an annual report sent to security holders pursuant to Rule X-14A-3 with respect to the same meeting as that to which the proxy statement relates, provided such financial statements substantially meet the requirements of this item.

Appendix F

REGULATION X–14 OF THE SECURITIES EXCHANGE ACT OF 1934, SCHEDULE 14B

INFORMATION TO BE INCLUDED IN STATEMENTS FILED
BY OR ON BEHALF OF A PARTICIPANT (OTHER THAN
THE ISSUER) IN A PROXY SOLICITATION
PURSUANT TO RULE X–14A–11(c)

Answer every item. If an item is inapplicable or the answer is in the negative, so state. The information called for by Items 2(a) and 3(a) or a fair summary thereof is required to be included in all preliminary soliciting material by Rule X–14A–11(d).

Item 1. *Issuer.* State the name and address of the issuer.

Item 2. *Identity and Background.*
  (a) State the following:
   (1) Your name and business address.
   (2) Your present principal occupation or employment and the name, principal business and address of any corporation or other organization in which such employment is carried on.

  (b) State the following:
   (1) Your residence address.
   (2) Information as to all material occupations, positions, offices or employments during the last ten years, giving starting and ending dates of each and the name, principal business and address of any business corporation or other business organization in which each such occupation, position, office or employment was carried on.

  (c) State whether or not you are or have been a participant in any other proxy contest involving this or other issuers within the past ten years. If so, identify the principals, the subject matter and your relationship to the parties and the outcome.

(d) State whether or not, during the past ten years, you have been convicted in a criminal proceeding (excluding traffic violations or similar misdemeanors) and, if so, give dates, nature of conviction, name and location of court, and penalty imposed or other disposition of the case. A negative answer to this sub-item need not be included in the proxy statement or other proxy soliciting material.

Item 3. *Interests in Securities of the Issuer.*

(a) State the amount of each class of securities of the issuer which you own beneficially, directly or indirectly.

(b) State the amount of each class of securities of the issuer which you own of record but not beneficially.

(c) State with respect to the securities specified in (a) and (b) the amounts acquired within the past two years, the dates of acquisition and the amounts acquired on each date.

(d) If any part of the purchase price or market value of any of the shares specified in paragraph (c) is represented by funds borrowed or otherwise obtained for the purpose of acquiring or holding such securities, so state and indicate the amount of the indebtedness as of the latest practicable date. If such funds were borrowed or obtained otherwise than pursuant to a margin account or bank loan in the regular course of business of a bank, broker or dealer, briefly describe the transaction, and state the names of the parties.

(e) State whether or not you are a party to any contracts, arrangements or understandings with any person with respect to any securities of the issuer, including but not limited to joint ventures, loan or option arrangements, puts or calls, guarantees against loss or guarantees of profits, division of losses or profits, or the giving or withholding of proxies. If so, name the persons with whom such contracts, arrangements, or understandings exist and give the details thereof.

(f) State the amount of securities of the issuer owned beneficially, directly or indirectly, by each of your associates and the name and address of each such associate.

(g) State the amount of each class of securities of any parent or subsidiary of the issuer which you own beneficially, directly or indirectly.

Item 4. *Further Matters.*

(a) Describe the time and circumstances under which you became a participant in the solicitation and state the nature and extent of your activities or proposed activities as a participant.

(b) Furnish for yourself and your associates the information required by Item 7(f) of Schedule 14A.

(c) State whether or not you or any of your associates have any arrangement or understanding with any person—

(1) with respect to any future employment by the issuer or its affiliates; or

(2) with respect to any future transactions to which the issuer or any of its affiliates will or may be a party.

If so, describe such arrangement or understanding and state the names of the parties thereto.

Item 5. *Signature.*

The statement shall be dated and signed in the following manner:

I certify that the statements made in this statement are true, complete, and correct, to the best of my knowledge and belief.

. . . .
(Date)

. . . .
(Signature of participant or authorized representative)

Instruction: If the statement is signed on behalf of a participant by the latter's authorized representative, evidence of the representative's authority to sign on behalf of such participant shall be filed with the statement.

Appendix G

FORM S-1 OF THE SECURITIES ACT OF 1933—
INSTRUCTIONS AS TO FINANCIAL STATEMENTS

These instructions specify the balance sheets and profit and loss statements required to be filed as a part of a registration statement on this form. Regulation S-X governs the certification, form and content of such balance sheets and profit and loss statements, including the basis of consolidation, and prescribes the statements of surplus and the schedules to be filed in support thereof. Item 21(a) above specifies the statements which are to be included in the prospectus. Attention is directed to Rule 411(b) regarding incorporation by reference of financial statements.

A. THE REGISTRANT

1. Balance Sheets of the Registrant.

(a) The registrant shall file a balance sheet as of a date within 90 days prior to the date of filing the registration statement. This balance sheet need not be certified. If all of the following conditions exist, this balance sheet may, however, be as of a date within six months prior to the date of filing.

    (1) The registrant files annual and other reports pursuant to Section 13 or 15(d) of the Securities Exchange Act of 1934;

    (2) The total assets of the registrant and its subsidiaries, as shown by the latest consolidated balance sheet filed, less any valuation or qualifying reserves, amount to $5,000,000 or more, exclusive of intangibles; and

    (3) No long-term debt of the registrant is in default as to principal, interest or sinking fund provisions.

(b) If the balance sheet required by paragraph (a) is not certified, there shall be filed in addition a certified balance sheet as of a date within one year unless the fiscal year of the registrant has ended within 90 days prior to the date of filing, in which case the certified balance sheet may be as of the end of the preceding fiscal year.

2. Profit and Loss Statements of the Registrant.

The registrant shall file a profit and loss statement for each of the three fiscal years preceding the date of the latest balance sheet filed, and for the period, if any, between the close of the latest of such fiscal years and the date of the latest balance sheet filed. These statements shall be certified up to the date of the latest certified balance sheet filed.

3. Omission of Registrant's Statements in Certain Cases.

Notwithstanding Instructions 1 and 2, the individual financial statements of the registrant may be omitted if (1) consolidated statements of the registrant and one or more of its subsidiaries are filed, (2) the conditions specified in either of the following paragraphs are met, and (3) the Commission is advised as to the reasons for such omission.

(a) The registrant is primarily an operating company and all subsidiaries included in the consolidated financial statements filed are totally-held subsidiaries; or

(b) The registrant's total assets, exclusive of investments in and advances to the consolidated subsidiaries, constitute 85% or more of the total assets shown by the consolidated balance sheets filed and the registrant's total gross revenues for the period for which its profit and loss statements would be filed, exclusive of interest and dividends received from the consolidated subsidiaries, constitute 85% or more of the total gross revenue shown by the consolidated profit and loss statements filed.

B. CONSOLIDATED STATEMENTS

4. Consolidated Balance Sheets.

There shall be filed a consolidated balance sheet of the registrant and its subsidiaries as of the same date as each balance sheet of the registrant filed pursuant to Instruction 1. The consolidated balance sheet shall be certified if the registrant's balance sheet as of the same date is certified. If the registrant's balance sheets are omitted pursuant to Instruction 3, the consolidated balance sheets filed shall be as of the same dates as the balance sheets of the registrant would be required and shall be certified if the corresponding balance sheet of the registrant would be required to be certified.

5. Consolidated Profit and Loss Statements.

There shall be filed consolidated profit and loss statements of the registrant and its subsidiaries for each of the three fiscal years preceding the date of the latest consolidated balance sheet filed, and for the period, if any, between the close of the latest of such fiscal years and the date of the latest consolidated balance sheet filed. These statements shall be certified up to the date of the latest related certified consolidated balance sheet filed.

C. UNCONSOLIDATED SUBSIDIARIES AND OTHER PERSONS

6. Unconsolidated Subsidiaries.

(a) Subject to Rule 4–03 of Regulation S–X regarding group statements of unconsolidated subsidiaries, there shall be filed for each majority-owned subsidiary of the registrant not consolidated the balance sheets and profit and loss statements which would be required if the subsidiary were itself a registrant. Insofar as practicable, these balance sheets and profit and loss statements shall be as of the same dates or for the same periods as those of the registrant.

(b) If it is impracticable to file a balance sheet of any unconsolidated subsidiary as of a date within 90 days prior to the date of filing, there may be filed in lieu thereof a certified balance sheet of the subsidiary as of the end of its latest annual or semi-annual fiscal period preceding the date of filing the registration statement, for which it is practicable to do so.

7. Fifty-Percent-Owned Persons.

If the registrant owns, directly or indirectly, approximately 50 per cent of the voting securities of any person and approximately 50 per cent of the voting securities of such person is owned, directly or indirectly, by another single interest, there shall be filed for each such person the financial statements which would be required if it were a registrant. The statements filed for each such person shall identify the other single interest.

8. Omission of Statements in Certain Cases.

Notwithstanding Instructions 6 and 7, there may be omitted from the registration statement all financial statements of any one or more unconsolidated subsidiaries or 50-per cent-owned persons if all such subsidiaries and 50-per cent-owned persons for which statements are so omitted, considered in the aggregate as a single subsidiary, would not constitute a significant subsidiary.

9. Affiliates Whose Securities Secure an Issue Being Registered.

(a) For each affiliate, securities of which constitute or are to constitute a substantial portion of the collateral securing any class of securities being registered, there shall be filed the financial statements that would be required if the affiliate were a registrant.

(b) For the purposes of this instruction, securities of a person shall be deemed to constitute a substantial portion of collateral if the aggregate principal amount, par value, or book value as shown by the books of the registrant, or market value, whichever is the greatest of such securities equals 20 per cent or more of the principal amount of the class secured thereby.

D. SPECIAL PROVISIONS

10. Reorganization of Registrant.

(a) If during the period for which its profit and loss statements are required, the registrant has emerged from a reorganization in which substantial changes occurred in its asset, liability, capital stock, surplus or reserve accounts, a brief explanation of such changes shall be set forth in a note or supporting schedule to the balance sheets filed.

(b) If the registrant is about to emerge from such a reorganization, there shall be filed, in addition to the balance sheets of the registrant otherwise required, a balance sheet giving effect to the plan of reorganization. These balance sheets shall be set forth in such form, preferably columnar, as will show in related manner the balance sheet of the registrant prior to the reorganization, the changes to be effected in the reorganization and the balance sheet of the registrant after giving effect to the plan of reorganization. By a footnote or otherwise a brief explanation of the changes shall be given.

11. Succession to Other Businesses.

(a) If during the period for which its profit and loss statements are required, the registrant has by merger, consolidation or otherwise succeeded to one or more businesses, the additions, eliminations and other changes effected in the succession shall be appropriately set forth in a note or supporting schedule to the balance sheets filed. In addition, profit and loss statements for each constituent business, or combined statements if appropriate, shall be filed for such period prior to the succession as may be necessary when added to the time, if any, for which profit and loss statements after the succession are filed to cover the equivalent of the period specified in Instruction 2 and 5 above.

(b) If the registrant by merger, consolidation or otherwise is about to succeed to one or more businesses, there shall be filed for the constituent businesses financial statements, combined if appropriate, which would be required if they were registering securities under the Act. In addition, there shall be filed a balance sheet of the registrant giving effect to the plan of succession. These balance sheets shall be set forth in such form, preferably columnar, as will show in related manner the balance sheets of the constituent businesses, the changes to be effected in the succession and the balance sheet of the registrant after giving effect to the plan of succession. By a footnote or otherwise, a brief explanation of the changes shall be given.

(c) This instruction shall not apply with respect to the registrant's succession to the business of any totally-held subsidiary or to any acquisition of a business by purchase.

12. Acquisition of Other Businesses.

(a) There shall be filed for any business directly or indirectly acquired by the registrant after the date of the latest balance sheet filed pursuant to Part A or B above and for any business to be directly or indirectly acquired by the registrant, the financial statements which would be required if such business were a registrant.

(b) The acquisition of securities shall be deemed to be the acquisition of a business if such securities give control of the business or combined with securities already held give such control. In addition, the acquisition of securities which will extend the registrant's control of a business shall be deemed the acquisition of the business if any of the securities being registered hereunder are to be offered in exchange for the securities to be acquired.

(c) No financial statements need be filed, however, for any business acquired or to be acquired from a totally-held subsidiary. In addition, the statements of any one or more businesses may be omitted if such businesses, considered in the aggregate as a single subsidiary, would not constitute a significant subsidiary, provided that the statements of any business may not be omitted where any of the securities being registered are to be offered in exchange for securities representing such business.

13. Filing of Other Statements in Certain Cases.

The Commission may, upon the request of the registrant, and where consistent with the protection of investors, permit the omission of one or more of the statements herein required or the filing in substitution therefor of appropriate statements of comparable character. The Commission may also require the filing of other statements in addition to, or in substitution for, the statements herein required in any case where such statements are necessary or appropriate for an adequate presentation of the financial condition of any person whose financial statements are required, or whose statements are otherwise necessary for the protection of investors.

E. HISTORICAL FINANCIAL INFORMATION

14. Scope of Part E.

The information required by Part E shall be furnished for the seven-year period preceding the period for which profit and loss statements are filed, as to the accounts of each person whose balance sheet is filed. The information is to be given as to all of the accounts specified whether they are presently carried on the books or not. Part E does not call for an audit, but only for a survey or review of the accounts specified. It should not be detailed beyond a point material to an investor. Information may be omitted, however, as to any person for whom equivalent information for the period has been filed with the Commission pursuant to the Securities Act of 1933 or the Securities Exchange Act of 1934.

15. Revaluation of Property.

(a) If there were any material increases or decreases in investments, in property, plant and equipment, or in intangible assets, resulting from revaluing such assets, state (1) in what year or years such revaluations were made; (2) the amounts of such increases or decreases, and the accounts affected, including all related entries; and (3) if in connection with such revaluations any related adjustments were made in reserve accounts, state the accounts and amounts with explanations.

(b) Information is not required as to adjustments made in the ordinary course of business, but only as to major revaluations made for the purpose of entering in the books current values, reproduction cost or any values other than original cost.

(c) No information need be furnished with respect to any revaluation entry which was subsequently reversed or with respect to the reversal of a revaluation entry recorded prior to the period if a statement as to the reversal is made.

16. Capital Shares.

(a) If there were any material restatements of capital shares which resulted in transfers from capital share liability to surplus or reserve, state the amount of each such restatement and all related entries. No statement need be made as to restatements resulting from the declaration of share dividends.

(b) If there was an original issue of capital shares, any part of the proceeds of which was credited to accounts other than capital share accounts, state the title of the class, the accounts and the respective amounts credited thereto.

17. Debt Discount and Expense Written Off.

If any material amount of debt discount and expense, on long-term debt still outstanding, was written off earlier than as required under any periodic amortization plan, give the following information: (1) title of the securities, (2) date of the write-off, (3) amount written off, and (4) to what account charged.

18. Premiums and Discount and Expense on Securities Retired.

If any material amount of long-term debt or preferred shares was retired, and if either the retirement was made at a premium or there remained, at the time of retirement, a material amount of unamortized discount and expense applicable to the securities retired, state for each class (1) title of the securities retired, (2) date of retirement, (3) amount of premium paid and of unamortized discount and expense, (4) to what account charged, and (5) whether being amortized and, if so, the plan of amortization.

19. Other Changes in Surplus.

If there were any material increases or decreases in surplus, other than those resulting from transactions specified above, the closing of the profit and loss account or the declaration or payment of dividends, state (1) the year or years in which such increases or decreases were made; (2) the nature and amounts thereof; and (3) the accounts affected, including all material related entries. Instruction 15(c) above shall also apply here.

20. Predecessors.

The information shall be furnished, to the extent it is material, as to any predecessor of the registrant from the beginning of the period to the date of succession, not only as to the entries made respectively in the books of the predecessor or the successor, but also as to the changes effected in the transfer of the assets from the predecessor. However, no information need be furnished as to any one or more predecessors which, considered in the aggregate, would not constitute a significant predecessor.

21. Omission of Certain Information.

(a) No information need be furnished as to any subsidiary, whether consolidated or unconsolidated, for the period prior to the date on which the subsidiary became a majority-owned subsidiary of the registrant or of a predecessor for which information is required above.

(b) No information need be furnished hereunder as to any one or more unconsolidated subsidiaries for which separate financial statements are filed if all subsidiaries for which the information is so omitted, considered in the aggregate as a single subsidiary, would not constitute a significant subsidiary.

(c) Only the information specified in Instruction 15 need be given as to any predecessor or any subsidiary thereof if immediately prior to the date of succession thereto by a person for which information is required, the predecessor or subsidiary was in insolvency proceedings.

Appendix H

FORM S–1 OF THE SECURITIES ACT OF 1933, ITEM 6—SUMMARY OF EARNINGS

Furnish in comparative columnar form a summary of earnings for the registrant or for the registrant and its subsidiaries consolidated, or both, as appropriate, for each of the last five fiscal years of the registrant (or for the life of the registrant and its immediate predecessors, if less) and for any period between the end of the latest of such fiscal years and the date of the latest balance sheet furnished, and for the corresponding period of the preceding fiscal year. In connection with such summary, whenever necessary, reflect information or explanation of material significance to investors in appraising the results shown, or refer to such information or explanation set forth elsewhere in the prospectus.

INSTRUCTIONS

1. Include comparable data for any additional fiscal years necessary to keep the summary from being misleading. Subject to appropriate variation to conform to the nature of the business or the purpose of the offering, the following items shall be included: net sales or operating revenues; cost of goods sold or operating expenses (or gross profit); interest charges; income taxes; net income; special items; and net income and special items. The summary shall reflect the retroactive adjustment of any material items affecting the comparability of the results. See Item 21 (b).

2. If common stock is being registered, the summary shall be prepared to present earnings applicable to common stock. Per share earnings and dividends declared for each period of the summary shall also be included unless inappropriate.

3. A registrant which is engaged primarily (i) in the generation, transmission or distribution of electricity, the manufacture, mixing, transmission or distribution of gas, the supplying or distribution of water or in furnishing telephone or telegraph services or (ii) in holding securities in such companes, may, at its option, include a sum-

mary for a twelve months period to the date of the latest balance sheet furnished, in lieu of both the summary for the interim period between the end of the last fiscal year and such balance sheet date and the summary for the corresponding period of the preceding fiscal year.

4. A registrant may, at its option, show in tabular form for each fiscal year or other period, the ratio of earnings (computed in accordance with generally accepted accounting principles after all operating and income deductions, except taxes based on income or profits and fixed charges) to fixed charges. The term "fixed charges" shall mean (i) interest and amortization of debt discount and expenses and premium on all indebtedness; (ii) an appropriate portion of rentals under long-term leases and, (iii) in case consolidated figures are used, preferred stock dividend requirements of consolidated subsidiaries, excluding in all cases, items eliminated in consolidation. In the case of utilities, interest credits charged to construction should be added to gross income and not deducted from interest. If the ratio is shown, the pro forma ratio of earnings to fixed charges adjusted to give effect to the issuance of securities being registered and to any presently proposed issuance, retirement or redemption of securities should be disclosed. Any registrant electing to show the ratio of earnings to fixed charges, in accordance with this instruction, shall file as an exhibit a statement setting forth in reasonable detail the computations of such ratios. For the purpose of this exhibit and the pro forma ratio referred to above, an assumed maximum interest rate may be used on securities as to which the interest rate has not yet been fixed, which assumed rate should be shown.

5. In connection with any unaudited summary for an interim period or periods between the end of the last fiscal year and the balance sheet date, and any comparable unaudited prior period, a statement shall be made that all adjustments necessary to a fair statement of the results for such interim period or periods, have been included. In addition, there shall be furnished in such cases, as supplemental information but not as a part of the registration statement, a letter describing in detail the nature and amount of any adjustments, other than normal recurring accruals, entering into the determination of the results shown.

6. If long term debt or preferred stock is being registered, there shall be shown the annual interest requirements on such long-term debt or the annual dividend requirements on such preferred stock. To the extent that an issue represents refunding or refinancing, only the additional annual interest or dividend requirements shall be stated.

Appendix I

BRIEF DESCRIPTION OF SCHEDULES I TO XVII UNDER REGULATION S–X OF THE 1933 AND 1934 ACTS, AND THE INVESTMENT COMPANY ACT OF 1940

Schedule I. *Marketable Securities—Other Security Investments.*

The schedule prescribed by Rule 12.02 shall be filed:

1. If the greater of the aggregate amount of marketable securities on the basis of current market quotations or the amount at which carried in such balance sheet constitutes 15 per cent or more of total assets
2. If the amount at which other security investments is carried in such balance sheet constitutes 15 per cent or more of total assets
3. If the amount at which other security investments is carried in such balance sheet plus the greater of the aggregate amount of marketable securities on the basis of current market quotations or the amount at which carried on such balance sheet constitutes 20 per cent or more of the total assets

Schedule II. *Amounts Due from Directors, Officers, and Principal Holders of Equity Securities Other Than Affiliates.*

The schedule prescribed by Rule 12.03 shall be filed with respect to each person among the directors, officers, and principal holders of equity securities other than affiliates, from whom an aggregate indebtedness of more than $20,000 or 1 per cent of total assets, whichever is less, is owed, or at any time during the period for which related profit and loss statements are filed, was owed. This excludes amounts due from such persons for purchases subject to usual trade terms, for ordinary travel and expense advances, and for other such items arising in the ordinary course of business.

Schedule III. *Investments in Securities of Affiliates.*

The schedule prescribed by Rule 12.04 shall be filed provided that this schedule may be omitted if (1) neither the sum of securities and non-current indebtedness of affiliates nor the amount of indebtedness to affiliates exceeds 5 per cent of total assets (exclusive of intangible assets) as shown by the related balance sheet at either the beginning or end of the period, or (2) there have been no changes in the information required to be filed from that last previously reported.

Schedule IV. *Indebtedness of Affiliates—Not Current.*

The schedule prescribed by Rule 12.05 shall be filed in support of such indebtedness. This schedule and Schedule X may be combined if desired and may be omitted under the same conditions as Schedule III.

Schedule V. *Property, Plant, and Equipment.*

The schedule prescribed by Rule 12.06 shall be filed in support of this item provided that this schedule may be omitted if the total does not exceed 5 per cent of total assets (exclusive of intangible assets) at both the beginning and end of the period and if neither the additions nor deductions during the period exceeded 5 per cent of total assets (exclusive of intangible assets).

Schedule VI. *Reserves for Depreciation, Depletion, and Amortization of Property, Plant, and Equipment.*

The schedule prescribed by Rule 12.07 shall be filed in support of this item. This schedule may be omitted if Schedule V is omitted.

Schedule VII. *Intangible Assets.*

The schedule prescribed by Rule 12.08 shall be filed in support of this item.

Schedule VIII. *Reserves for Depreciation and Amortization of Intangible Assets.*

The schedule prescribed by Rule 12.07 shall be filed in support of this item.

Schedule IX. *Bonds, Mortgages and Similar Debt.*

The schedule prescribed by Rule 12.10 shall be filed in support of this item.

Schedule X. *Indebtedness to Affiliates—Not Current.*

The schedule prescribed by Rule 12.11 shall be filed in support of this item. This schedule and Schedule IV may be combined if desired and may be omitted under the same conditions as Schedules III and IV.

Schedule XI. *Guarantees of Securities of Other Issuers.*

The schedule prescribed by Rule 12.12 shall be filed with respect to any guarantees of securities of other issuers by the person for which the statement is filed.

Schedule XII. *Reserves.*

The schedule prescribed by Rule 12.13 shall be filed in support of reserves included in the balance sheet but not included in Schedules VI and VIII.

Schedule XIII. *Capital Shares.*

The schedule prescribed by Rule 12.14 shall be filed in support of this item.

Schedule XIV. *Warrants or Rights.*

The schedule prescribed by Rule 12.15 shall be filed with respect to warrants or rights granted by the person for which the statement is filed to subscribe for or purchase securities to be issued by such person.

Schedule XV. *Other Securities.*

If there are any classes of securities not included in Schedules IX, XI, XIII, or XIV, set forth in this schedule information concerning such securities corresponding to that required for the securities included in such schedules. Information need not be set forth, however, as to notes, drafts, bills of exchange, or bankers' acceptances having a maturity at the time of issuance of not exceeding one year.

Schedule XVI. *Supplementary Profit and Loss Information.*

The schedule prescribed by Rule 12.16 shall be filed in support of each profit and loss statement in which sales or operating revenues were of significant amount. This schedule may also be omitted if the information required is furnished in the profit and loss or income statement or in a footnote thereto.

Schedule XVII. *Income from Dividends—Equity in Net Profit and Loss of Affiliates.*

The schedule prescribed by Rule 12.17 shall be filed for each period for which a profit and loss statement is filed. This schedule may be omitted if neither the sum of investments in and indebtedness to affiliates nor the amount of indebtedness to affiliates exceeds 5 per cent of total assets (exclusive of intangible assets) as shown by the related balance sheet at either the beginning or end of the period.

Appendix J

SECURITIES ACT OF 1933
RELEASE NO. 4552

NON-PUBLIC OFFERING EXEMPTION

The [Securities and Exchange] Commission today [November 6, 1962] announced the issuance of a statement regarding the availability of the exemption from the registration requirements of Section 5 of the Securities Act of 1933 afforded by the second clause of Section 4(1) of the Act for "transactions by an issuer not involving any public offering," the so-called "private offering exemption." Traditionally, the second clause of Section 4(1) has been regarded as providing an exemption from registration for bank loans, private placements of securities with institutions, and the promotion of a business venture by a few closely related persons. However, an increasing tendency to rely upon the exemption for offerings of speculative issues to unrelated and uninformed persons prompts this statement to point out the limitations on its availability.

Whether a transaction is one not involving any public offering is essentially a question of fact and necessitates a consideration of all surrounding circumstances, including such factors as the relationship between the offerees and the issuer, the nature, scope, size, type and manner of the offering.

The Supreme Court in *S.E.C.* v. *Ralston Purina Co.*, 346 U.S. 119, 124, 125 (1953), noted that the exemption must be interpreted in the light of the statutory purpose to "protect investors by promoting full disclosure of information thought necessary to informed investment decisions" and held that "the applicability of Section 4(1) should turn on whether the particular class of persons affected need the protection of the Act." The Court stated that the number of offerees is not conclusive as to the availability of the exemption, since the statute seems to apply to an offering "whether to few or many." [1] However, the Court indicated that "nothing prevents the Commission, in enforcing

---

[1] See, also, *Gilligan, Will & Co.* v. *S.E.C.*, 267 F.2d 461, 467 (C.A. 2, 1959), *cert. denied,* 361 U.S. 896 (1960).

the statute, from using some kind of numerical test in deciding when to investigate particular exemption claims." It should be emphasized, therefore, that the number of persons to whom the offering is extended is relevant only to the question whether they have the requisite association with and knowledge of the issuer which make the exemption available.

Consideration must be given not only to the identity of the actual purchasers but also to the offerees. Negotiations or conversations with or general solicitations of an unrestricted and unrelated group of prospective purchasers for the purpose of ascertaining who would be willing to accept an offer of securities is inconsistent with a claim that the transaction does not involve a public offering even though ultimately there may only be a few knowledgeable purchasers.[2]

A question frequently arises in the context of an offering to an issuer's employees. Limitation of an offering to certain employees designated as key employees may not be a sufficient showing to qualify for the exemption. As the Supreme Court stated in the *Ralston Purina* case: "The exemption as we construe it, does not deprive corporate employees, as a class, of the safeguards of the Act. We agree that some employee offerings may come within Section 4(1), e.g., one made to executive personnel who because of their position have access to the same kind of information that the Act would make available in the form of a registration statement. Absent such a showing of special circumstances, employees are just as much members of the investing 'public' as any of their neighbors in the community." The Court's concept is that the exemption is necessarily narrow. The exemption does not become available simply because offerees are voluntarily *furnished* information about the issuer. Such a construction would give each issuer the choice of registering or making its own voluntary disclosures without regard to the standards and sanctions of the Act.

The sale of stock to promoters who take the initiative in founding or organizing the business would come within the exemption. On the other hand, the transaction tends to become public when the promoters begin to bring in a diverse group of uninformed friends, neighbors and associates.

The size of the offering may also raise questions as to the probability

---

[2] Reference is made to the so-called "investment clubs" which have been organized under claim of an exemption from the registration provisions of the Securities Act of 1933 as well as the Investment Company Act of 1940. It should not be assumed that so long as the investment club, which is an investment company within the meaning of the latter Act, does not *obtain* more than 100 members, a public offering of its securities, namely the memberships, will not be involved. An investment company may be exempt from the provisions of the Investment Company Act if its securities are owned by not more than 100 persons *and* it is not making and does not presently propose to make a public offering of its securities. (Section 3(c)(1)). Both elements must be considered in determining whether the exemption is available.

that the offering will be completed within the strict confines of the exemption. An offering of millions of dollars to non-institutional and non-affiliated investors or one divided, or convertible, into many units would suggest that a public offering may be involved.

When the services of an investment banker, or other facility through which public distributions are normally effected, are used to place the securities, special care must be taken to avoid a public offering. If the investment banker places the securities with discretionary accounts and other customers without regard to the ability of such customers to meet the tests implicit in the *Ralston Purina* case, the exemption may be lost. Public advertising of the offerings would, of course, be incompatible with a claim of a private offering. Similarly, the use of the facilities of a securities exchange to place the securities necessarily involves an offering to the public.

An important factor to be considered is whether the securities offered have come to rest in the hands of the initial informed group or whether the purchasers are merely conduits for a wider distribution. Persons who act in this capacity, whether or not engaged in the securities business, are deemed to be "underwriters" within the meaning of Section 2(11) of the Act. If the purchasers do in fact acquire the securities with a view to public distribution, the seller assumes the risk of possible violation of the registration requirements of the Act and consequent civil liabilities.[3] This has led to the practice whereby the issuer secures from the initial purchasers representations that they have acquired the securities for investment. Sometimes a legend to this effect is placed on the stock certificates and stop-transfer instructions issued to the transfer agent. However, a statement by the initial purchaser, at the time of his acquisition, that the securities are taken for investment and not for distribution is necessarily self-serving and not conclusive as to his actual intent. Mere acceptance at face value of such assurances will not provide a basis for reliance on the exemption when inquiry would suggest to a reasonable person that these assurances are formal rather than real. The additional precautions of placing a legend on the security and issuing stop-transfer orders have proved in many cases to be an effective means of preventing illegal distributions. Nevertheless, these are only precautions and are not to be regarded as a basis for exemption from registration. The nature of the purchaser's past investment and trading practices or the character and scope of his business may be inconsistent with the purchase of large blocks of securities for investment. In particular, purchases by persons engaged in the business of buying and selling securities require careful scrutiny for the purpose of determining whether such person may be acting as an underwriter for the issuer.

The view is occasionally expressed that, solely by reason of con-

[3] See Release No. 33–4445.

tinued holding of a security for the six-month capital-gain period specified in the income-tax laws, or for a year from the date of purchase, the security may be sold without registration. There is no statutory basis for such assumption. Of course, the longer the period of retention, the more persuasive would be the argument that the resale is not at variance with an original investment intent, but the length of time between acquisition and resale is merely one evidentiary fact to be considered. The weight to be accorded this evidentiary fact must, of necessity, vary with the circumstances of each case. Further, a limitation upon resale for a stated period of time or under certain circumstances would tend to raise a question as to original intent even though such limitation might otherwise recommend itself as a policing device. There is no legal justification for the assumption that holding a security in an "investment account" rather than a "trading account," holding for a deferred sale, for a market rise, for sale if the market does not rise, or for a statutory escrow period, without more, establishes a valid basis for an exemption from registration under the Securities Act.[4]

An unforeseen change of circumstances since the date of purchase may be a basis for an opinion that the proposed resale is not inconsistent with an investment representation. However, such claim must be considered in the light of all of the relevant facts. Thus, an advance or decline in market price or a change in the issuer's operating results are normal investment risks and do not usually provide an acceptable basis for such claim of changed circumstances. Possible inability of the purchaser to pay off loans incurred in connection with the purchase of the stock would ordinarily not be deemed an unforeseeable change of circumstances. Further, in the case of securities pledged for a loan, the pledgee should not assume that he is free to distribute without registration. The Congressional mandate of disclosure to investors is not to be avoided to permit a public distribution of unregistered securities because the pledgee took the securities from a purchaser, subsequently delinquent.[5]

The view is sometimes expressed that investment companies and other institutional investors are not subject to any restrictions regarding disposition of securities stated to be taken for investment and that any securities so acquired may be sold by them whenever the investment decision to sell is made, no matter how brief the holding period. Institutional investors are, however, subject to the same restrictions on sale of securities acquired from an issuer or a person in a control relationship with an issuer insofar as compliance with the registration requirements of the Securities Act is concerned.

---

[4] See Release No. 33–3825 re The Crowell-Collier Publishing Company.
[5] *S.E.C.* v. *Guild Films Company, Inc., et al.,* 279 F.2d 485 (C.A. 2, 1960), *cert. denied sub nom., Santa Monica Bank* v. *S.E.C.,* 364 U.S. 819 (1960).

Integration of Offerings

A determination whether an offering is public or private would also include a consideration of the question whether it should be regarded as a part of a larger offering made or to be made. The following factors are relevant to such question of integration: whether (1) the different offerings are part of a single plan of financing, (2) the offerings involve issuance of the same class of security, (3) the offerings are made at or about the same time, (4) the same type of consideration is to be received, (5) the offerings are made for the same general purpose.

What may appear to be a separate offering to a properly limited group will not be so considered if it is one of a related series of offerings. A person may not separate parts of a series of related transactions, the sum total of which is really one offering, and claim that a particular part is a non-public transaction. Thus, in the case of offerings of fractional undivided interests in separate oil or gas properties where the promoters must constantly find new participants for each new venture, it would appear to be appropriate to consider the entire series of offerings to determine the scope of this solicitation.

As has been emphasized in other releases discussing exemptions from the registration and prospectus requirements of the Securities Act, the terms of an exemption are to be strictly construed against the claimant who also has the burden of proving its availability.[6] Moreover, persons receiving advice from the staff of the Commission that no action will be recommended if they proceed without registration in reliance upon the exemption should do so only with full realization that the tests so applied may not be proof against claims by purchasers of the security that registration should have been effected. Finally, Sections 12(2) and 17 of the Act, which provide civil liabilities and criminal sanctions for fraud in the sale of a security, are applicable to the transactions notwithstanding the availability of an exemption from registration.

[6] *S.E.C.* v. *Sunbeam Gold Mining Co.*, 95 F.2d 699, 701 (C.A. 9, 1938); *Gilligan, Will & Co.* v. *S.E.C.*, 267 F.2d 461, 466 (C.A. 2, 1959); *S.E.C.* v. *Ralston Purina Co.*, 346 U.S. 119, 126 (1953); *S.E.C.* v. *Culpepper et al.*, 270 F.2d 241, 246 (C.A. 2, 1959).

Appendix K

ORIGINAL LISTING QUALIFICATIONS OF THE NEW YORK STOCK EXCHANGE

Standards of Eligibility for Listing

By reason of their nature and the necessity for flexibility, the qualifications for listing on the New York Stock Exchange can better be described in general terms than as exact formulae.

The company must be a going concern, or be the successor to a going concern, and must have substantial assets or demonstrated earning power, or both. While the amount of assets and earnings, and the aggregate market value of the company's junior securities, are considerations, greater emphasis is placed on such questions as degree of national interest in the company, its standing in its particular field, the character of the market for its products, its relative stability and position in its industry, and whether or not it is engaged in an expanding industry, with prospects of maintaining its position.

The particular securities for which listing is sought must have a sufficiently wide distribution to offer reasonable assurance that an adequate auction market in the securities will exist.

Guides as to Standards of Size, Earnings and Distribution

In applying the above principles to individual cases, certain minimum "yardsticks" have been developed with respect to those standards which can be expressed in such terms. These are not intended to be inflexible mathematical formulae but are merely guides. It should be understood that all of the standards are considered collectively and that weight may be given to compensating factors. The "yardsticks" referred to are as follows:

Size and Earnings: The company should have a demonstrated earning power, under competitive conditions, of $1,000,000 annually, after all charges, including Federal Income and Excess Profits taxes. As to size, net tangible assets should be at least $10,000,000, but greater emphasis will be placed on the aggregate market value of the Common Stock, where $10,000,000 or more at the time of listing will be looked for.

[*Exception:* An exception to these general yardsticks applies only to companies registered under the Investment Company Act of 1940 and the Small Business Investment Act of 1958, where the following alternate size and earnings yardsticks apply:

1. The $1,000,000 earnings requirement will be modified to the extent appropriate for companies of this character.
2. Net tangible assets applicable to common stock shall be at least $16,000,000 including a minimum of $8,000,000 composed of paid-in capital or capitalized cash earnings. The company will be asked for an undertaking not to take action that would significantly reduce its net assets below this $16,000,000 level. In this connection, unusual and special circumstances will be considered on their merits.
3. The company shall have operated for a minimum of three years.

All other original listing standards will be applicable.]

Distribution: In the case of Common Stock issues, a broad distribution of at least 500,000 shares (exclusive of concentrated or family holdings) among not less than 1,500 holders will be looked for, after substantially discounting the number of holders of less than 100 shares.

Voting Rights—Stock

Since 1926, the Exchange has refused to authorize the listing of non-voting common stock, or of any non-voting stock, however designated, which by its terms is in effect a common stock. The Exchange will also refuse to list the common voting stock of a company which also has outstanding in public hands a non-voting stock, however designated, which by its terms is in effect a common stock.

In line with the above-stated policy, the Exchange usually has refused to authorize listing of voting trust certificates. Exception has been made in the case of voting trusts established pursuant to reorganization proceedings under Court direction.

The Exchange will also refuse to list common stock (or other voting stock) where the voting rights of shareholders in stock to be issued for assets or sold for cash would be restricted by the use of a voting trust, irrevocable proxy, or any similar arrangement to which the company or any of its officers or directors is a party, either directly or indirectly. This also applies to original listings where a voting trust has arisen in this manner and the voting restrictions are still present.

The Exchange also takes into account, when considering listing, the effect of concentrated holdings upon the voting position of the publicly held stock, the proportionate distribution of voting power as between classes of stock, and unusual voting provisions which, in effect, tend to permit one class to nullify or veto the vote of another class.

Further, as a matter of policy adopted in 1940, the Exchange may refuse to list preferred stock not having certain minimum voting rights.

. . . [A] more complete statement of Exchange policies in respect of the above matters, and the circumstances under which certain exceptions to those policies may be made, . . . appears in Section A 15 of . . . [the Exchange's Company] Manual, entitled *Voting Rights—Stock*.

Informal Preliminary Review as to Eligibility

In the case of a company contemplating presentation of an application for the listing of its securities on the Exchange, and particularly where there is any doubt as to its eligibilty for listing in the light of the considerations outlined above, it is recommended that data first be presented, informally, for confidential study by the Exchange prior to the preparation of a complete formal application. Data submitted should include as much of the following as is available or may readily be obtained:

1. Brief description of the company's business, its products, date of organization, markets where securities to be listed are traded in, available data as to recent price range and volume of trading;
2. Latest available income account, surplus account and balance sheet, together with copies of annual reports for the past ten years, or a statement of net earnings for any of such years as to which annual reports are not available;
3. Detailed schedule showing distribution of the security in accordance with the Exchange's tabulated form, which appears in Section B 5 of . . . [the Company] Manual, under the heading *Stock Distribution Schedule;*
4. Copy of the Charter and By-Laws.

Appendix L

ORIGINAL LISTING QUALIFICATIONS OF THE AMERICAN STOCK EXCHANGE

ORIGINAL LISTING STANDARDS

The American Stock Exchange has adopted the following minimum standards for the determination of whether an applicant will qualify for listing:

Size (Net Worth):

The applicant must have net tangible assets of at least $1,000,000.

Earnings:

The applicant must have net earnings of at least $150,000 after all charges, including Federal income taxes, in the fiscal year immediately preceding the filing of the listing application, and net earnings averaging at least $100,000 for the past three fiscal years.

In special situations the Exchange may consider applications of companies which do not meet the above net earnings standards but which have substantially larger net worth than the minimum of $1,000,000 specified above. These special situations will be considered on their merits, and will include companies such as the following:

(a) Companies licensed under the Small Business Investment Act of 1958 or qualified as real estate investment trusts under the so-called "Real Estate Investment Act of 1960," provided that the companies have been in operation for at least one year.

(b) Real estate companies operating under the "cash flow" concept, provided that the companies have a "cash flow" income substantially greater than the minimum net after tax earnings specified above for other types of companies.

(c) Companies not yet on a sustained producing and earnings basis which are engaged in the development and/or construction of plants or other facilities and are fully financed to complete such program, provided that such companies submit satisfactory evidence of their ability to exceed the above minimum net earnings standard within a reasonable period of time after completion of such fully financed program.

Distribution of Common Stock Issues:

In the case of common stock issues the Exchange requires a minimum public distribution of 200,000 shares (exclusive of the holdings of officers and directors and other concentrated or family holdings) among not less than 750 holders, of whom not less than 500 must be holders of lots of 100 shares or more.

The total number of outstanding shares of common stock must have a minimum aggregate market value of $2,000,000, and the publicly distributed shares a minimum aggregate market value of $1,000,000.

Preliminary Opinion Prior to Preparation of Complete Listing Application

An informal and confidential opinion as to the eligibility of a particular issue for listing may be obtained in advance of the preparation and filing of a complete listing application, by sending to the Division of Securities of the Exchange (a) copy of the latest prospectus of the company (if comparatively recent), (b) copies of printed annual reports distributed to stockholders for the past three years (if available) or financial statements for such periods, and (c) a certificate showing a breakdown of the extent of the public distribution of the stock, the latter on a printed form (Listing Form K) which will be supplied by the Exchange upon request.

VOTING RIGHTS

The American Stock Exchange will not view favorably applications for the listing of (a) Common Stocks which are non-voting or which have unduly restricted voting rights, and (b) non-voting Preferred Stocks which do not acquire voting rights upon specified defaults (maximum two years) in the payment of fixed dividend requirements. However, in applying the above policy the Exchange will consider each case individually and on its own merits, and may make certain exceptions thereto depending upon the circumstances in each case. A statement of the Exchange's policy (and possible exceptions thereto) will be furnished upon request. The staff of the Division of Securities will discuss this policy and furnish an opinion in any particular case.

INDEX

344 INDEX